RIVERS OF LONDON

CRY FOX

Titan
COMICS

RIVERS OF LONDON: CRY FOX
ISBN: 9781785861727
FP HC ISBN: 9781785866210

TITAN COMICS

EDITOR STEVE WHITE
SENIOR DESIGNER ANDREW LEUNG

Managing & Launch Editor Andrew James
Production Controller Peter James
Production Supervisor Maria Pearson
Senior Production Controller Jackie Flook
Art Director Oz Browne
Sales & Circulation Manager Santosh Maharaj
Press Officer Will O'Mullane
Brand Manager Lucy Ripper
Direct Sales and Marketing Manager Ricky Claydon
Commercial Manager Michelle Fairlamb
Head of Rights Jenny Boyce
Publishing Manager Darryl Tothill
Publishing Director Chris Teather
Operations Director Leigh Baulch
Executive Director Vivian Cheung
Publisher Nick Landau

Published by Titan Comics
A division of Titan Publishing Group, Ltd.
144 Southwark St.
London
SE1 0UP

A CIP catalogue record for this title is available from the British Library.

First edition: June 2018
10 9 8 7 6 5 4 3 2 1

Printed in China.
Titan Comics.

For rights information contact jenny.boyce@titanemail.com

WWW.TITAN-COMICS.COM

Become a fan on Facebook.com/comicstitan

Follow us on Twitter @ComicsTitan

RIVERS OF LONDON

CRY FOX

WRITTEN BY
ANDREW CARTMEL & BEN AARONOVITCH

ART BY
LEE SULLIVAN

COLORS BY
LUIS GUERRERO

LETTERING BY
ROB STEEN

TITAN®
COMICS

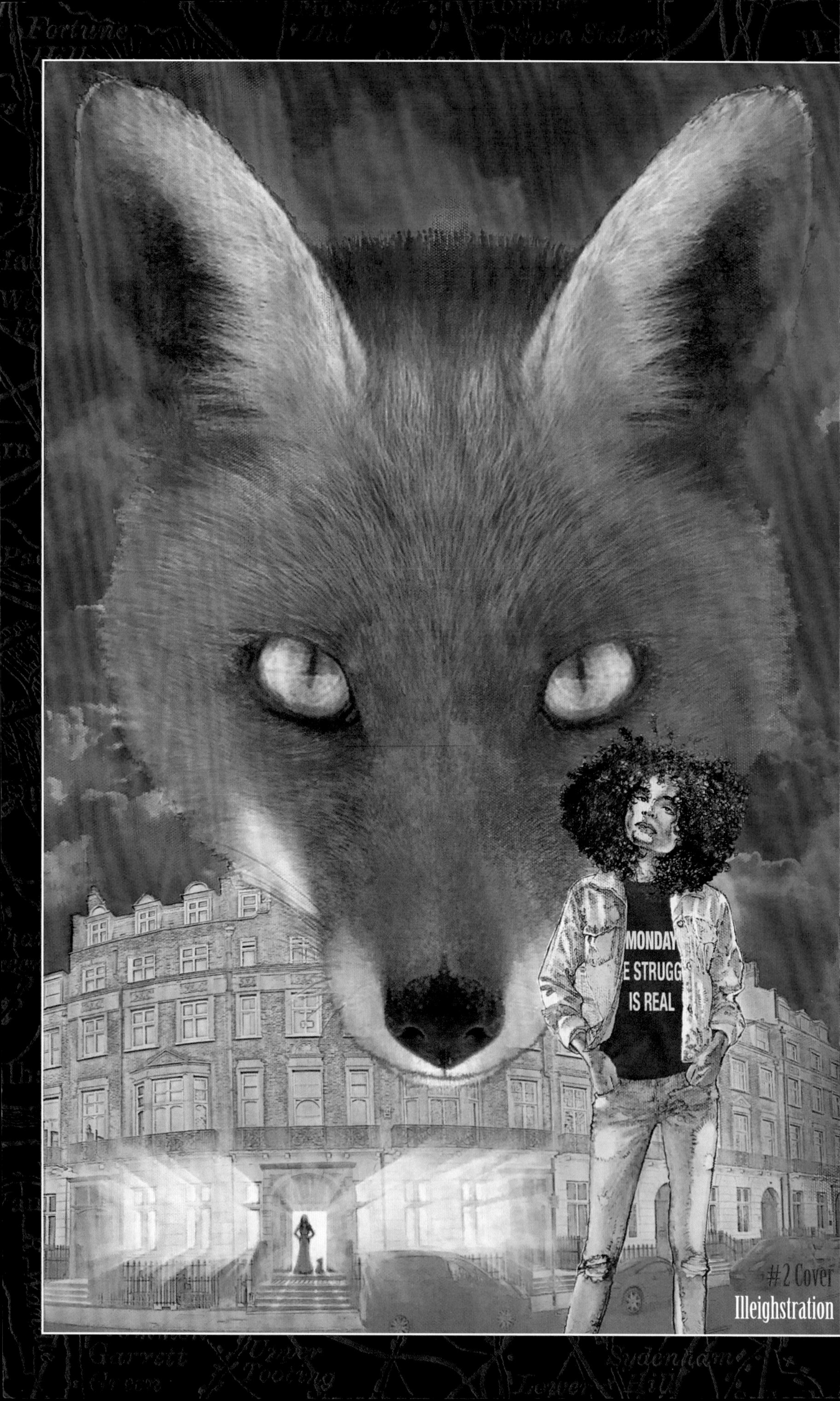
MONDAY
IS REAL
#2 Cover
Illeighstration

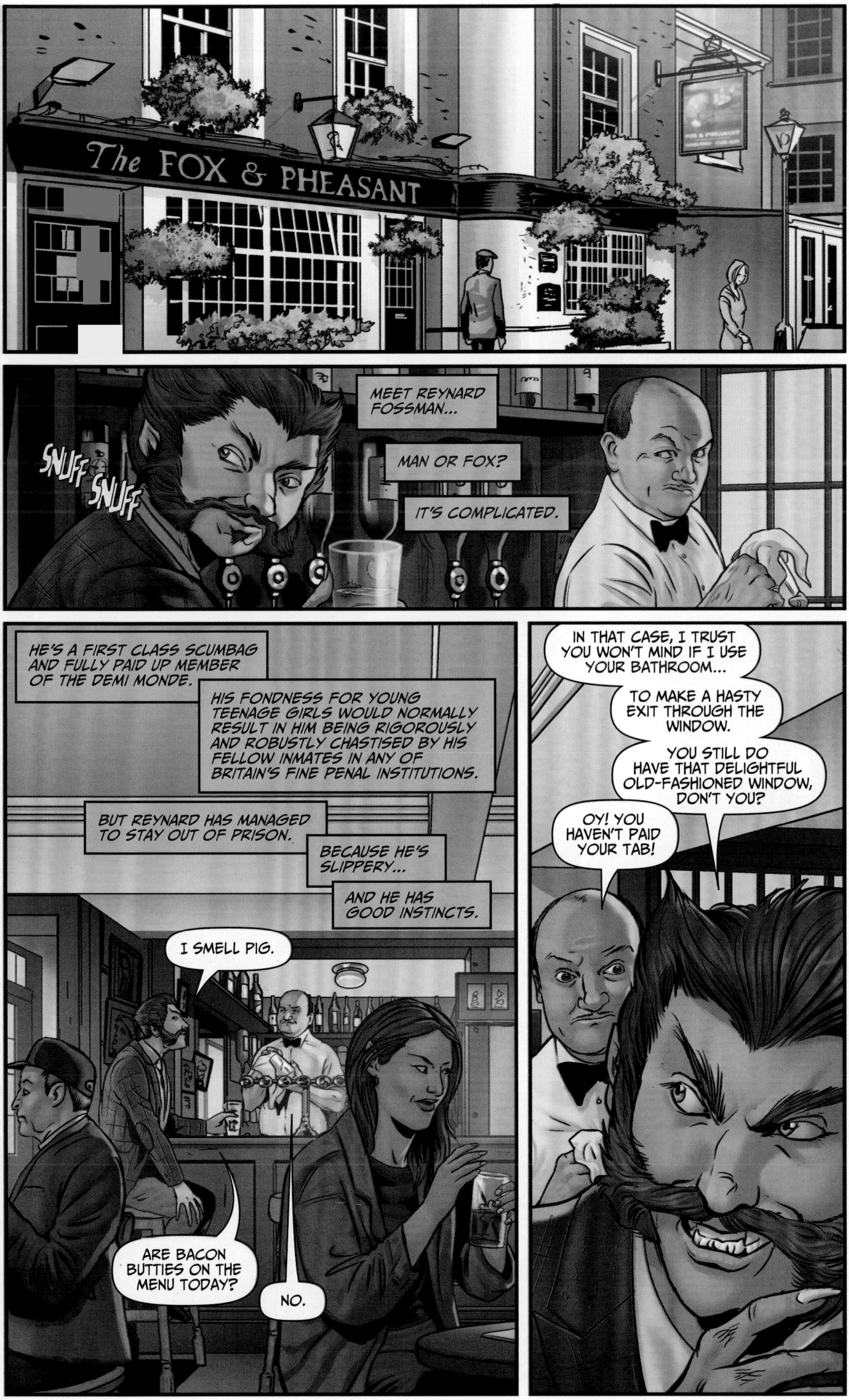

The FOX & PHEASANT
MEET REYNARD FOSSMAN...
MAN OR FOX?
IT'S COMPLICATED.
SNUFF SNUFF
HE'S A FIRST CLASS SCUMBAG AND FULLY PAID UP MEMBER OF THE DEMI MONDE.
HIS FONDNESS FOR YOUNG TEENAGE GIRLS WOULD NORMALLY RESULT IN HIM BEING RIGOROUSLY AND ROBUSTLY CHASTISED BY HIS FELLOW INMATES IN ANY OF BRITAIN'S FINE PENAL INSTITUTIONS.
BUT REYNARD HAS MANAGED TO STAY OUT OF PRISON.
BECAUSE HE'S SLIPPERY...
AND HE HAS GOOD INSTINCTS.
I SMELL PIG.
ARE BACON BUTTIES ON THE MENU TODAY?
NO.
IN THAT CASE, I TRUST YOU WON'T MIND IF I USE YOUR BATHROOM...
TO MAKE A HASTY EXIT THROUGH THE WINDOW.
YOU STILL DO HAVE THAT DELIGHTFUL OLD-FASHIONED WINDOW, DON'T YOU?
OY! YOU HAVEN'T PAID YOUR TAB!

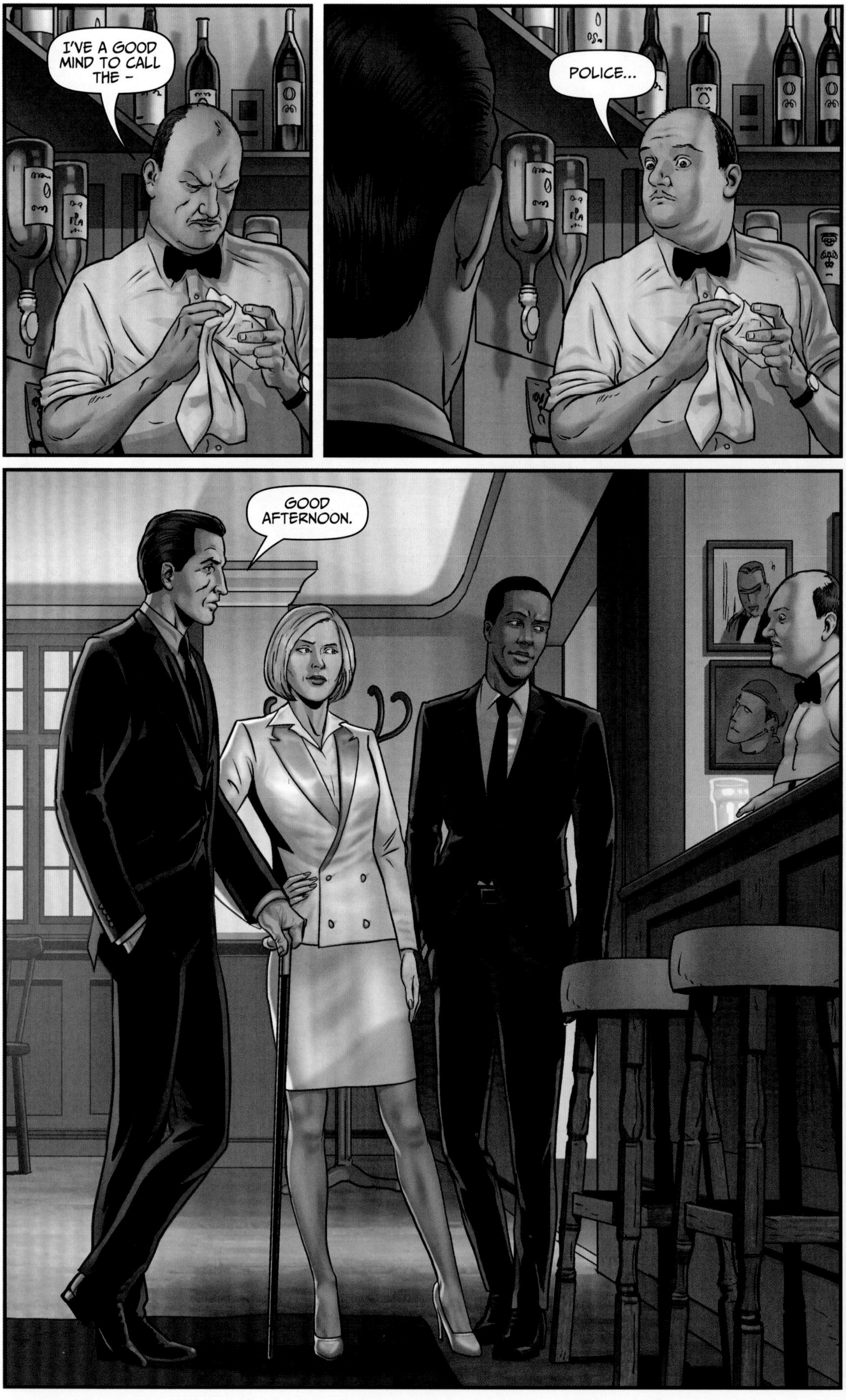
I'VE A GOOD MIND TO CALL THE -
POLICE...
GOOD AFTERNOON.

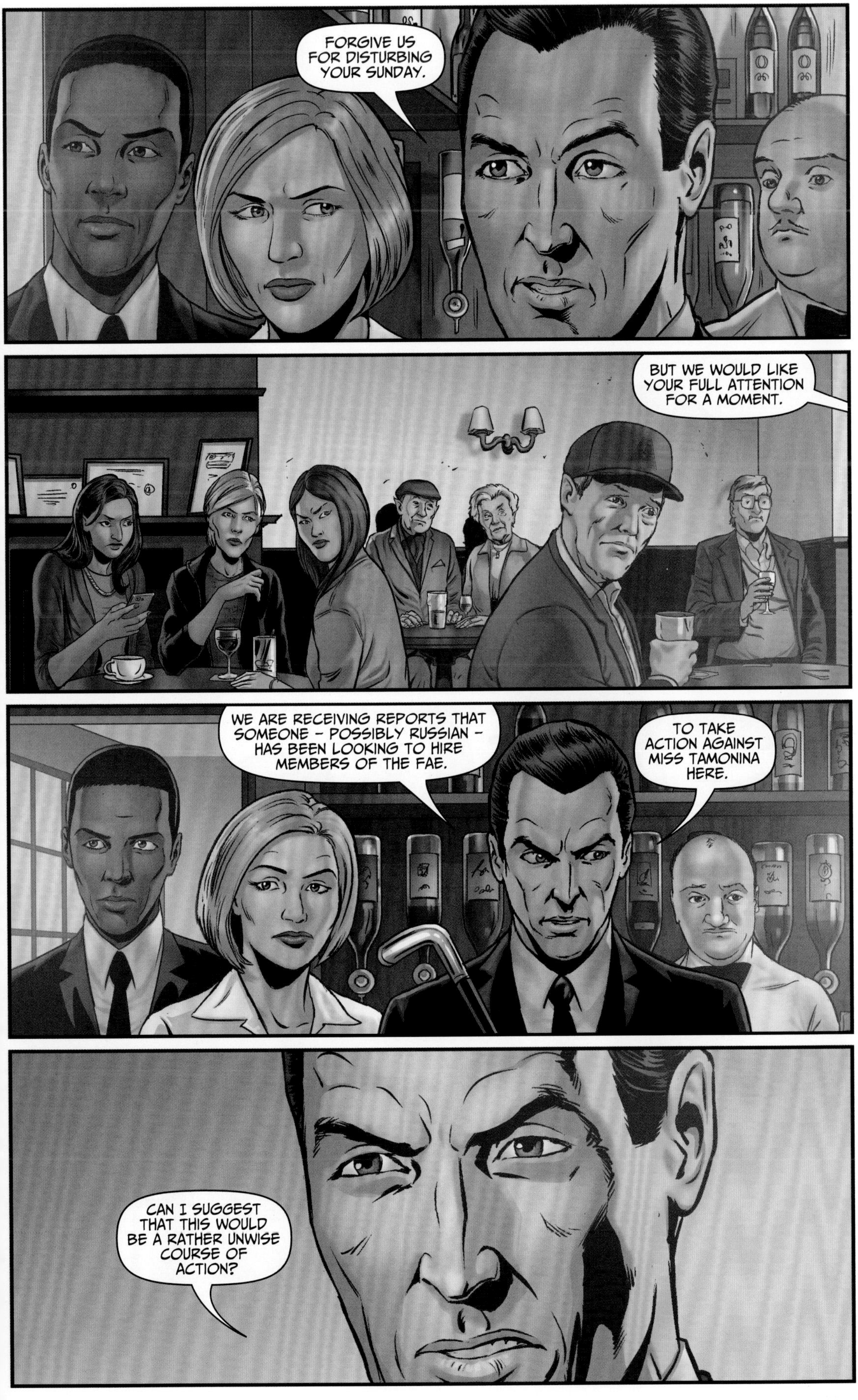
FORGIVE US FOR DISTURBING YOUR SUNDAY.
BUT WE WOULD LIKE YOUR FULL ATTENTION FOR A MOMENT.
WE ARE RECEIVING REPORTS THAT SOMEONE – POSSIBLY RUSSIAN – HAS BEEN LOOKING TO HIRE MEMBERS OF THE FAE.
TO TAKE ACTION AGAINST MISS TAMONINA HERE.
CAN I SUGGEST THAT THIS WOULD BE A RATHER UNWISE COURSE OF ACTION?

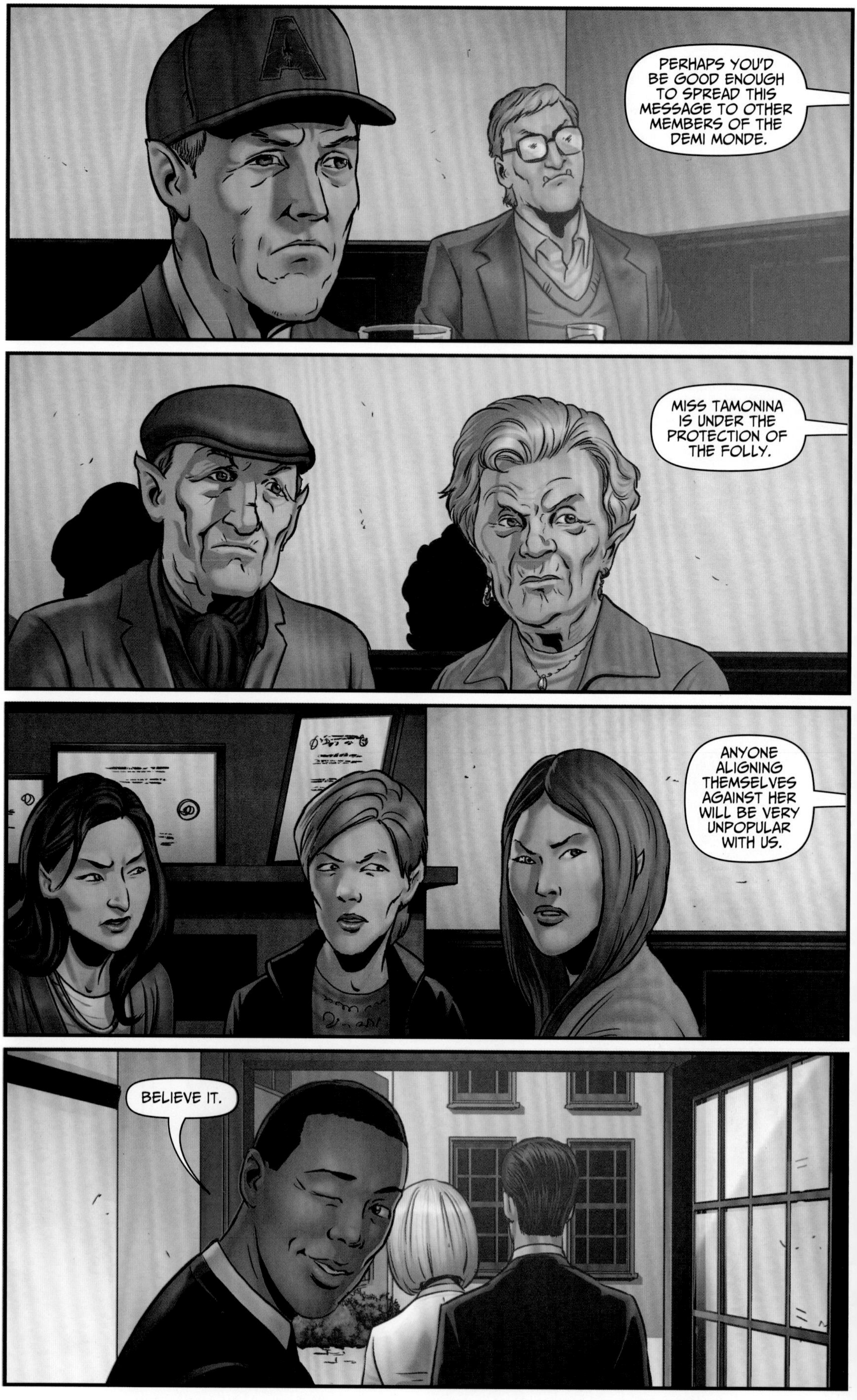
PERHAPS YOU'D BE GOOD ENOUGH TO SPREAD THIS MESSAGE TO OTHER MEMBERS OF THE DEMI MONDE.
MISS TAMONINA IS UNDER THE PROTECTION OF THE FOLLY.
ANYONE ALIGNING THEMSELVES AGAINST HER WILL BE VERY UNPOPULAR WITH US.
BELIEVE IT.

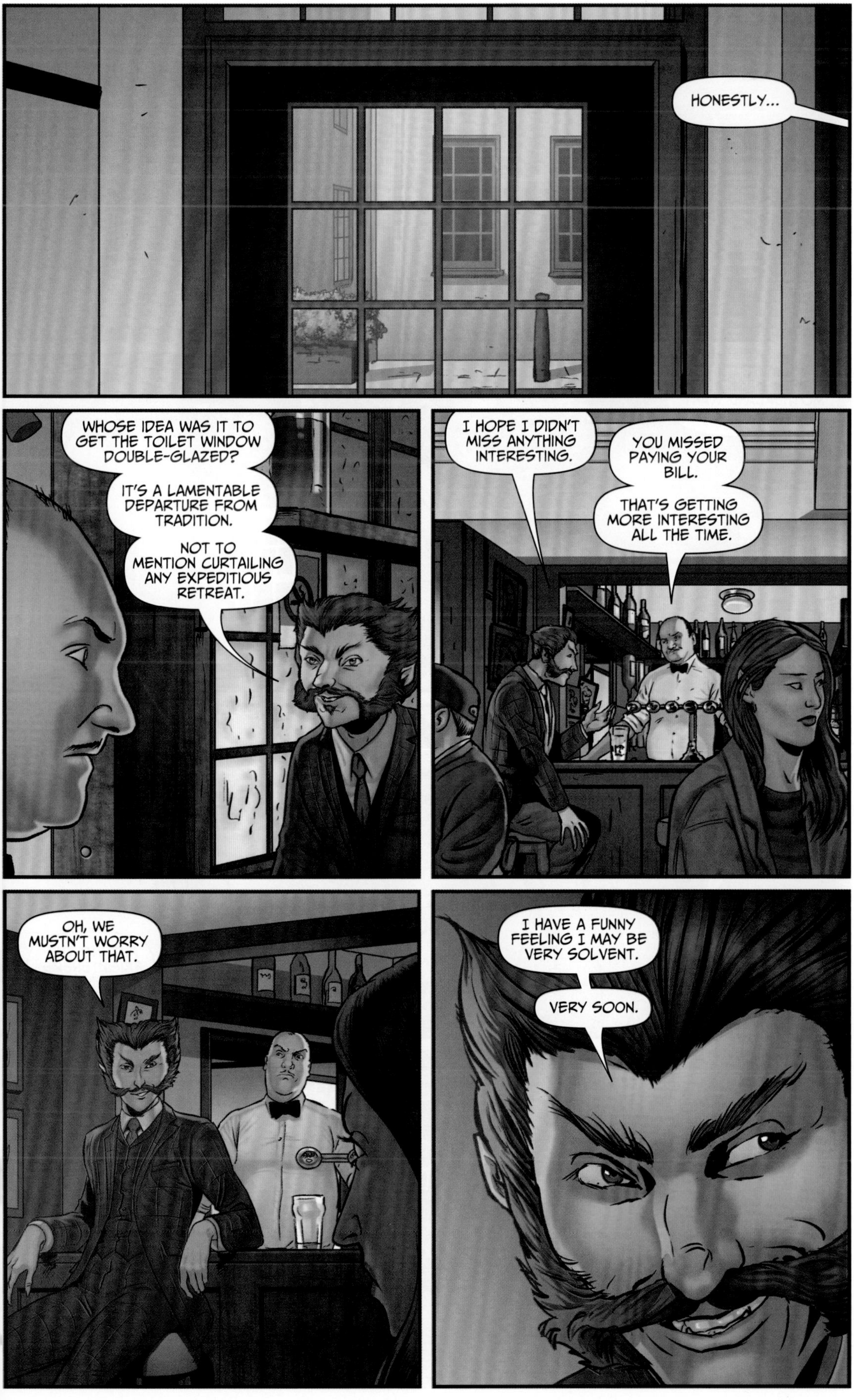
HONESTLY...
WHOSE IDEA WAS IT TO GET THE TOILET WINDOW DOUBLE-GLAZED?
IT'S A LAMENTABLE DEPARTURE FROM TRADITION.
NOT TO MENTION CURTAILING ANY EXPEDITIOUS RETREAT.
I HOPE I DIDN'T MISS ANYTHING INTERESTING.
YOU MISSED PAYING YOUR BILL.
THAT'S GETTING MORE INTERESTING ALL THE TIME.
OH, WE MUSTN'T WORRY ABOUT THAT.
I HAVE A FUNNY FEELING I MAY BE VERY SOLVENT.
VERY SOON.

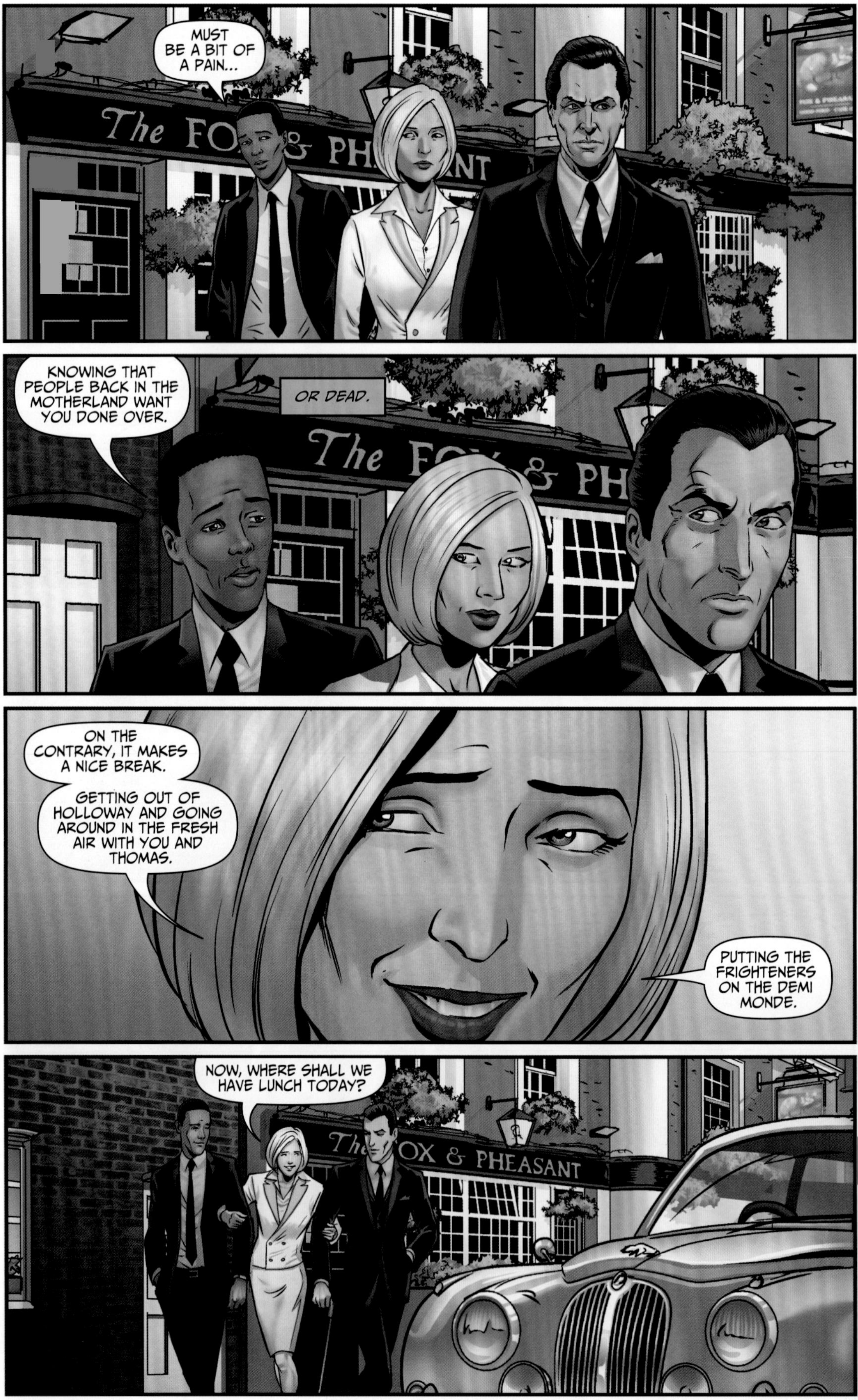
MUST BE A BIT OF A PAIN...
The FOX & PHEASANT
KNOWING THAT PEOPLE BACK IN THE MOTHERLAND WANT YOU DONE OVER.
OR DEAD.
ON THE CONTRARY, IT MAKES A NICE BREAK.
GETTING OUT OF HOLLOWAY AND GOING AROUND IN THE FRESH AIR WITH YOU AND THOMAS.
PUTTING THE FRIGHTENERS ON THE DEMI MONDE.
NOW, WHERE SHALL WE HAVE LUNCH TODAY?
The FOX & PHEASANT

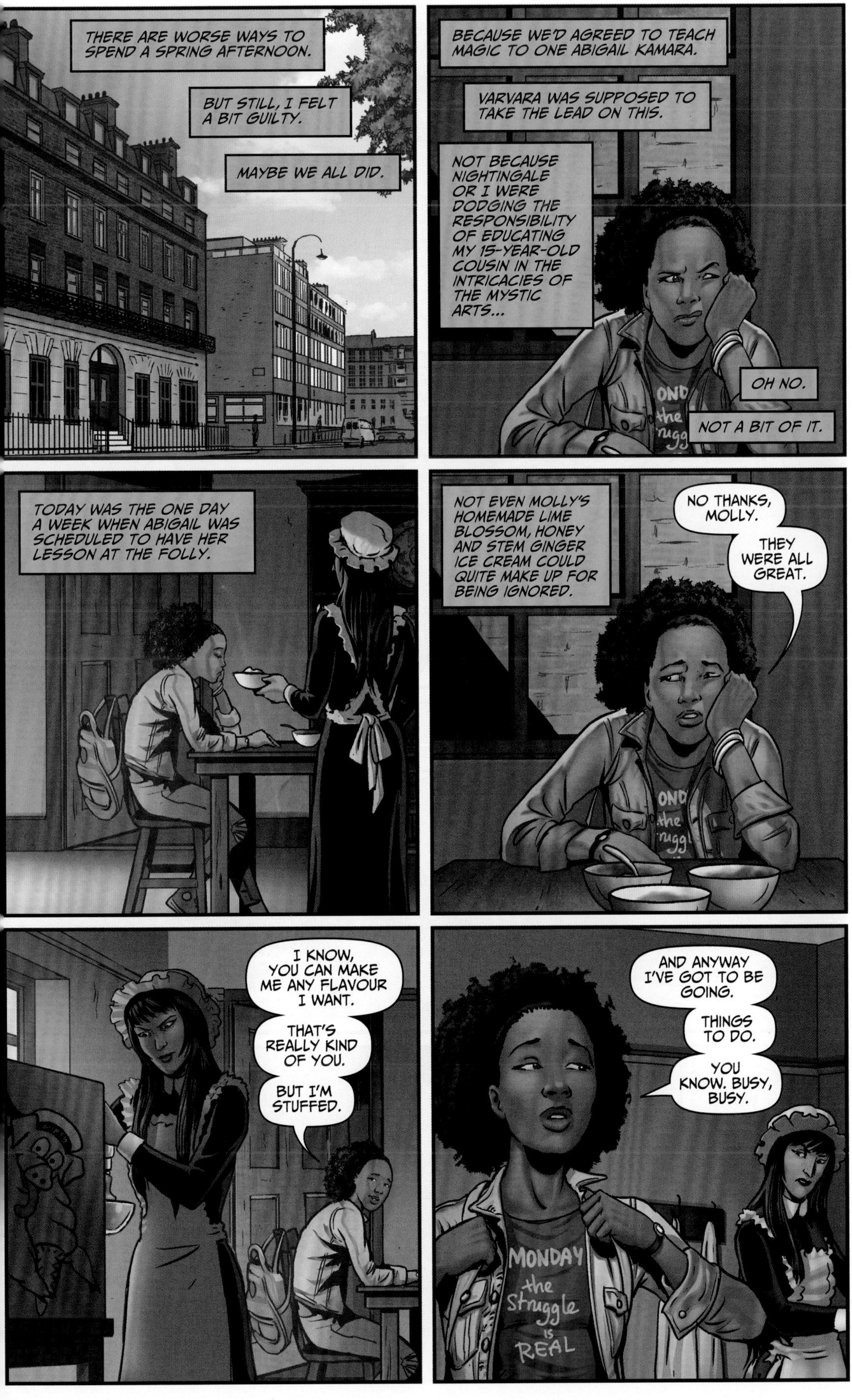
THERE ARE WORSE WAYS TO SPEND A SPRING AFTERNOON.
BUT STILL, I FELT A BIT GUILTY.
MAYBE WE ALL DID.
BECAUSE WE'D AGREED TO TEACH MAGIC TO ONE ABIGAIL KAMARA.
VARVARA WAS SUPPOSED TO TAKE THE LEAD ON THIS.
NOT BECAUSE NIGHTINGALE OR I WERE DODGING THE RESPONSIBILITY OF EDUCATING MY 15-YEAR-OLD COUSIN IN THE INTRICACIES OF THE MYSTIC ARTS...
OH NO.
NOT A BIT OF IT.
TODAY WAS THE ONE DAY A WEEK WHEN ABIGAIL WAS SCHEDULED TO HAVE HER LESSON AT THE FOLLY.
NOT EVEN MOLLY'S HOMEMADE LIME BLOSSOM, HONEY AND STEM GINGER ICE CREAM COULD QUITE MAKE UP FOR BEING IGNORED.
NO THANKS, MOLLY.
THEY WERE ALL GREAT.
I KNOW, YOU CAN MAKE ME ANY FLAVOUR I WANT.
THAT'S REALLY KIND OF YOU.
BUT I'M STUFFED.
AND ANYWAY I'VE GOT TO BE GOING.
THINGS TO DO.
YOU KNOW. BUSY, BUSY.
MONDAY the Struggle is REAL

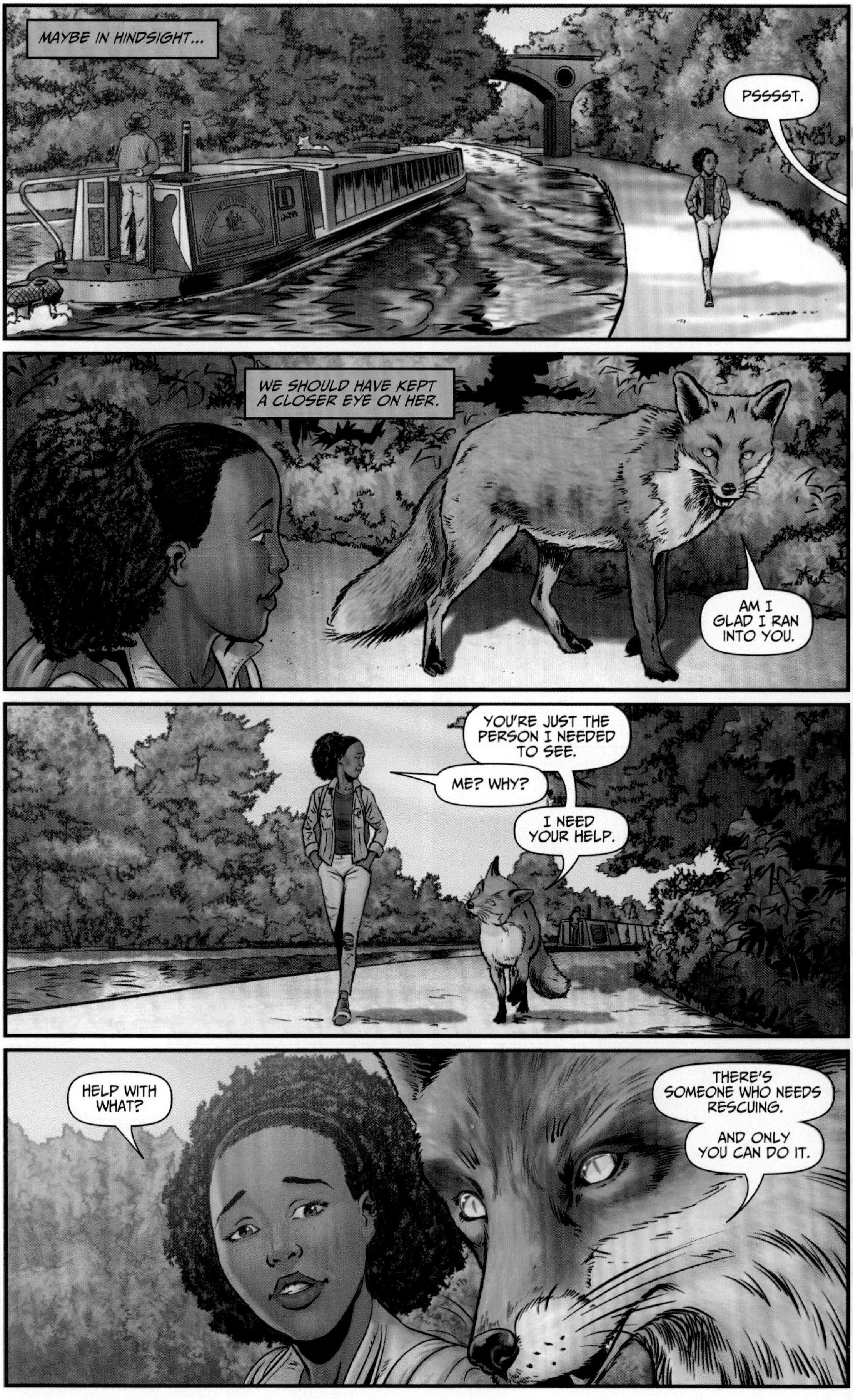
MAYBE IN HINDSIGHT...
PSSSST.
WE SHOULD HAVE KEPT A CLOSER EYE ON HER.
AM I GLAD I RAN INTO YOU.
YOU'RE JUST THE PERSON I NEEDED TO SEE.
ME? WHY?
I NEED YOUR HELP.
HELP WITH WHAT?
THERE'S SOMEONE WHO NEEDS RESCUING.
AND ONLY YOU CAN DO IT.

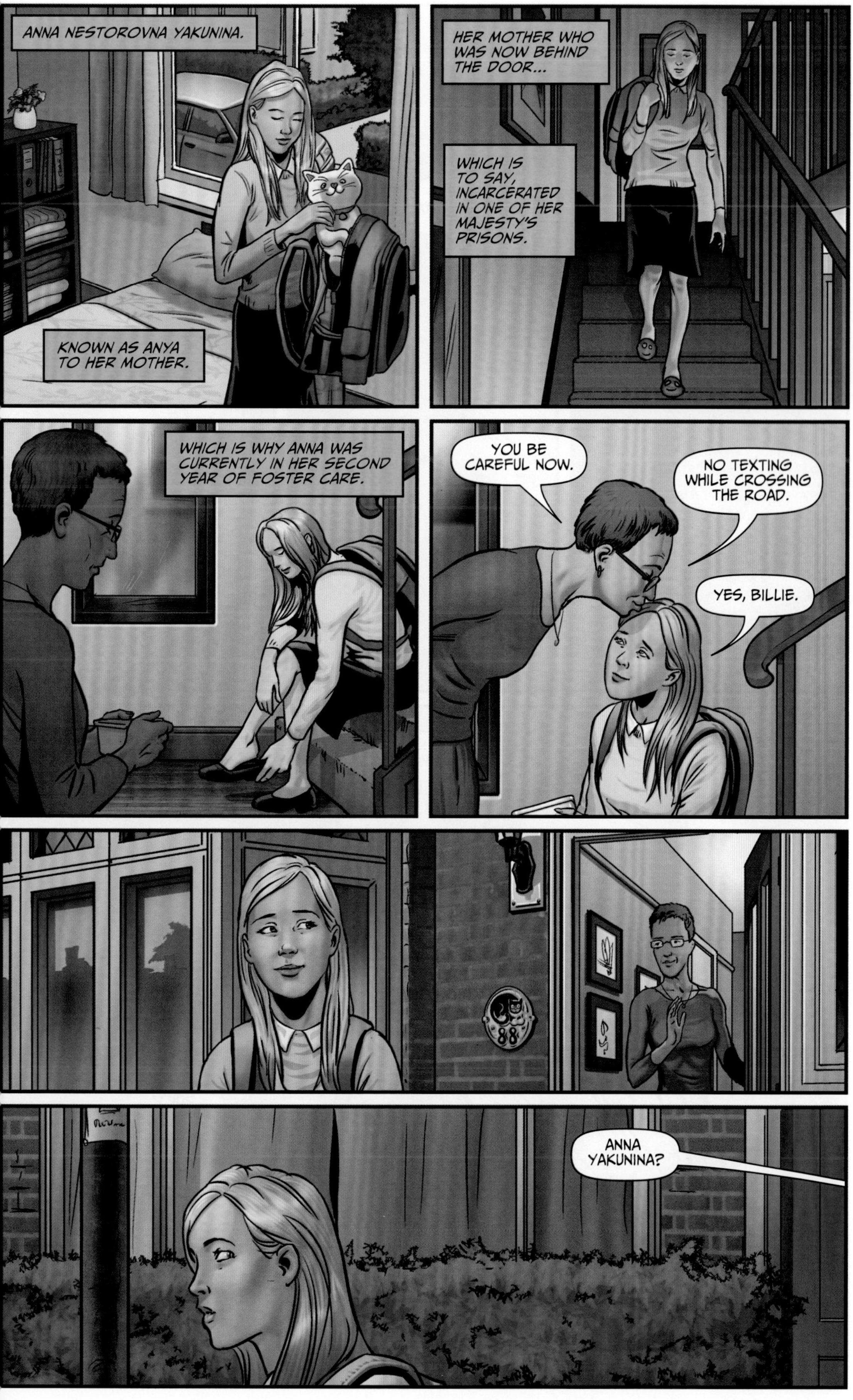
ANNA NESTOROVNA YAKUNINA.
KNOWN AS ANYA TO HER MOTHER.
HER MOTHER WHO WAS NOW BEHIND THE DOOR...
WHICH IS TO SAY, INCARCERATED IN ONE OF HER MAJESTY'S PRISONS.
WHICH IS WHY ANNA WAS CURRENTLY IN HER SECOND YEAR OF FOSTER CARE.
YOU BE CAREFUL NOW.
NO TEXTING WHILE CROSSING THE ROAD.
YES, BILLIE.
88
ANNA YAKUNINA?

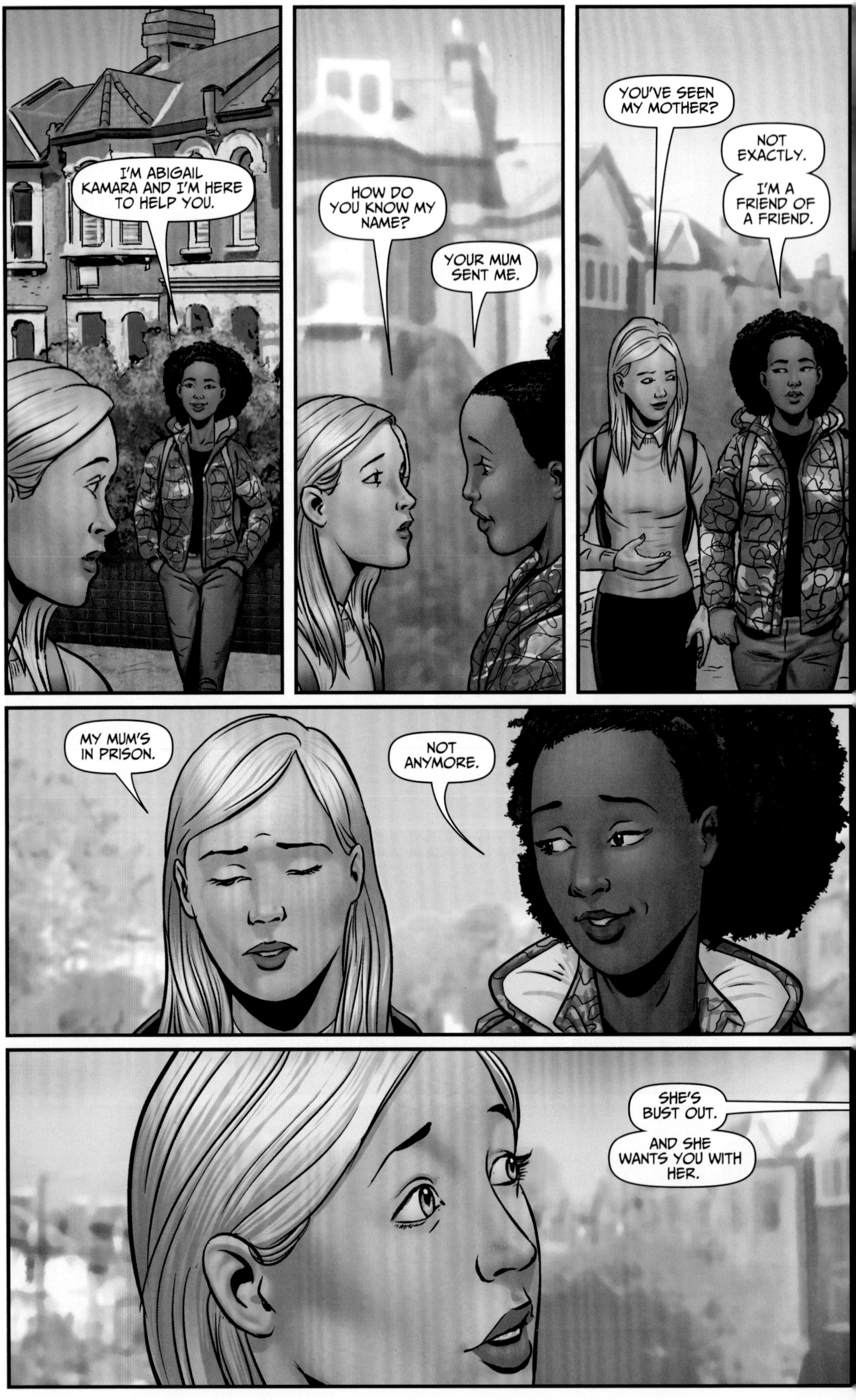
I'M ABIGAIL KAMARA AND I'M HERE TO HELP YOU.
HOW DO YOU KNOW MY NAME?
YOUR MUM SENT ME.
YOU'VE SEEN MY MOTHER?
NOT EXACTLY.
I'M A FRIEND OF A FRIEND.
MY MUM'S IN PRISON.
NOT ANYMORE.
SHE'S BUST OUT.
AND SHE WANTS YOU WITH HER.

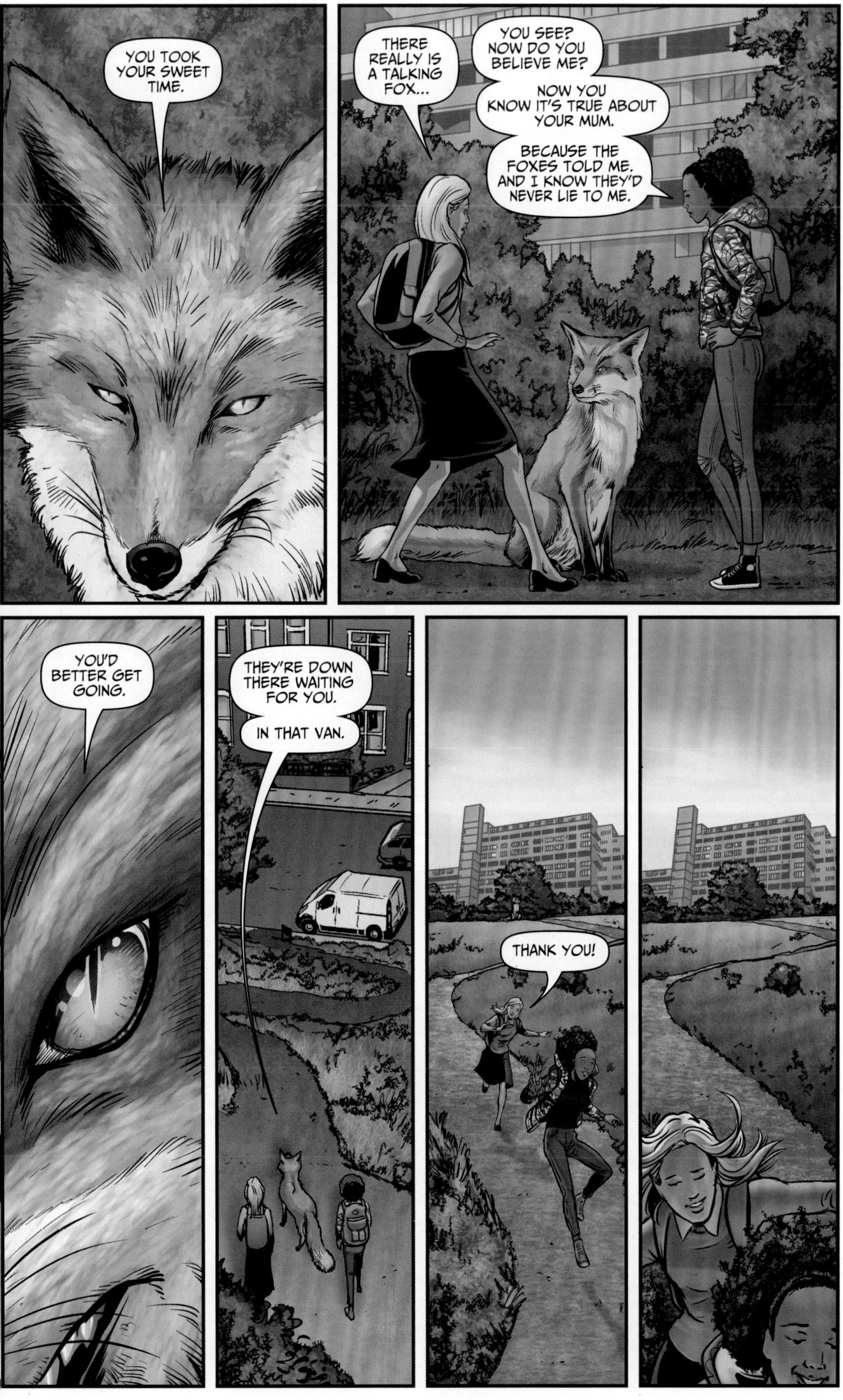
YOU TOOK YOUR SWEET TIME.
THERE REALLY IS A TALKING FOX...
YOU SEE? NOW DO YOU BELIEVE ME?
NOW YOU KNOW IT'S TRUE ABOUT YOUR MUM.
BECAUSE THE FOXES TOLD ME. AND I KNOW THEY'D NEVER LIE TO ME.
YOU'D BETTER GET GOING.
THEY'RE DOWN THERE WAITING FOR YOU.
IN THAT VAN.
THANK YOU!

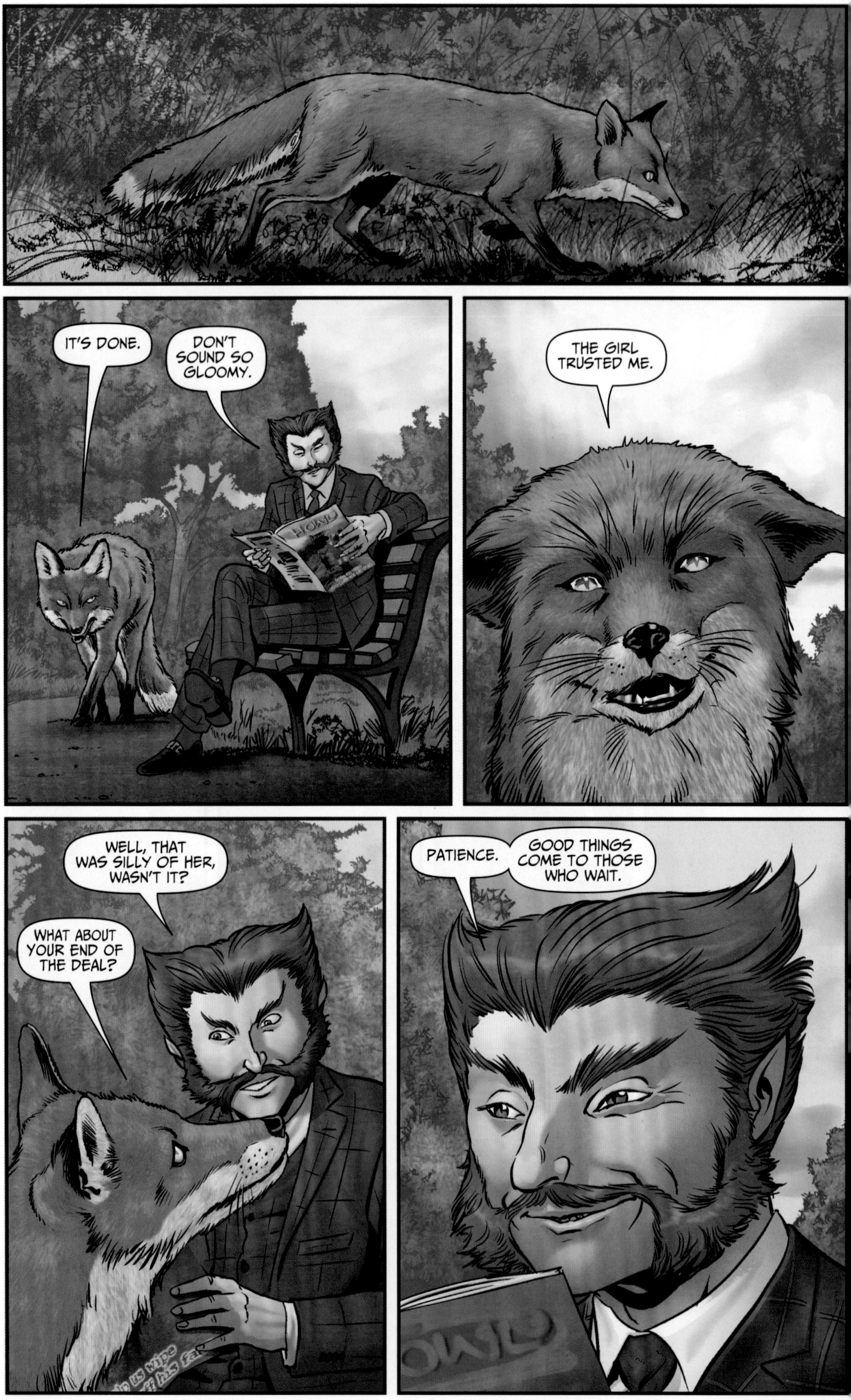
IT'S DONE.
DON'T SOUND SO GLOOMY.
THE GIRL TRUSTED ME.
WELL, THAT WAS SILLY OF HER, WASN'T IT?
WHAT ABOUT YOUR END OF THE DEAL?
PATIENCE.
GOOD THINGS COME TO THOSE WHO WAIT.

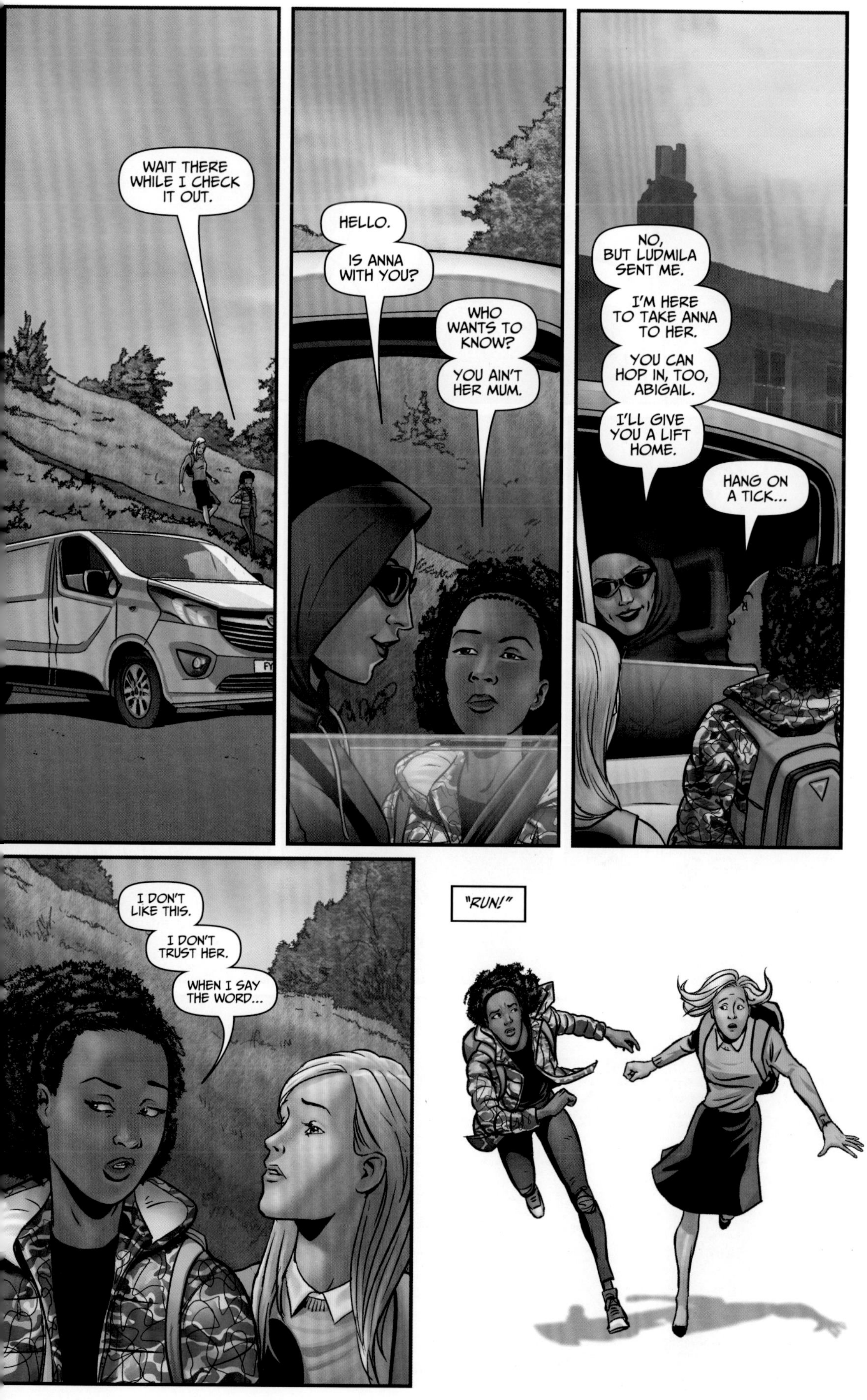
WAIT THERE WHILE I CHECK IT OUT.
HELLO.
IS ANNA WITH YOU?
WHO WANTS TO KNOW?
YOU AIN'T HER MUM.
NO, BUT LUDMILA SENT ME.
I'M HERE TO TAKE ANNA TO HER.
YOU CAN HOP IN, TOO, ABIGAIL.
I'LL GIVE YOU A LIFT HOME.
HANG ON A TICK...
I DON'T LIKE THIS.
I DON'T TRUST HER.
WHEN I SAY THE WORD...
"RUN!"

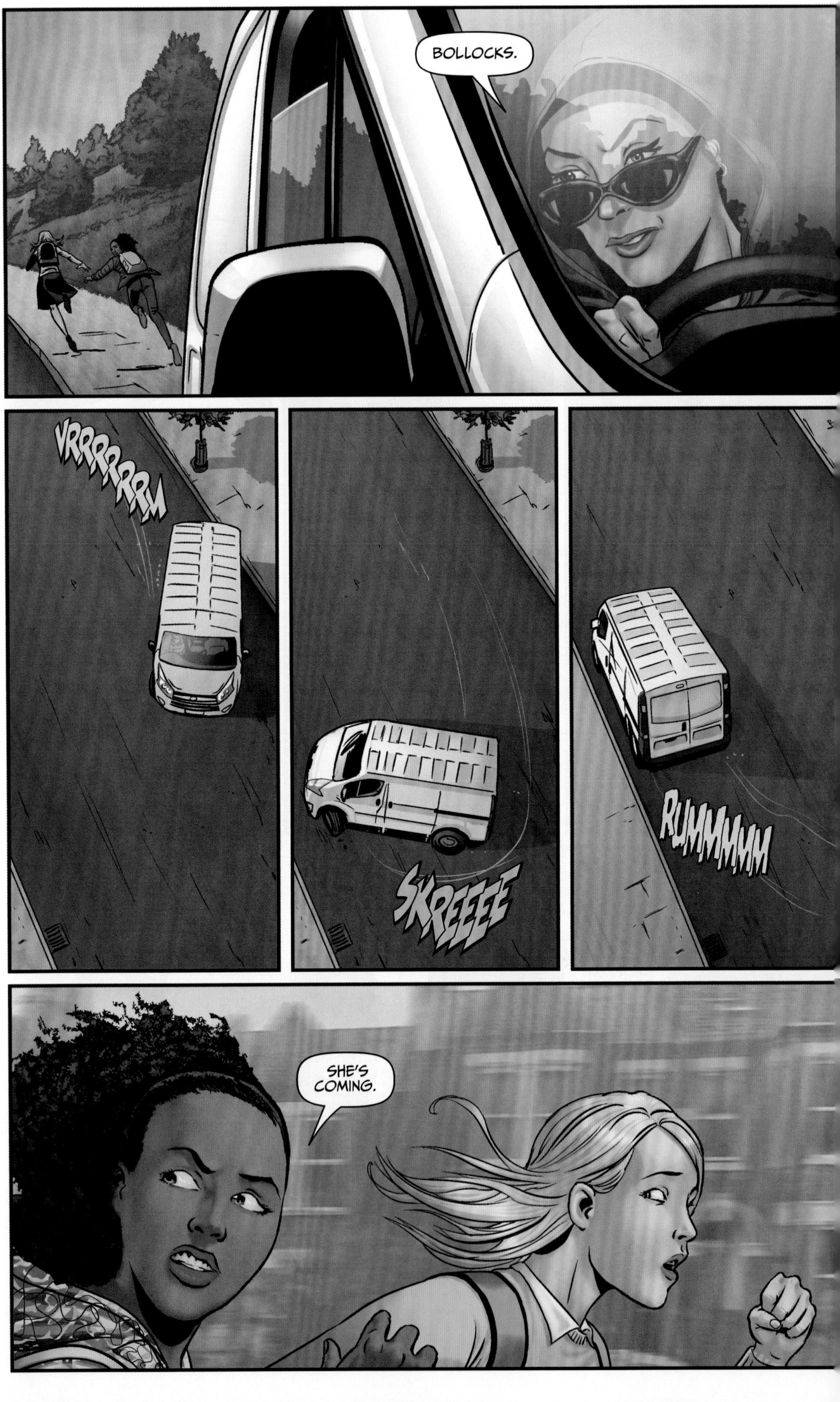
BOLLOCKS.
VRRRRRRRM
SKREEEEE
RUMMMMM
SHE'S COMING.

IN HERE!

WAIT...

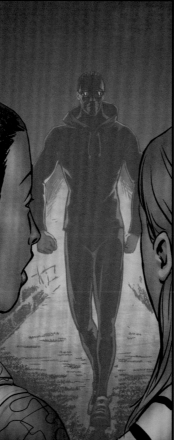

HEY GIRLS. GOOD TO SEE YOU.

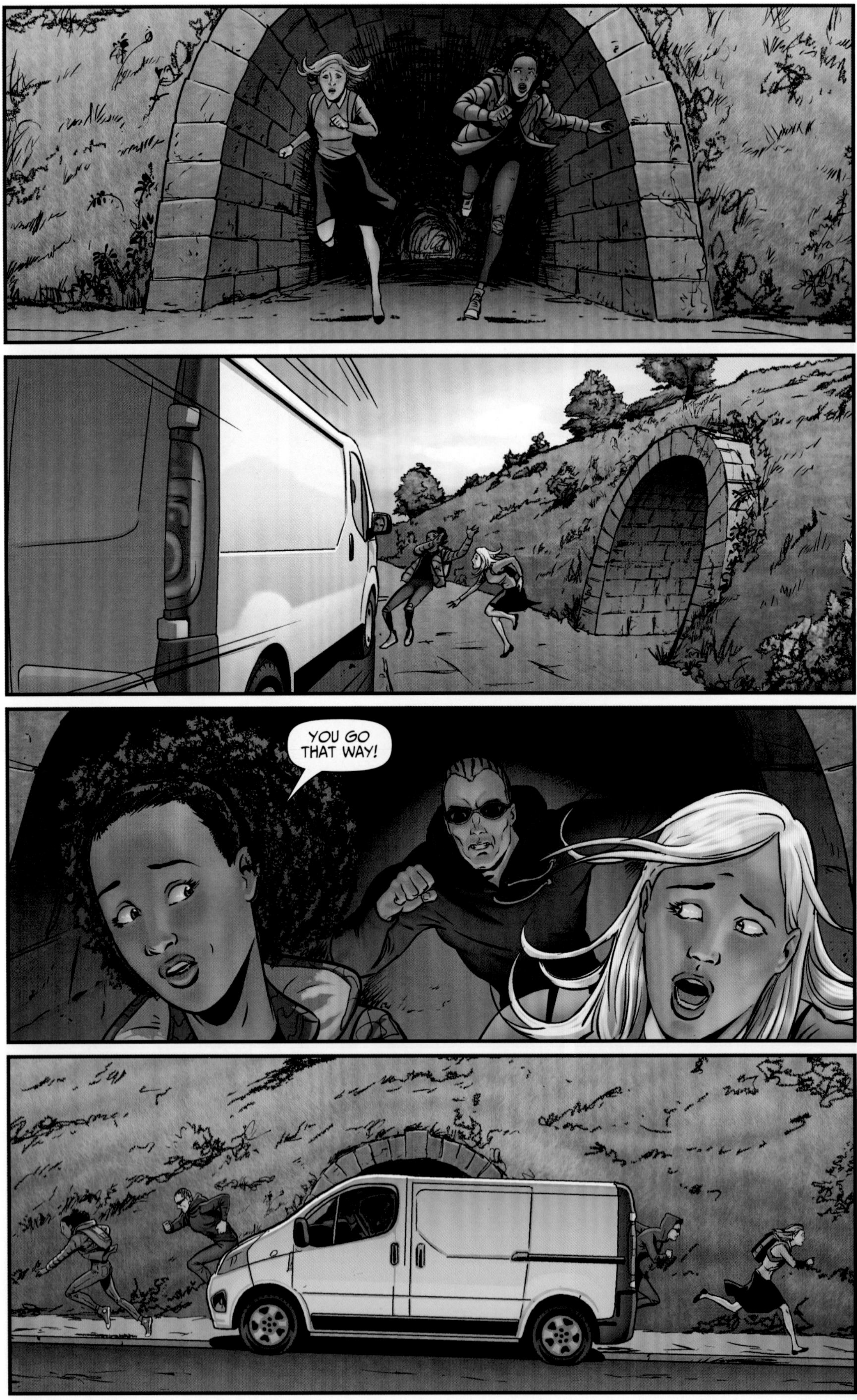
YOU GO THAT WAY!

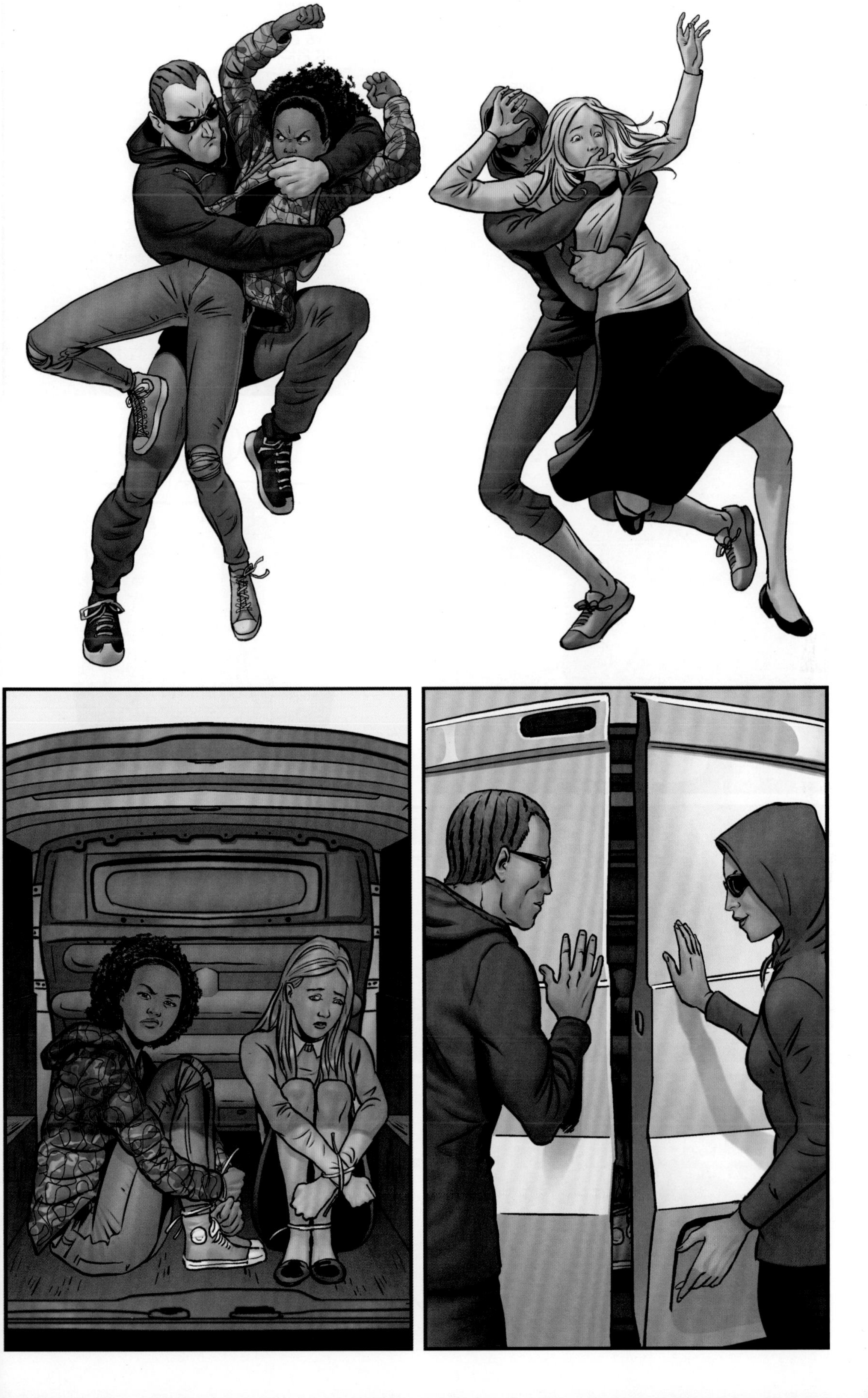

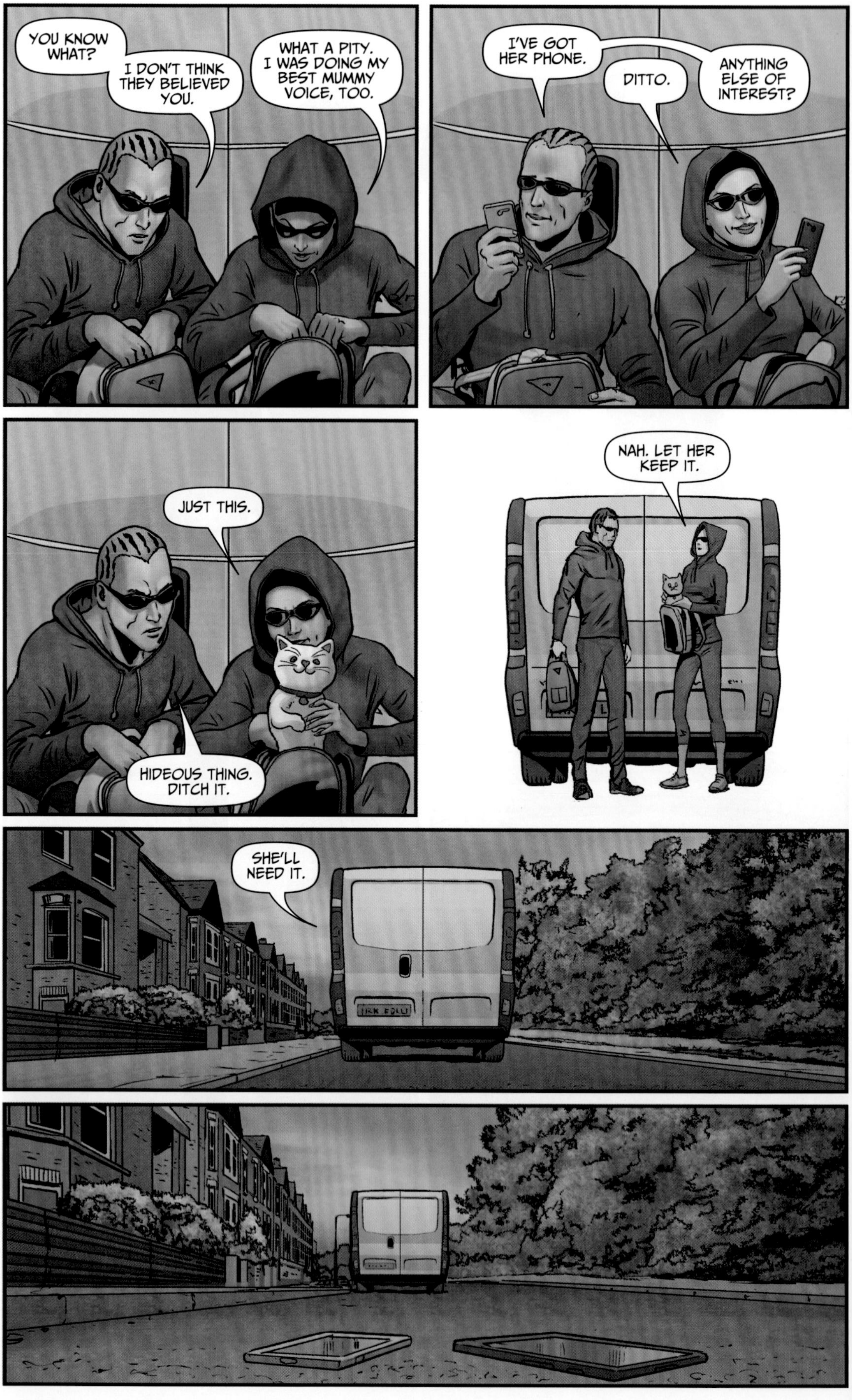
YOU KNOW WHAT?
I DON'T THINK THEY BELIEVED YOU.
WHAT A PITY. I WAS DOING MY BEST MUMMY VOICE, TOO.
I'VE GOT HER PHONE.
DITTO.
ANYTHING ELSE OF INTEREST?
JUST THIS.
HIDEOUS THING. DITCH IT.
NAH. LET HER KEEP IT.
SHE'LL NEED IT.

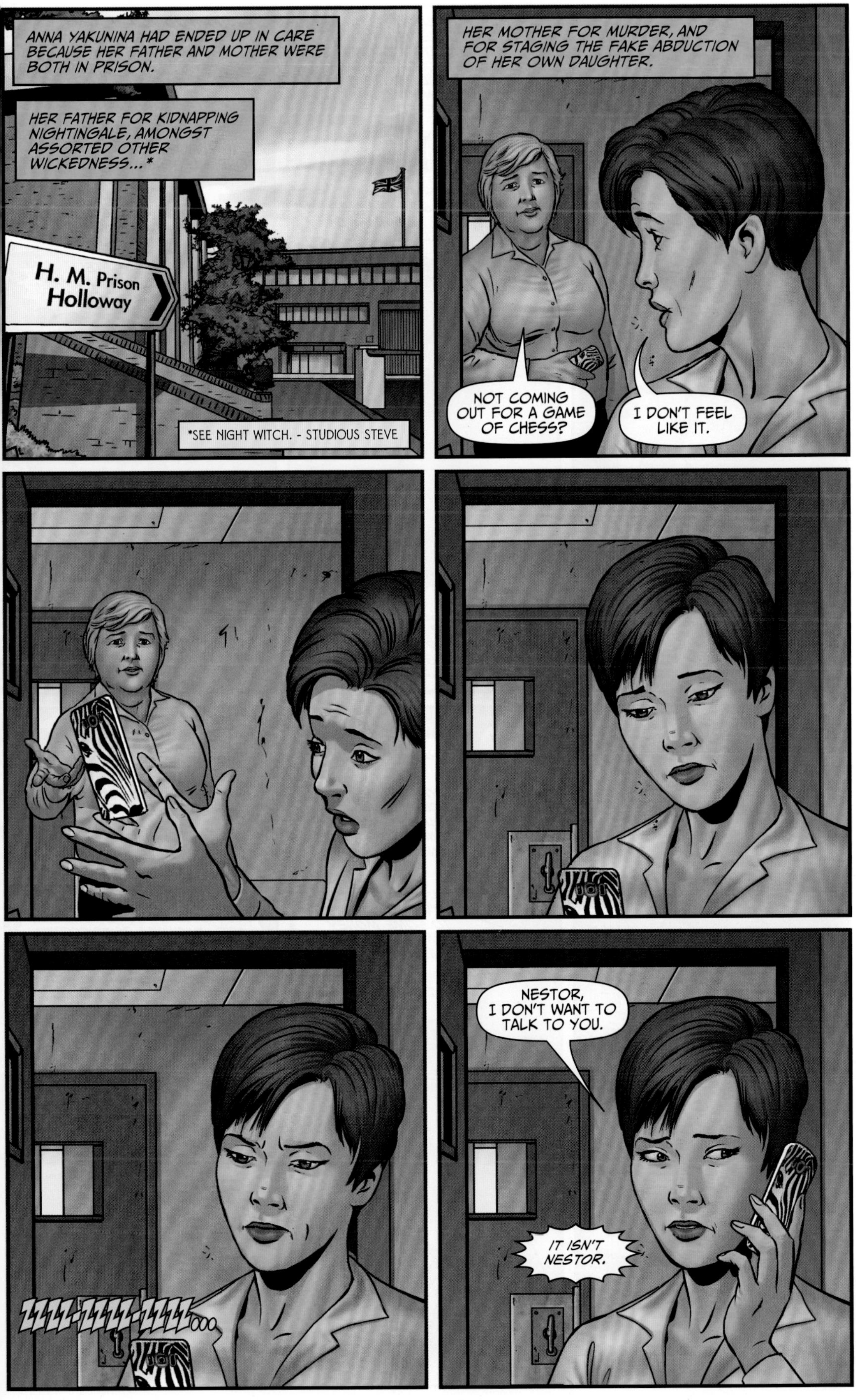
ANNA YAKUNINA HAD ENDED UP IN CARE BECAUSE HER FATHER AND MOTHER WERE BOTH IN PRISON.
HER FATHER FOR KIDNAPPING NIGHTINGALE, AMONGST ASSORTED OTHER WICKEDNESS...*
H. M. Prison Holloway
*SEE NIGHT WITCH. - STUDIOUS STEVE
HER MOTHER FOR MURDER, AND FOR STAGING THE FAKE ABDUCTION OF HER OWN DAUGHTER.
NOT COMING OUT FOR A GAME OF CHESS?
I DON'T FEEL LIKE IT.
ZZZZ-ZZZZ-ZZZZ...
NESTOR, I DON'T WANT TO TALK TO YOU.
IT ISN'T NESTOR.

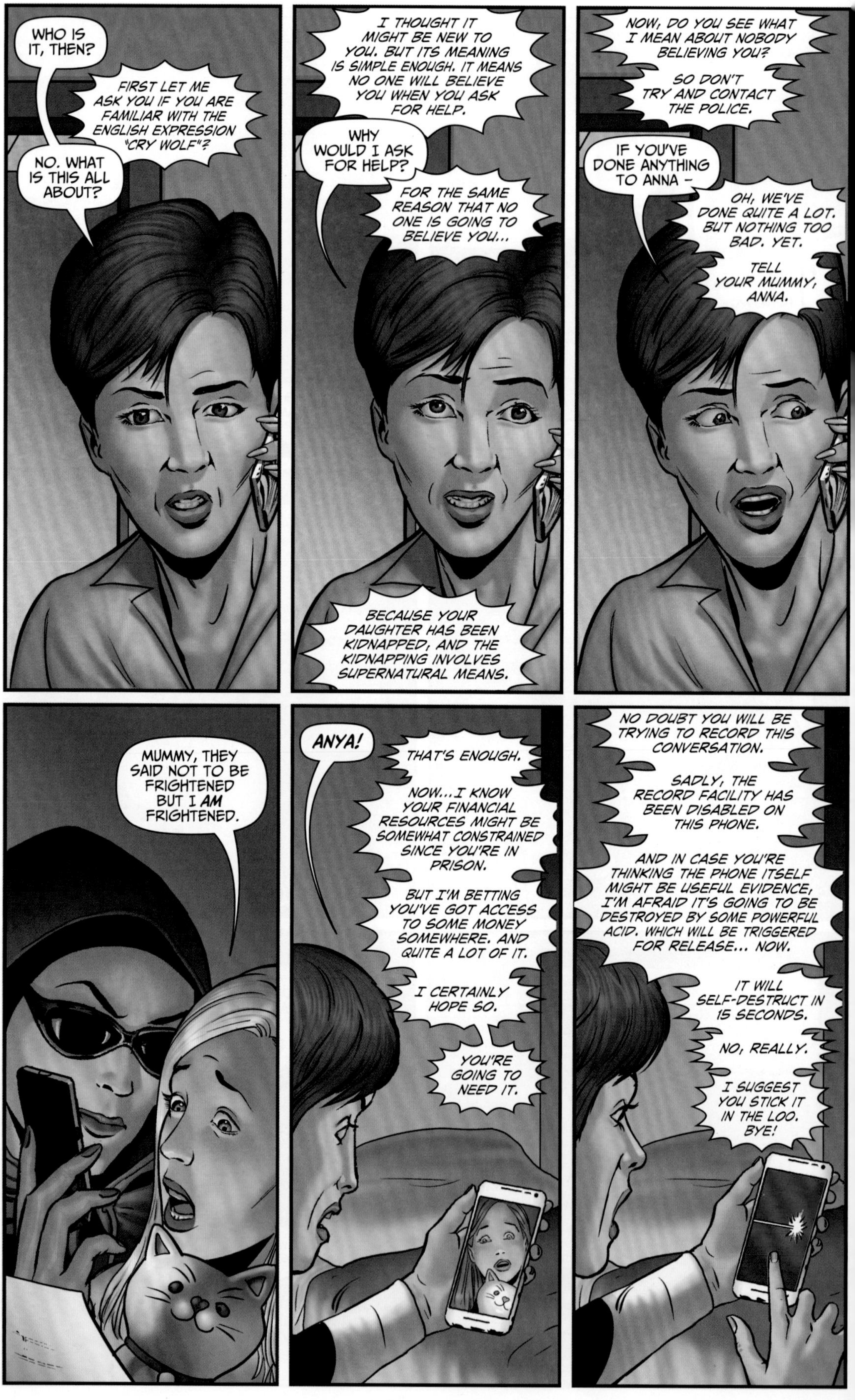
WHO IS IT, THEN?
FIRST LET ME ASK YOU IF YOU ARE FAMILIAR WITH THE ENGLISH EXPRESSION "CRY WOLF"?
NO. WHAT IS THIS ALL ABOUT?
I THOUGHT IT MIGHT BE NEW TO YOU. BUT ITS MEANING IS SIMPLE ENOUGH. IT MEANS NO ONE WILL BELIEVE YOU WHEN YOU ASK FOR HELP.
WHY WOULD I ASK FOR HELP?
FOR THE SAME REASON THAT NO ONE IS GOING TO BELIEVE YOU...
BECAUSE YOUR DAUGHTER HAS BEEN KIDNAPPED; AND THE KIDNAPPING INVOLVES SUPERNATURAL MEANS.
NOW, DO YOU SEE WHAT I MEAN ABOUT NOBODY BELIEVING YOU?
SO DON'T TRY AND CONTACT THE POLICE.
IF YOU'VE DONE ANYTHING TO ANNA –
OH, WE'VE DONE QUITE A LOT. BUT NOTHING TOO BAD. YET.
TELL YOUR MUMMY, ANNA.
MUMMY, THEY SAID NOT TO BE FRIGHTENED BUT I AM FRIGHTENED.
ANYA!
THAT'S ENOUGH.
NOW...I KNOW YOUR FINANCIAL RESOURCES MIGHT BE SOMEWHAT CONSTRAINED SINCE YOU'RE IN PRISON.
BUT I'M BETTING YOU'VE GOT ACCESS TO SOME MONEY SOMEWHERE. AND QUITE A LOT OF IT.
I CERTAINLY HOPE SO.
YOU'RE GOING TO NEED IT.
NO DOUBT YOU WILL BE TRYING TO RECORD THIS CONVERSATION.
SADLY, THE RECORD FACILITY HAS BEEN DISABLED ON THIS PHONE.
AND IN CASE YOU'RE THINKING THE PHONE ITSELF MIGHT BE USEFUL EVIDENCE, I'M AFRAID IT'S GOING TO BE DESTROYED BY SOME POWERFUL ACID. WHICH WILL BE TRIGGERED FOR RELEASE... NOW.
IT WILL SELF-DESTRUCT IN 15 SECONDS.
NO, REALLY.
I SUGGEST YOU STICK IT IN THE LOO. BYE!

SSSSSSSSSSSS

SPLISH

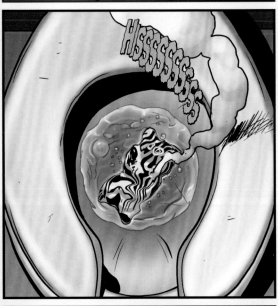

HISSSSSSSSS

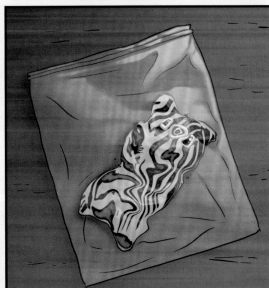

THEY TOLD ME NOT TO CONTACT THE POLICE.

THEY SAID IT WOULD DO NO GOOD. THEY USED THE ENGLISH EXPRESSION "CRY WOLF".

VERY APPROPRIATE. HERE'S ANOTHER GOOD OLD ENGLISH EXPRESSION...

"PULL THE OTHER ONE. IT'S GOT BELLS ON IT."

THAT MEANS YOU DON'T BELIEVE ME?

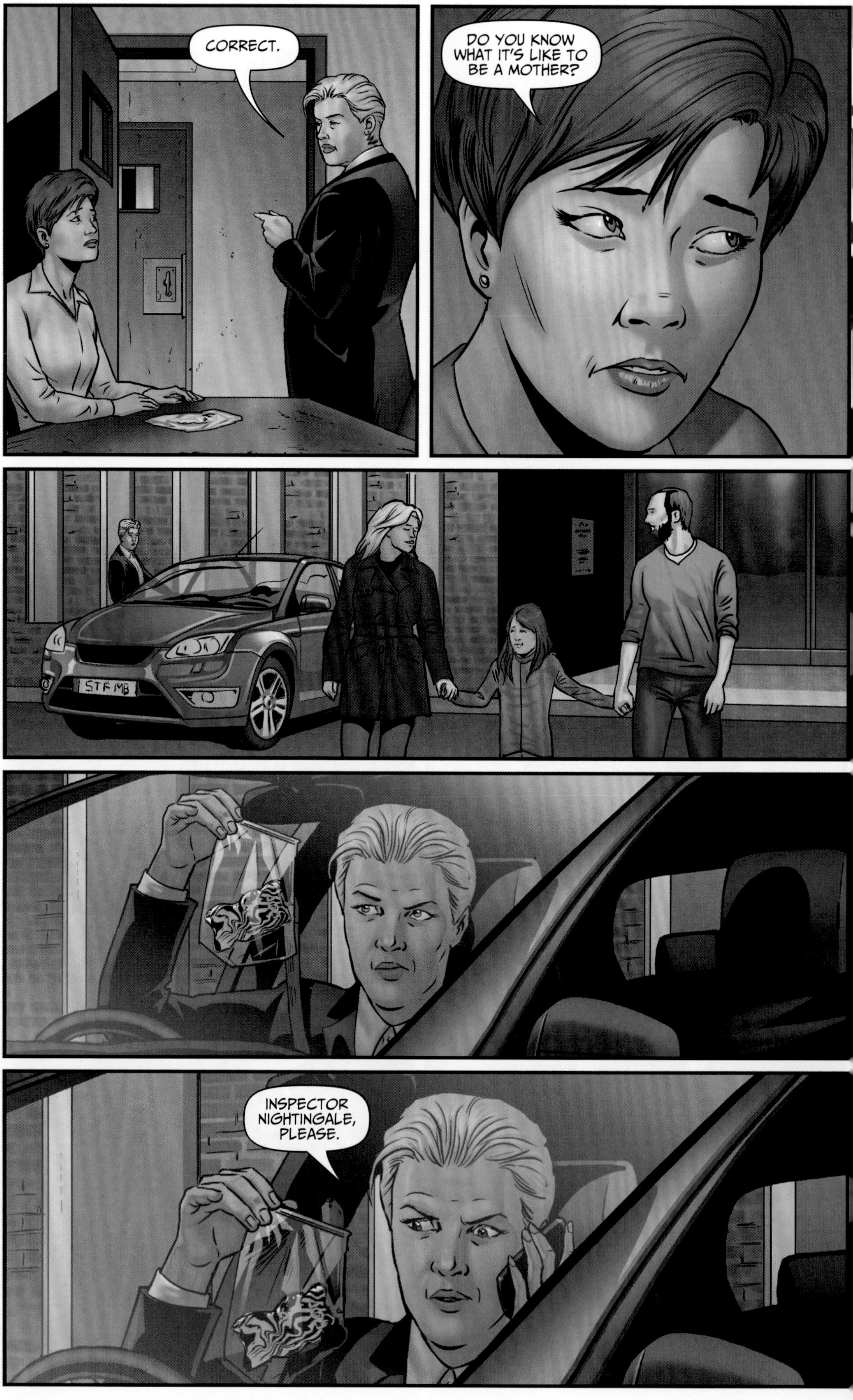
CORRECT.
DO YOU KNOW WHAT IT'S LIKE TO BE A MOTHER?
STF MB
INSPECTOR NIGHTINGALE, PLEASE.

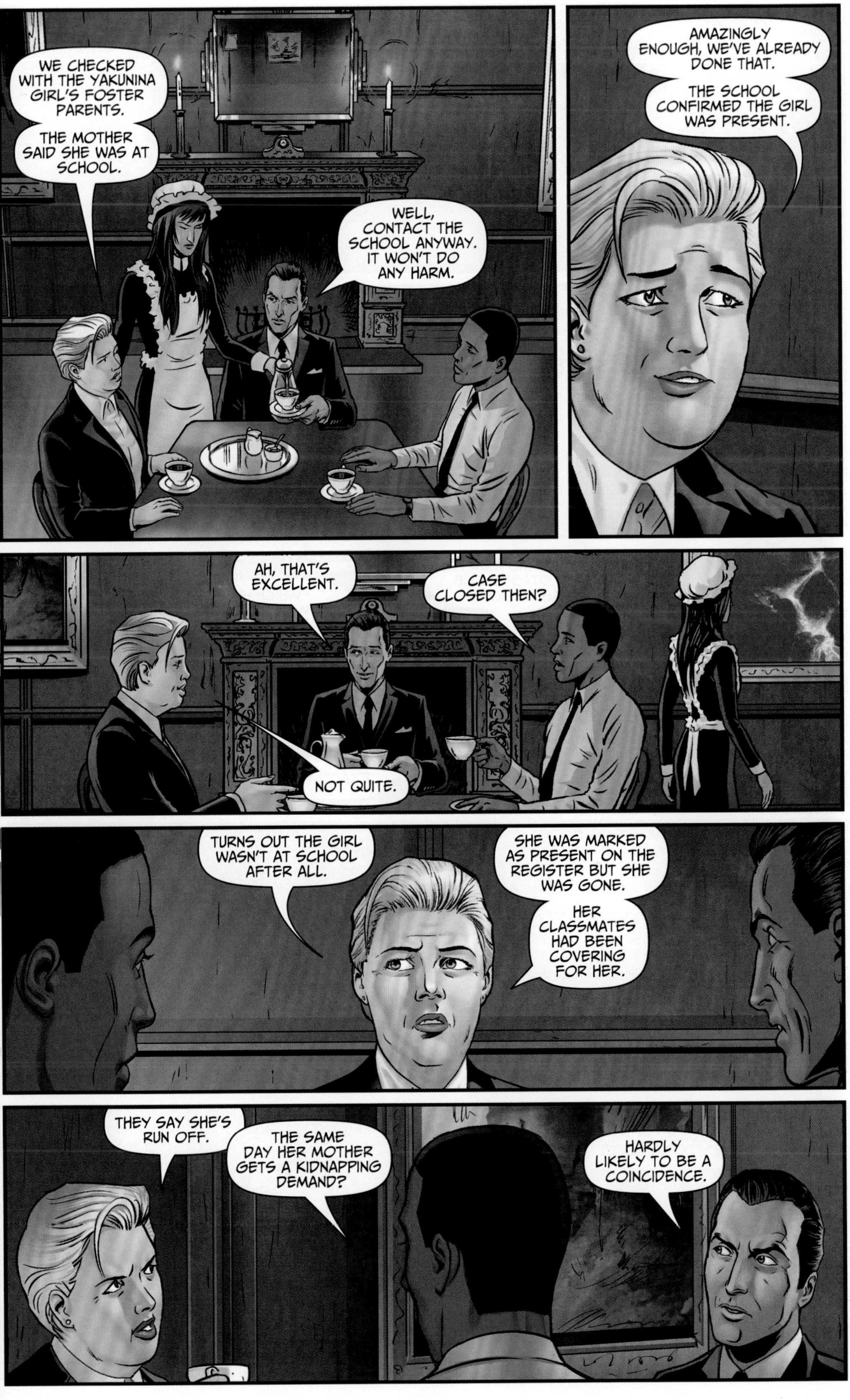
WE CHECKED WITH THE YAKUNINA GIRL'S FOSTER PARENTS.
THE MOTHER SAID SHE WAS AT SCHOOL.
WELL, CONTACT THE SCHOOL ANYWAY. IT WON'T DO ANY HARM.
AMAZINGLY ENOUGH, WE'VE ALREADY DONE THAT.
THE SCHOOL CONFIRMED THE GIRL WAS PRESENT.
AH, THAT'S EXCELLENT.
CASE CLOSED THEN?
NOT QUITE.
TURNS OUT THE GIRL WASN'T AT SCHOOL AFTER ALL.
SHE WAS MARKED AS PRESENT ON THE REGISTER BUT SHE WAS GONE.
HER CLASSMATES HAD BEEN COVERING FOR HER.
THEY SAY SHE'S RUN OFF.
THE SAME DAY HER MOTHER GETS A KIDNAPPING DEMAND?
HARDLY LIKELY TO BE A COINCIDENCE.

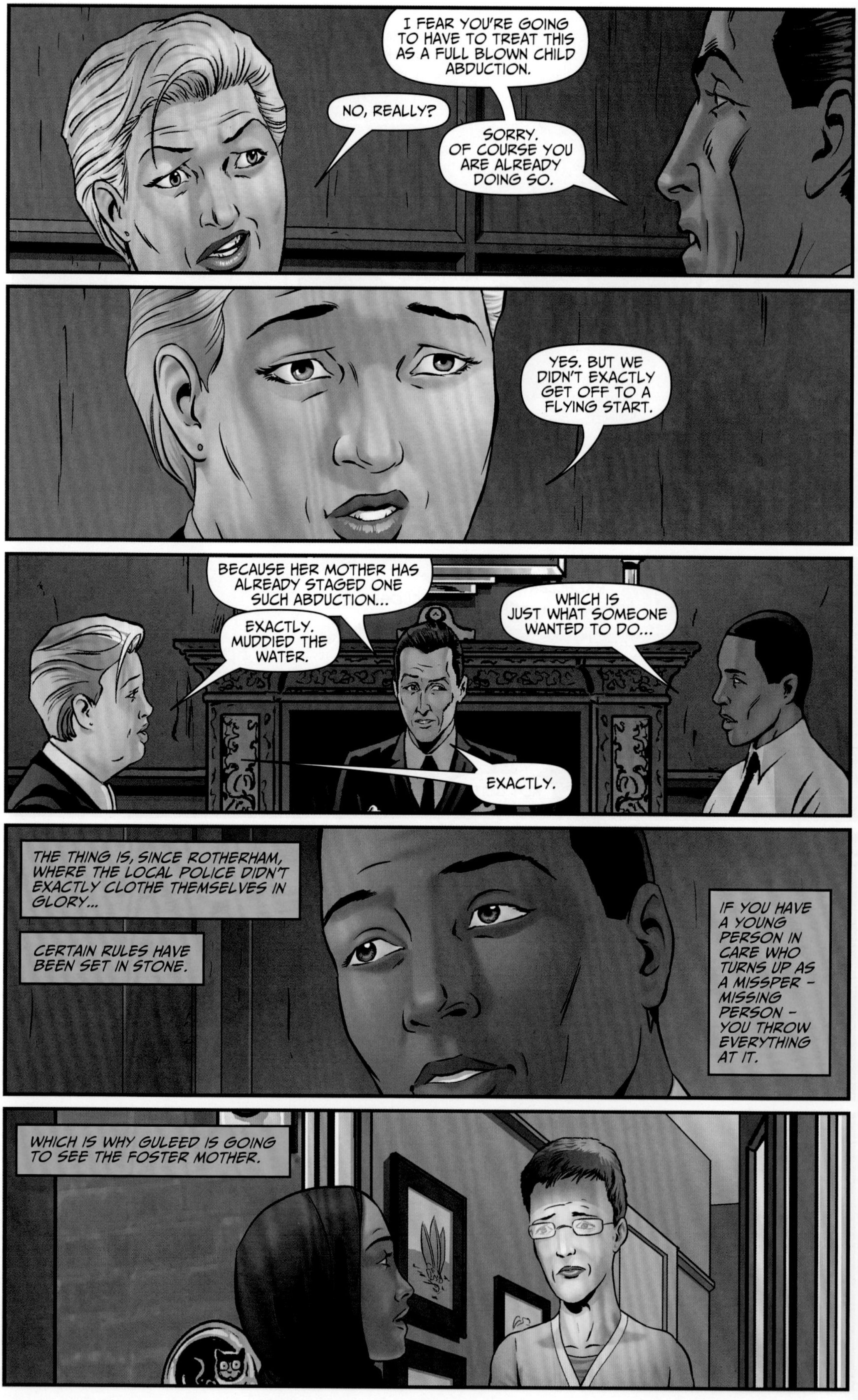
I FEAR YOU'RE GOING TO HAVE TO TREAT THIS AS A FULL BLOWN CHILD ABDUCTION.
NO, REALLY?
SORRY. OF COURSE YOU ARE ALREADY DOING SO.
YES. BUT WE DIDN'T EXACTLY GET OFF TO A FLYING START.
BECAUSE HER MOTHER HAS ALREADY STAGED ONE SUCH ABDUCTION...
EXACTLY. MUDDIED THE WATER.
WHICH IS JUST WHAT SOMEONE WANTED TO DO...
EXACTLY.
THE THING IS, SINCE ROTHERHAM, WHERE THE LOCAL POLICE DIDN'T EXACTLY CLOTHE THEMSELVES IN GLORY...
CERTAIN RULES HAVE BEEN SET IN STONE.
IF YOU HAVE A YOUNG PERSON IN CARE WHO TURNS UP AS A MISSPER - MISSING PERSON - YOU THROW EVERYTHING AT IT.
WHICH IS WHY GULEED IS GOING TO SEE THE FOSTER MOTHER.

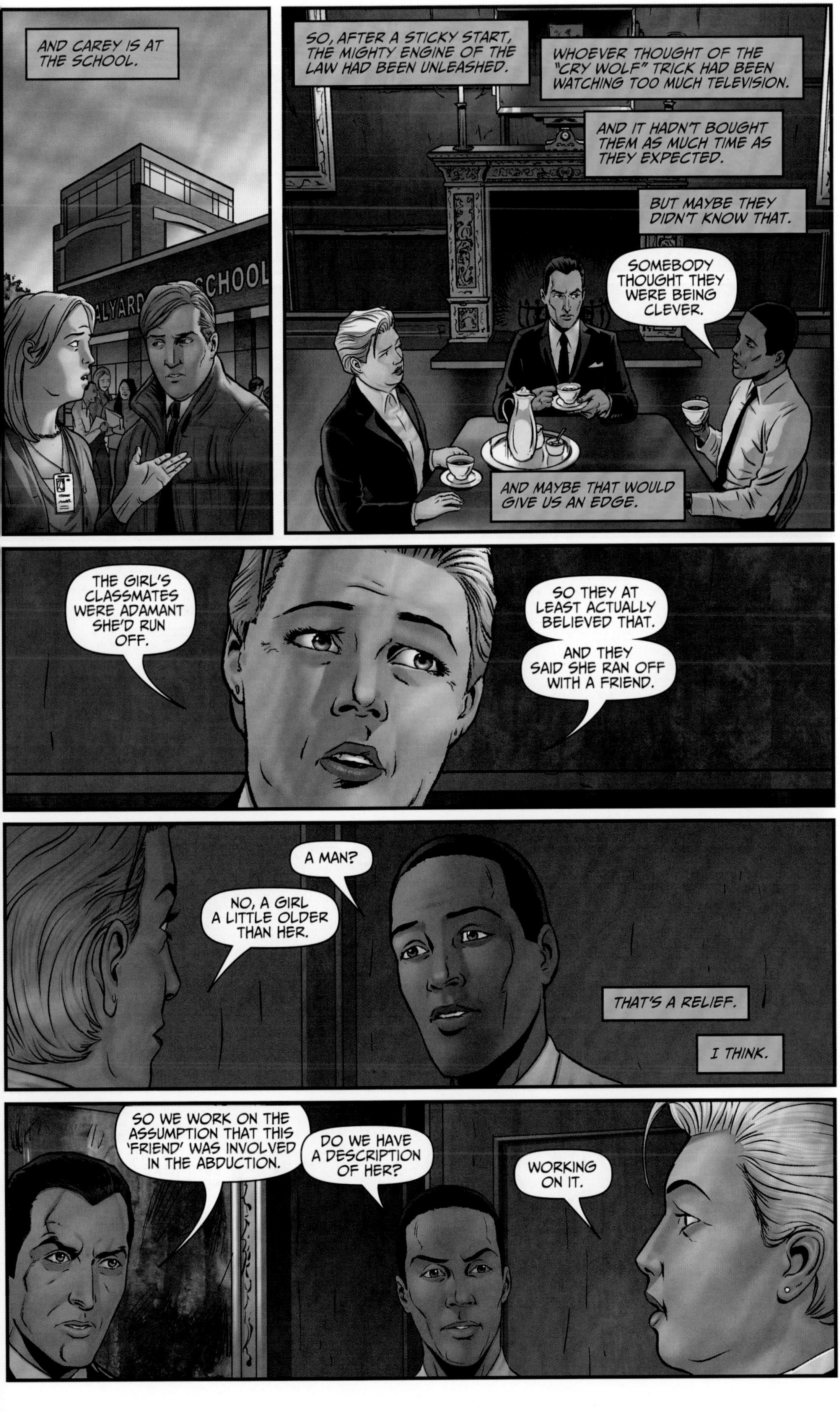
AND CAREY IS AT THE SCHOOL.
SCHOOL
SO, AFTER A STICKY START, THE MIGHTY ENGINE OF THE LAW HAD BEEN UNLEASHED.
WHOEVER THOUGHT OF THE "CRY WOLF" TRICK HAD BEEN WATCHING TOO MUCH TELEVISION.
AND IT HADN'T BOUGHT THEM AS MUCH TIME AS THEY EXPECTED.
BUT MAYBE THEY DIDN'T KNOW THAT.
SOMEBODY THOUGHT THEY WERE BEING CLEVER.
AND MAYBE THAT WOULD GIVE US AN EDGE.
THE GIRL'S CLASSMATES WERE ADAMANT SHE'D RUN OFF.
SO THEY AT LEAST ACTUALLY BELIEVED THAT.
AND THEY SAID SHE RAN OFF WITH A FRIEND.
A MAN?
NO, A GIRL A LITTLE OLDER THAN HER.
THAT'S A RELIEF.
I THINK.
SO WE WORK ON THE ASSUMPTION THAT THIS 'FRIEND' WAS INVOLVED IN THE ABDUCTION.
DO WE HAVE A DESCRIPTION OF HER?
WORKING ON IT.

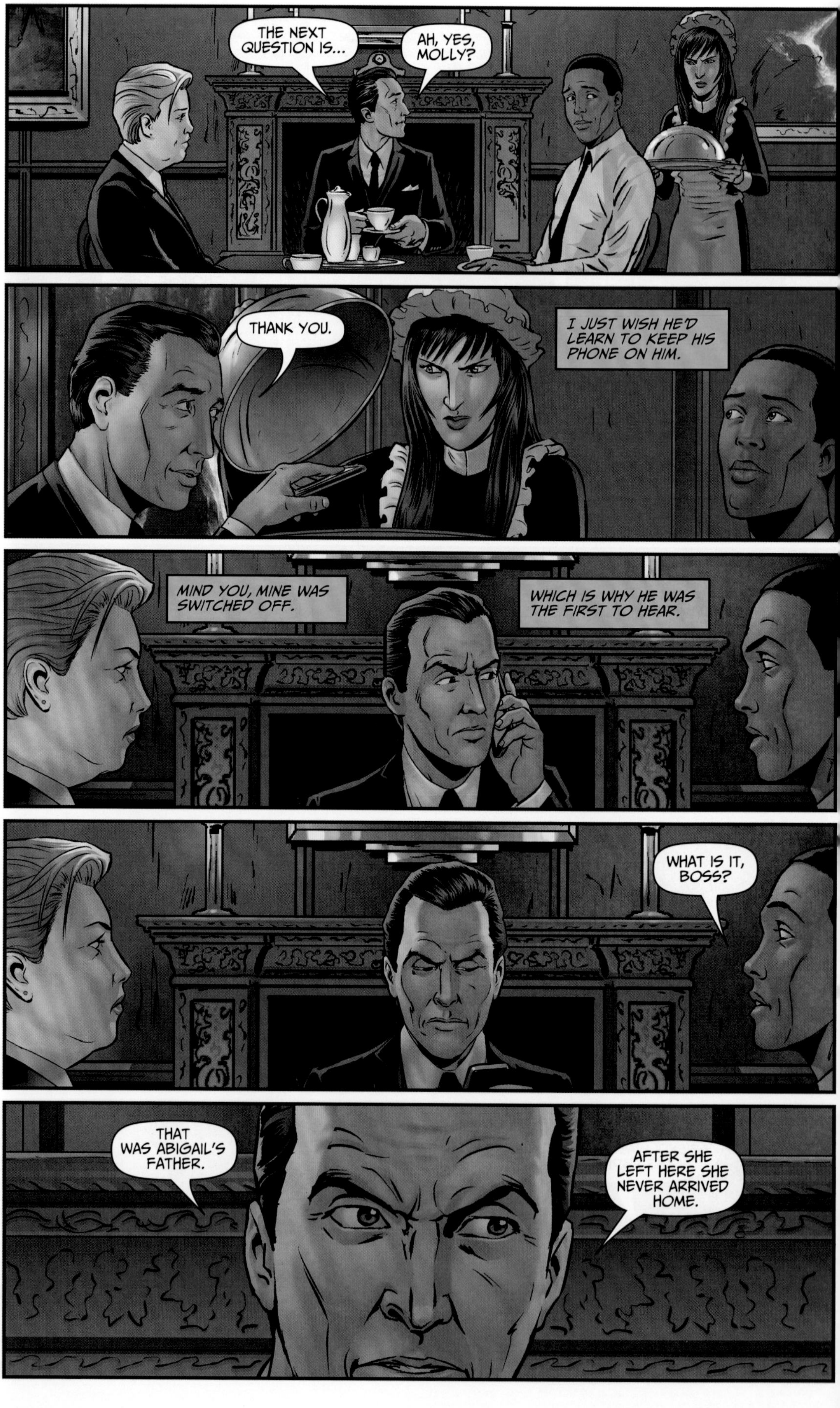
THE NEXT QUESTION IS...
AH, YES, MOLLY?
THANK YOU.
I JUST WISH HE'D LEARN TO KEEP HIS PHONE ON HIM.
MIND YOU, MINE WAS SWITCHED OFF.
WHICH IS WHY HE WAS THE FIRST TO HEAR.
WHAT IS IT, BOSS?
THAT WAS ABIGAIL'S FATHER.
AFTER SHE LEFT HERE SHE NEVER ARRIVED HOME.

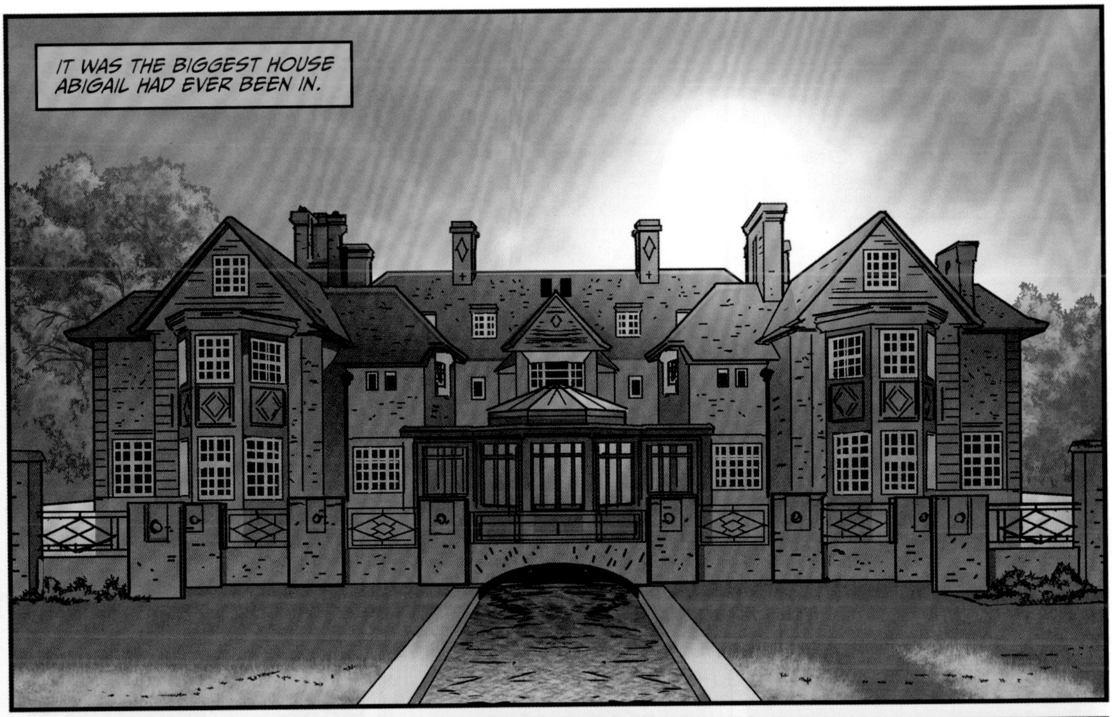
IT WAS THE BIGGEST HOUSE ABIGAIL HAD EVER BEEN IN.

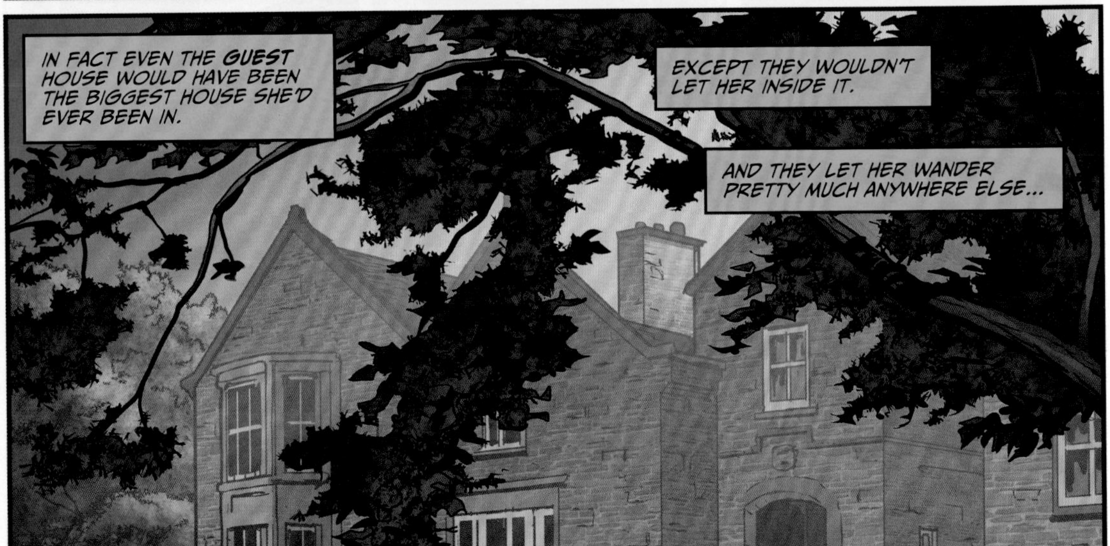
IN FACT EVEN THE GUEST HOUSE WOULD HAVE BEEN THE BIGGEST HOUSE SHE'D EVER BEEN IN.
EXCEPT THEY WOULDN'T LET HER INSIDE IT.
AND THEY LET HER WANDER PRETTY MUCH ANYWHERE ELSE...

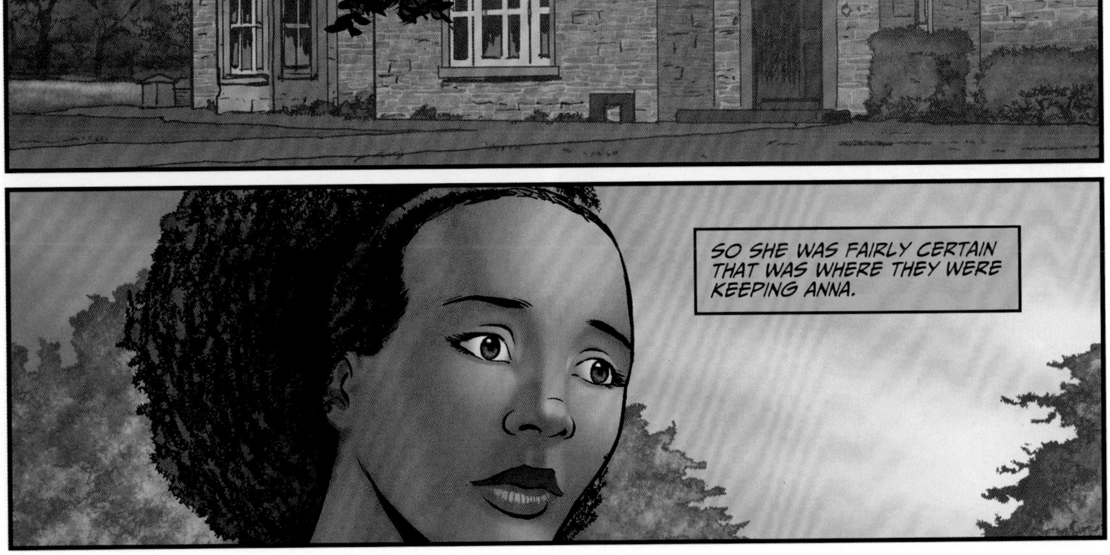
SO SHE WAS FAIRLY CERTAIN THAT WAS WHERE THEY WERE KEEPING ANNA.

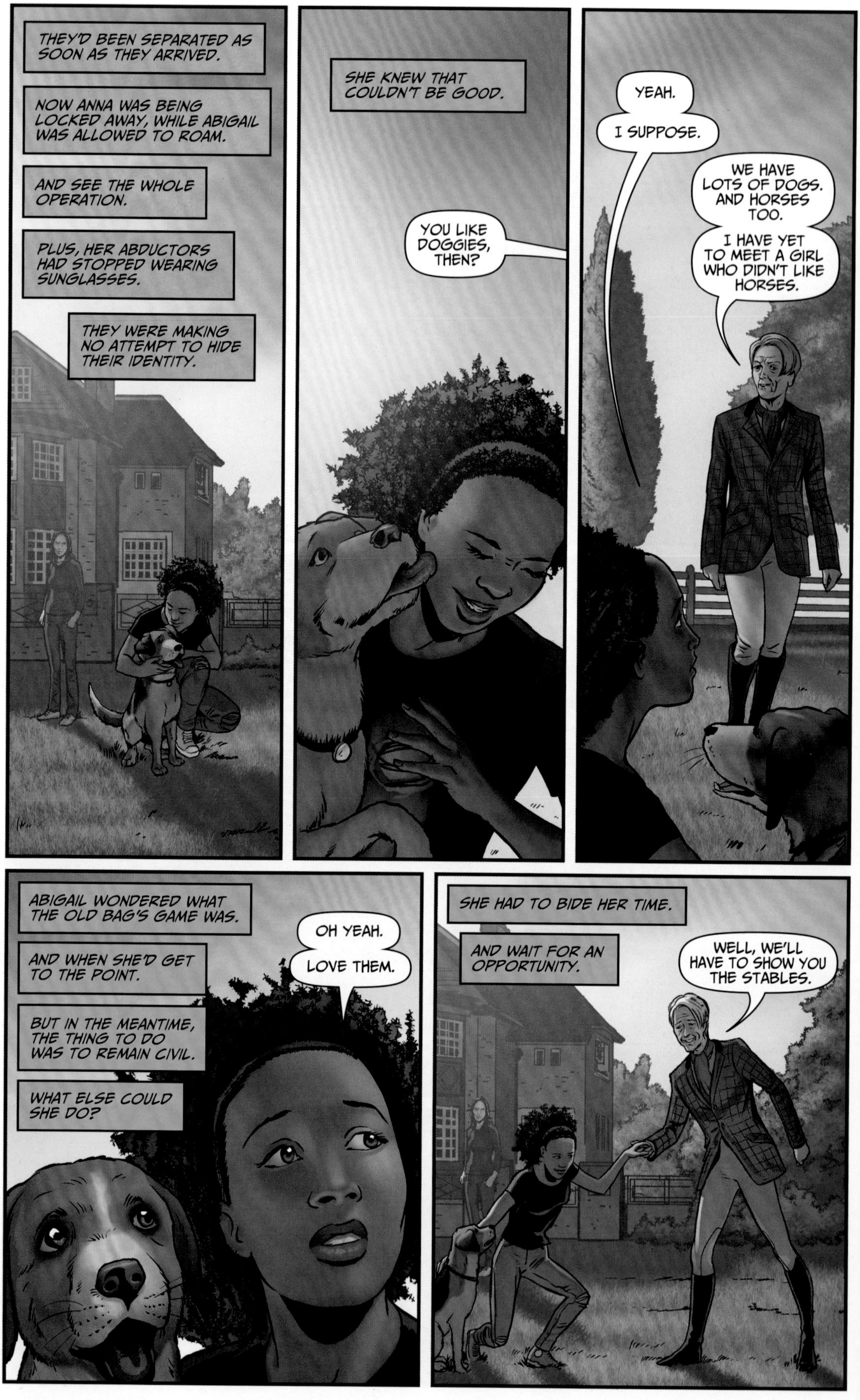
THEY'D BEEN SEPARATED AS SOON AS THEY ARRIVED.
NOW ANNA WAS BEING LOCKED AWAY, WHILE ABIGAIL WAS ALLOWED TO ROAM.
AND SEE THE WHOLE OPERATION.
PLUS, HER ABDUCTORS HAD STOPPED WEARING SUNGLASSES.
THEY WERE MAKING NO ATTEMPT TO HIDE THEIR IDENTITY.
SHE KNEW THAT COULDN'T BE GOOD.
YOU LIKE DOGGIES, THEN?
YEAH.
I SUPPOSE.
WE HAVE LOTS OF DOGS. AND HORSES TOO.
I HAVE YET TO MEET A GIRL WHO DIDN'T LIKE HORSES.
ABIGAIL WONDERED WHAT THE OLD BAG'S GAME WAS.
AND WHEN SHE'D GET TO THE POINT.
BUT IN THE MEANTIME, THE THING TO DO WAS TO REMAIN CIVIL.
WHAT ELSE COULD SHE DO?
OH YEAH.
LOVE THEM.
SHE HAD TO BIDE HER TIME.
AND WAIT FOR AN OPPORTUNITY.
WELL, WE'LL HAVE TO SHOW YOU THE STABLES.

BUT FIRST MY SON WOULD LIKE TO MEET YOU.

SON?

ABIGAIL WONDERED HOW MANY OTHER PEOPLE WERE LURKING IN THE BIG HOUSE.

CREEPY OLD BAG

SKINNY BITCH

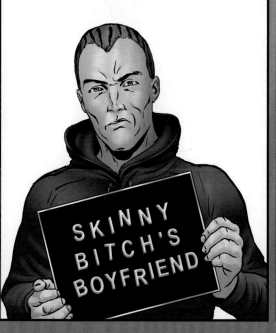

SKINNY BITCH'S BOYFRIEND

AND NOW...

CHUBBY WANKER

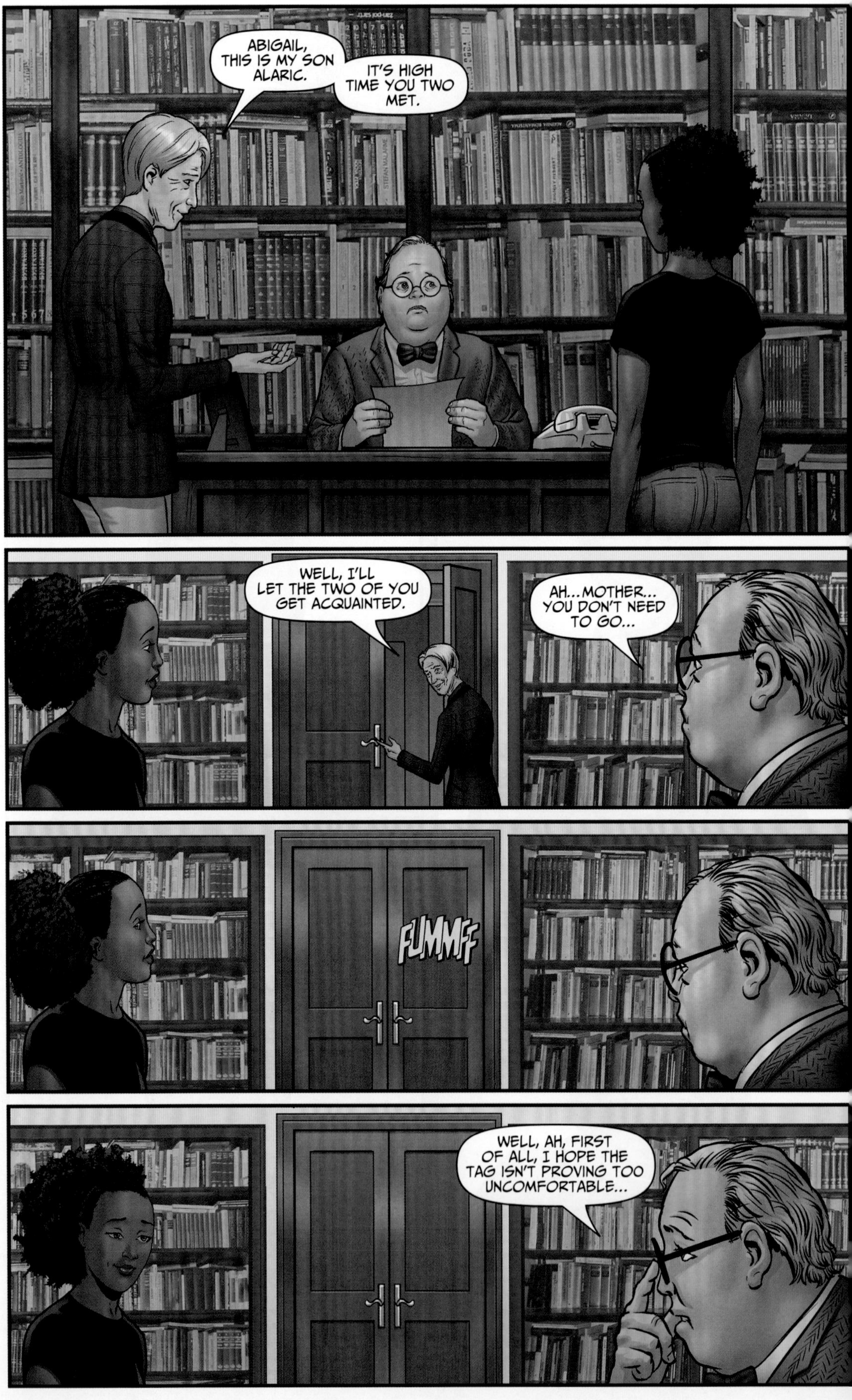
ABIGAIL, THIS IS MY SON ALARIC.
IT'S HIGH TIME YOU TWO MET.
WELL, I'LL LET THE TWO OF YOU GET ACQUAINTED.
AH...MOTHER... YOU DON'T NEED TO GO...
FUMMFF
WELL, AH, FIRST OF ALL, I HOPE THE TAG ISN'T PROVING TOO UNCOMFORTABLE...

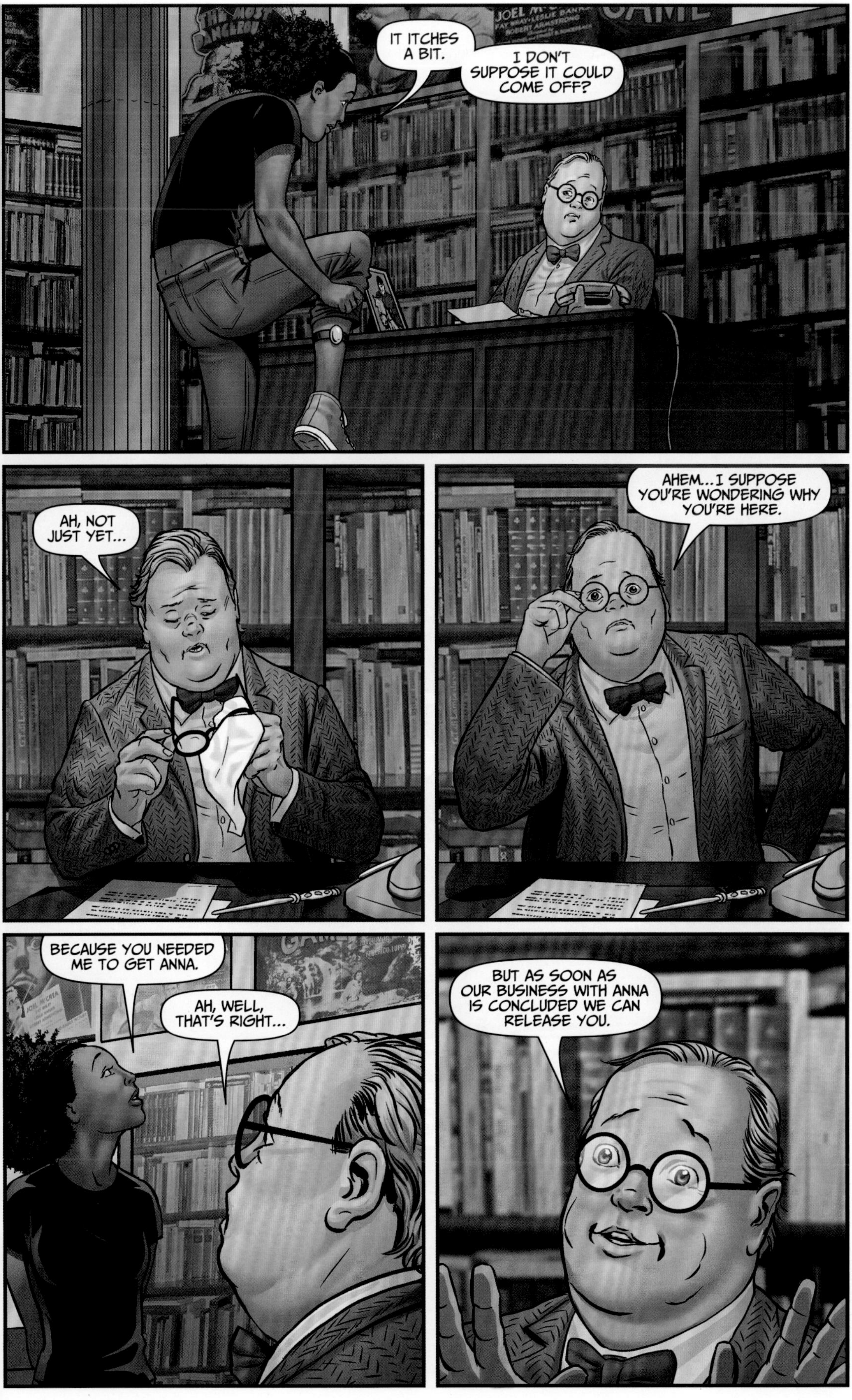
IT ITCHES A BIT.
I DON'T SUPPOSE IT COULD COME OFF?
AH, NOT JUST YET...
AHEM...I SUPPOSE YOU'RE WONDERING WHY YOU'RE HERE.
BECAUSE YOU NEEDED ME TO GET ANNA.
AH, WELL, THAT'S RIGHT...
BUT AS SOON AS OUR BUSINESS WITH ANNA IS CONCLUDED WE CAN RELEASE YOU.

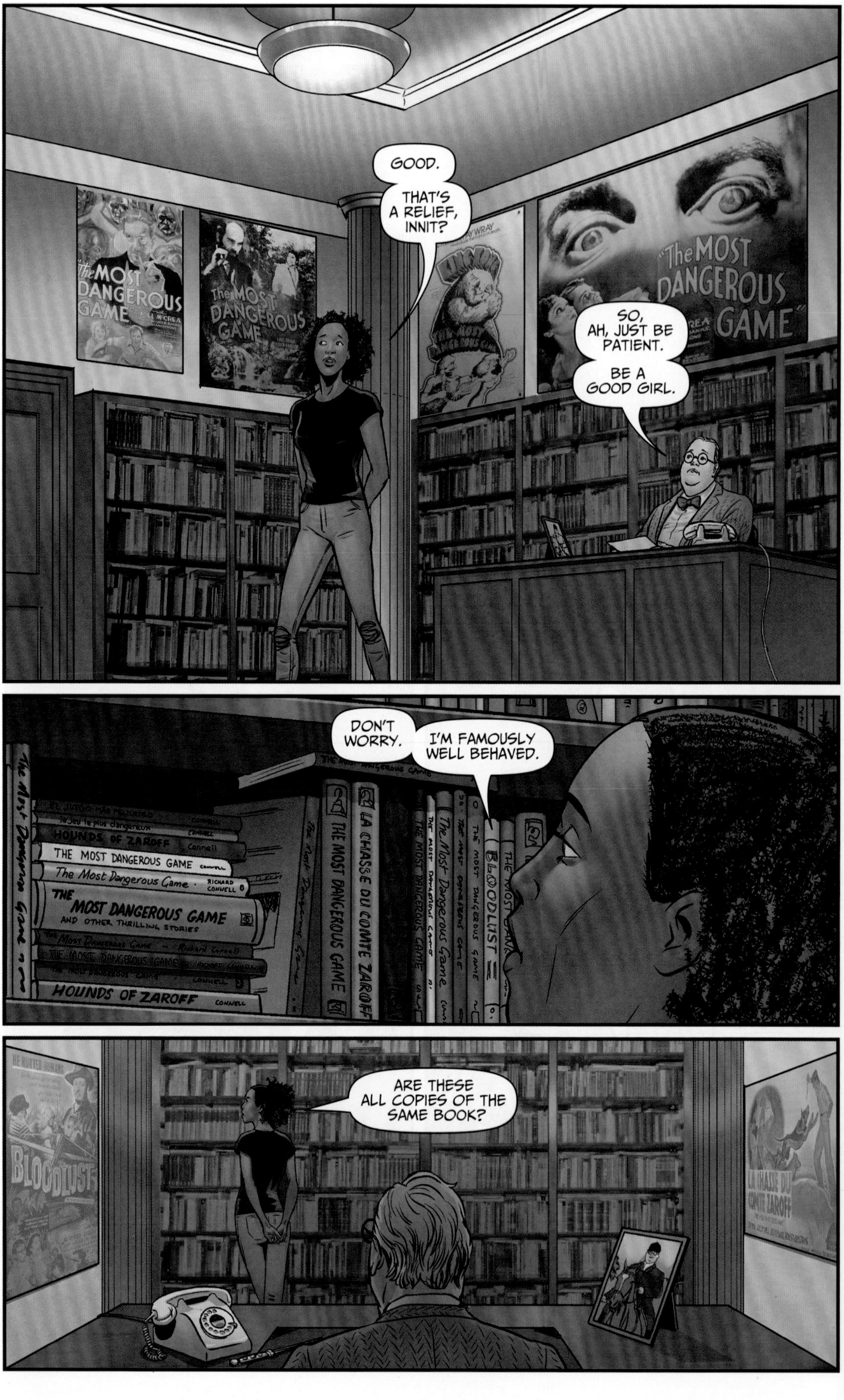

"The MOST DANGEROUS GAME"
The MOST DANGEROUS GAME
The MOST DANGEROUS GAME
"The MOST DANGEROUS GAME"
GOOD.
THAT'S A RELIEF, INNIT?
SO, AH, JUST BE PATIENT.
BE A GOOD GIRL.
DON'T WORRY.
I'M FAMOUSLY WELL BEHAVED.
HOUNDS OF ZAROFF
THE MOST DANGEROUS GAME
The Most Dangerous Game
THE MOST DANGEROUS GAME AND OTHER THRILLING STORIES
HOUNDS OF ZAROFF
THE MOST DANGEROUS GAME
LA CHASSE DU COMTE ZAROFF
BLOODLUST
ARE THESE ALL COPIES OF THE SAME BOOK?
BLOODLUST
LA CHASSE DU COMTE ZAROFF

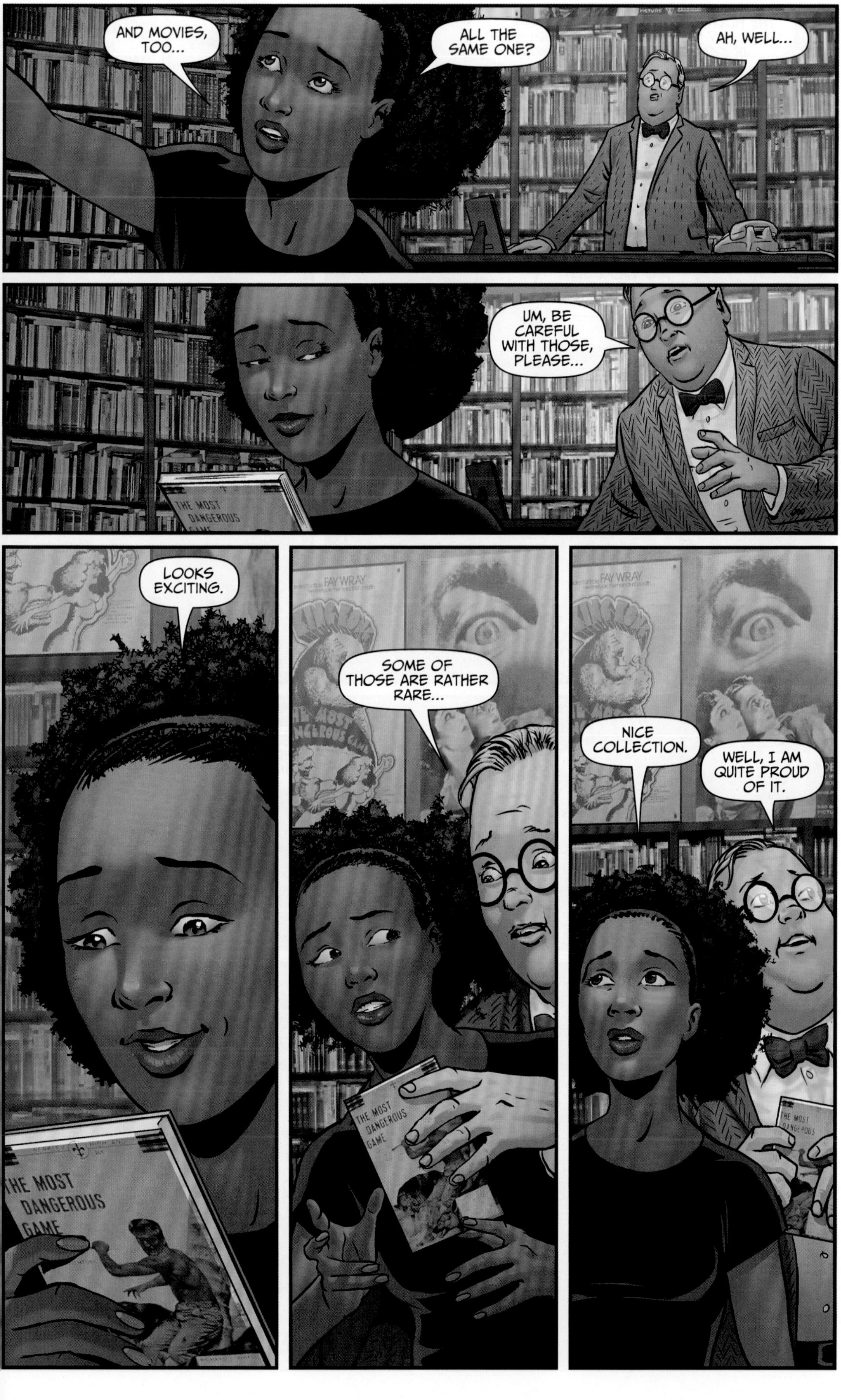
AND MOVIES, TOO...
ALL THE SAME ONE?
AH, WELL...
UM, BE CAREFUL WITH THOSE, PLEASE...
THE MOST DANGEROUS GAME
LOOKS EXCITING.
THE MOST DANGEROUS GAME
FAY WRAY
SOME OF THOSE ARE RATHER RARE...
THE MOST DANGEROUS GAME
FAY WRAY
NICE COLLECTION.
WELL, I AM QUITE PROUD OF IT.

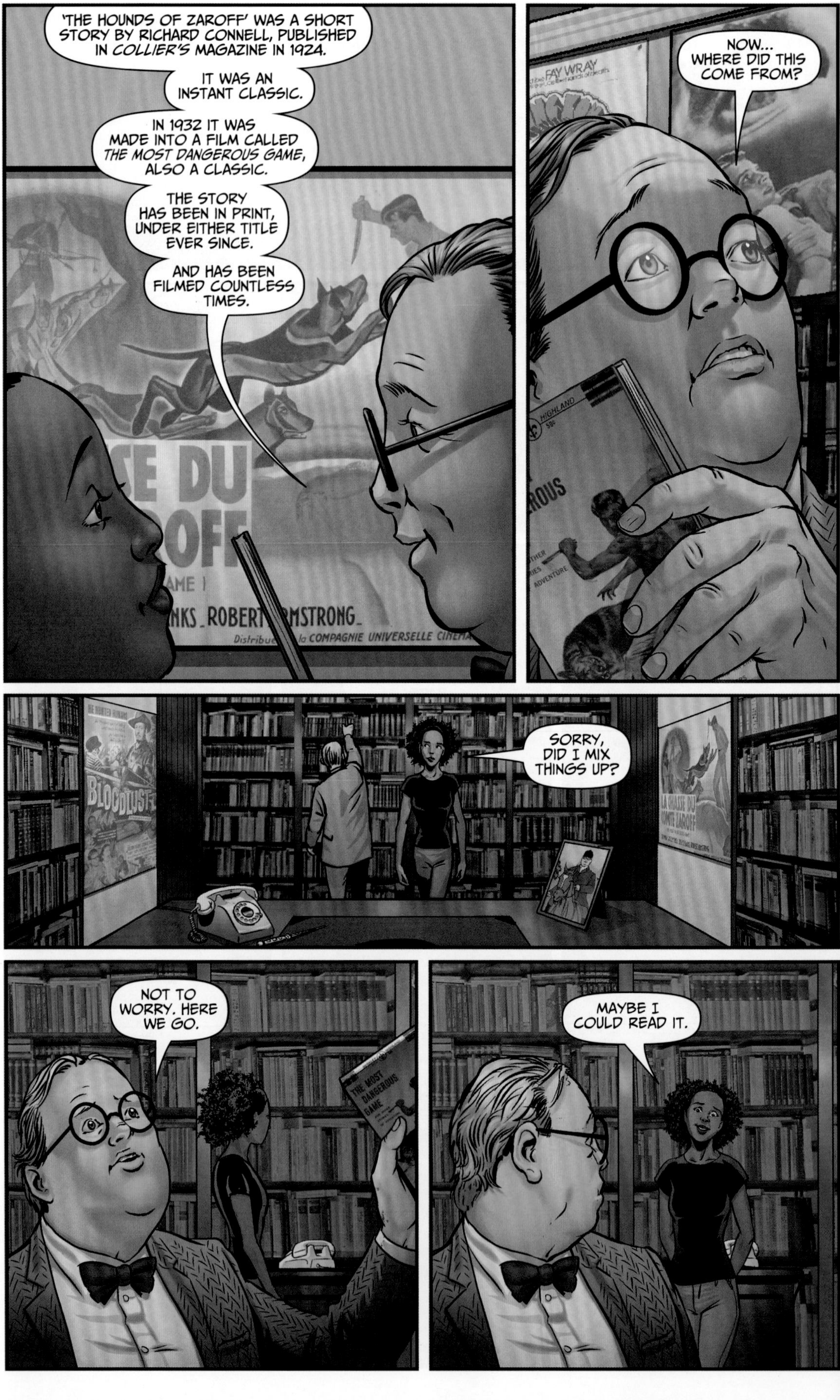

'THE HOUNDS OF ZAROFF' WAS A SHORT STORY BY RICHARD CONNELL, PUBLISHED IN *COLLIER'S* MAGAZINE IN 1924.
IT WAS AN INSTANT CLASSIC.
IN 1932 IT WAS MADE INTO A FILM CALLED *THE MOST DANGEROUS GAME*, ALSO A CLASSIC.
THE STORY HAS BEEN IN PRINT, UNDER EITHER TITLE EVER SINCE.
AND HAS BEEN FILMED COUNTLESS TIMES.
NOW... WHERE DID THIS COME FROM?
SORRY, DID I MIX THINGS UP?
NOT TO WORRY. HERE WE GO.
THE MOST DANGEROUS GAME
MAYBE I COULD READ IT.

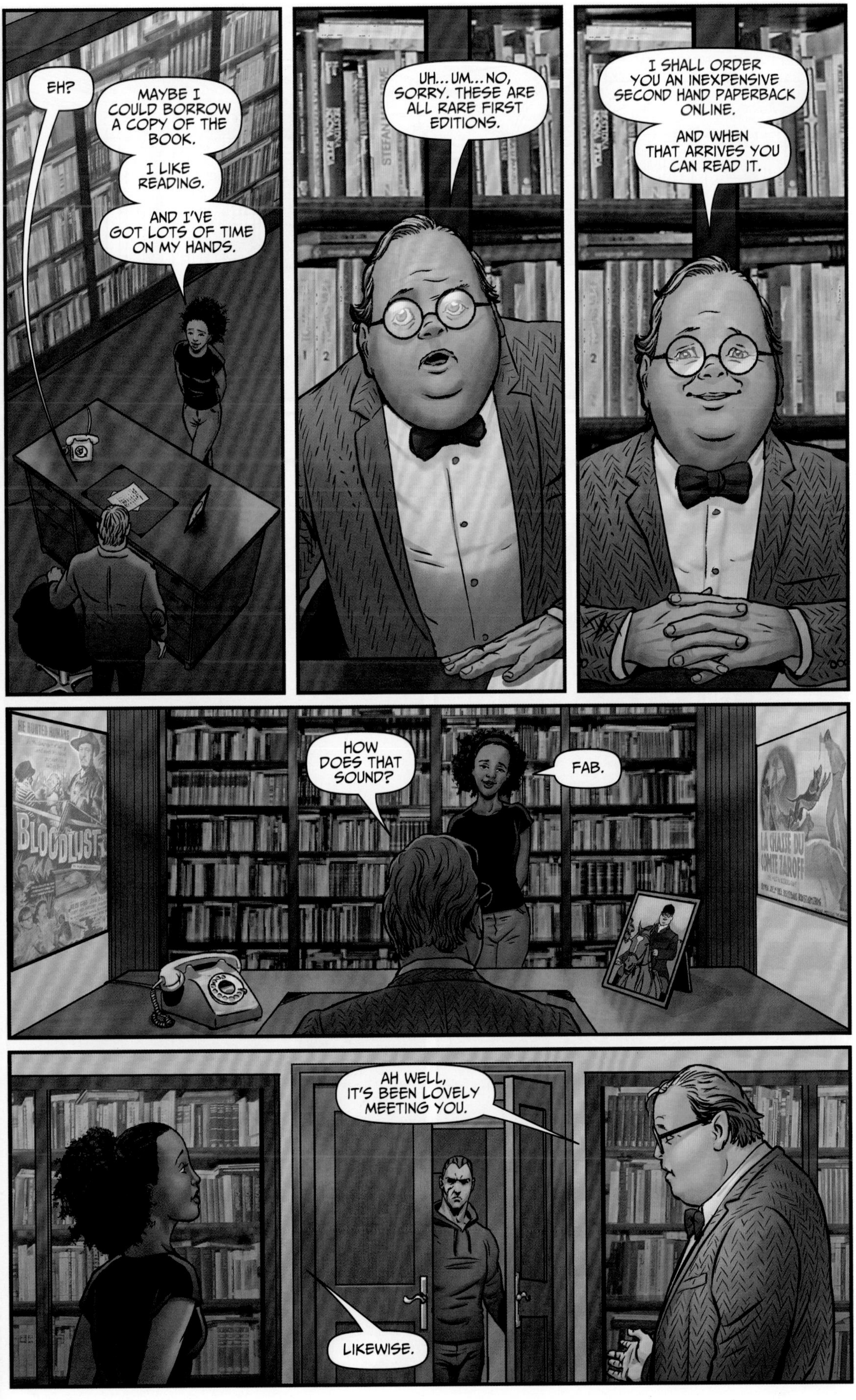
EH?
MAYBE I COULD BORROW A COPY OF THE BOOK.
I LIKE READING.
AND I'VE GOT LOTS OF TIME ON MY HANDS.
UH...UM...NO, SORRY. THESE ARE ALL RARE FIRST EDITIONS.
I SHALL ORDER YOU AN INEXPENSIVE SECOND HAND PAPERBACK ONLINE.
AND WHEN THAT ARRIVES YOU CAN READ IT.
HE HUNTED HUMANS
BLOODLUST!
HOW DOES THAT SOUND?
FAB.
LA CHASSE DU COMTE ZAROFF
AH WELL, IT'S BEEN LOVELY MEETING YOU.
LIKEWISE.

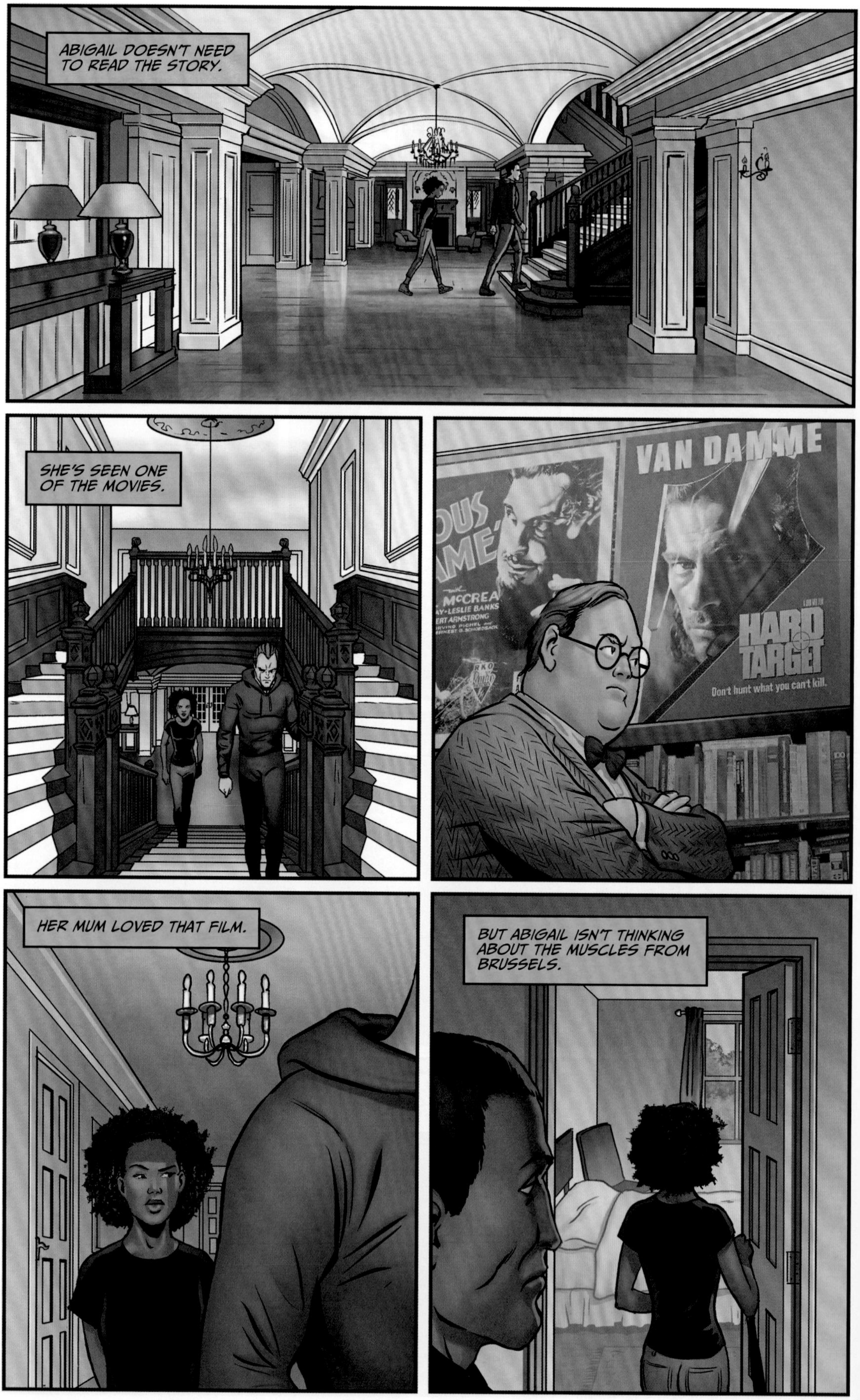
ABIGAIL DOESN'T NEED TO READ THE STORY.
SHE'S SEEN ONE OF THE MOVIES.
VAN DAMME
HARD TARGET
Don't hunt what you can't kill.
HER MUM LOVED THAT FILM.
BUT ABIGAIL ISN'T THINKING ABOUT THE MUSCLES FROM BRUSSELS.

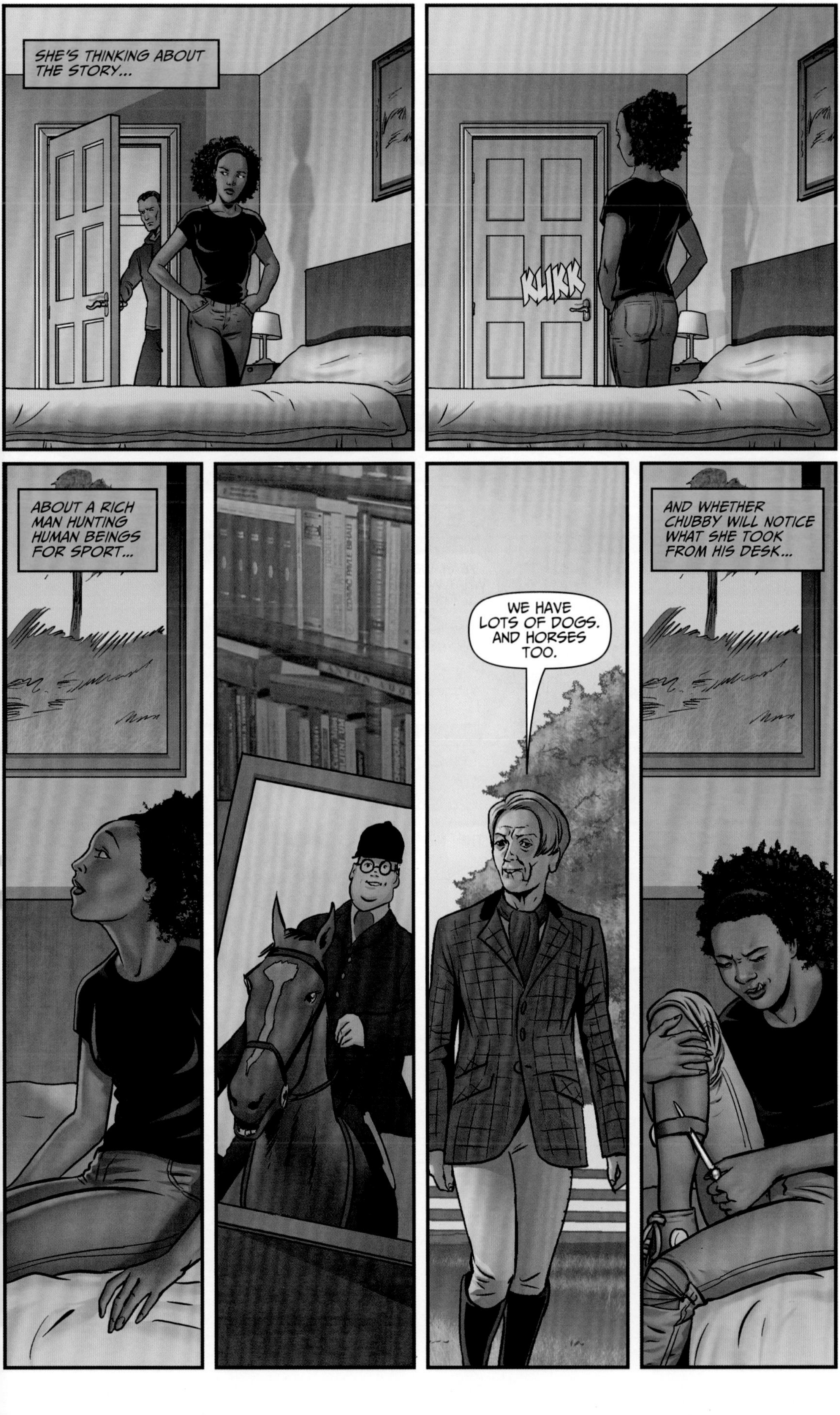
SHE'S THINKING ABOUT THE STORY...
KLIKK
ABOUT A RICH MAN HUNTING HUMAN BEINGS FOR SPORT...
WE HAVE LOTS OF DOGS. AND HORSES TOO.
AND WHETHER CHUBBY WILL NOTICE WHAT SHE TOOK FROM HIS DESK...

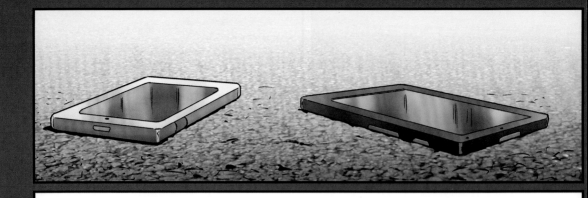

YEAH, WE'VE LOCATED WHAT WE BELIEVE TO BE THE SITE OF THE ABDUCTION.

THEY'VE CHOSEN CAREFULLY.

ISOLATED.

NO CCTV IN THE VICINITY.

YEAH, I'LL KEEP YOU POSTED.

THEY USED ABIGAIL TO REACH OUT TO ANNA.

BUT WHO DID THEY USE TO REACH OUT TO ABIGAIL?

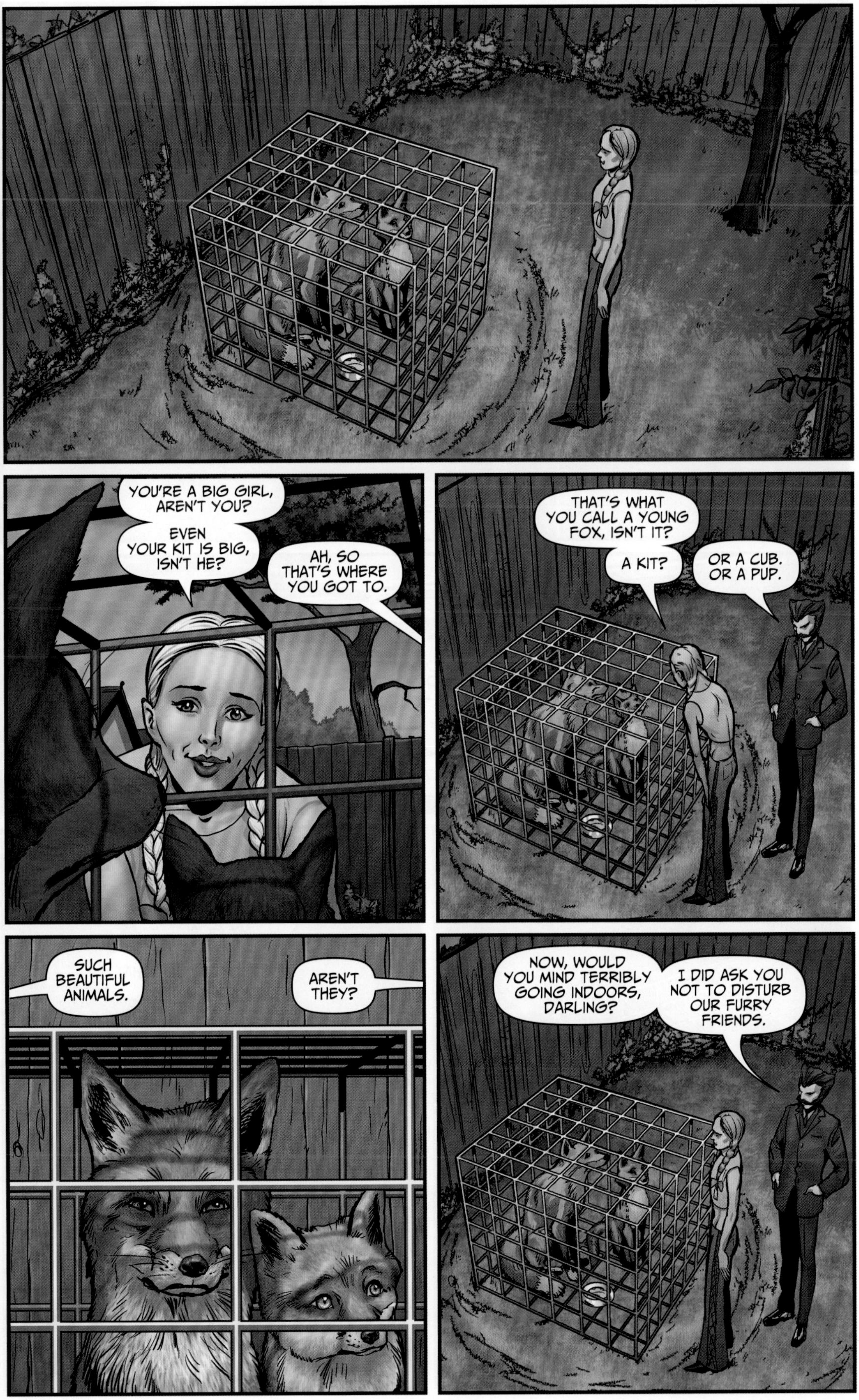

YOU'RE A BIG GIRL, AREN'T YOU?
EVEN YOUR KIT IS BIG, ISN'T HE?
AH, SO THAT'S WHERE YOU GOT TO.
THAT'S WHAT YOU CALL A YOUNG FOX, ISN'T IT?
A KIT?
OR A CUB. OR A PUP.
SUCH BEAUTIFUL ANIMALS.
AREN'T THEY?
NOW, WOULD YOU MIND TERRIBLY GOING INDOORS, DARLING?
I DID ASK YOU NOT TO DISTURB OUR FURRY FRIENDS.

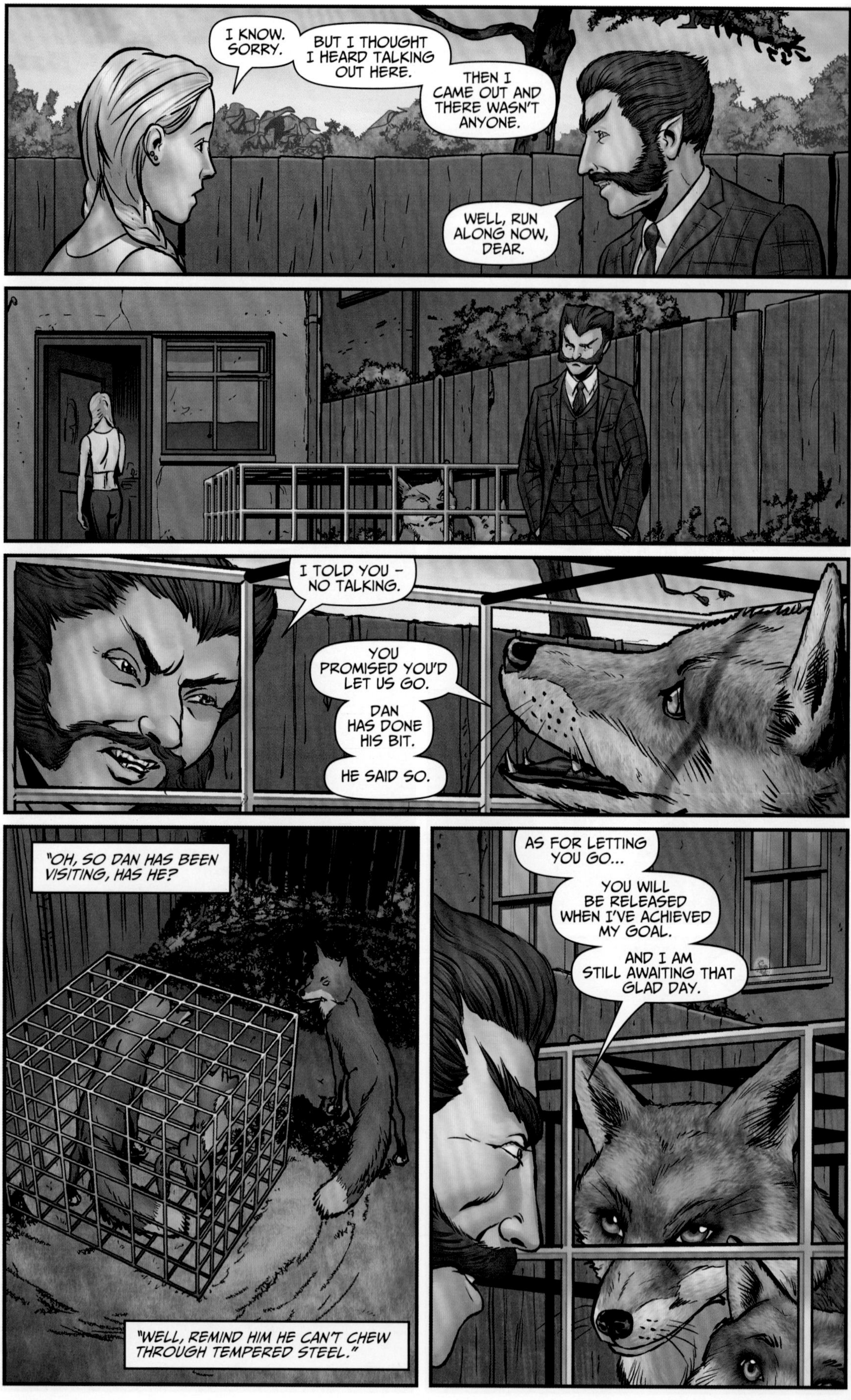
I KNOW. SORRY.
BUT I THOUGHT I HEARD TALKING OUT HERE.
THEN I CAME OUT AND THERE WASN'T ANYONE.
WELL, RUN ALONG NOW, DEAR.
I TOLD YOU – NO TALKING.
YOU PROMISED YOU'D LET US GO.
DAN HAS DONE HIS BIT.
HE SAID SO.
"OH, SO DAN HAS BEEN VISITING, HAS HE?
"WELL, REMIND HIM HE CAN'T CHEW THROUGH TEMPERED STEEL."
AS FOR LETTING YOU GO...
YOU WILL BE RELEASED WHEN I'VE ACHIEVED MY GOAL.
AND I AM STILL AWAITING THAT GLAD DAY.

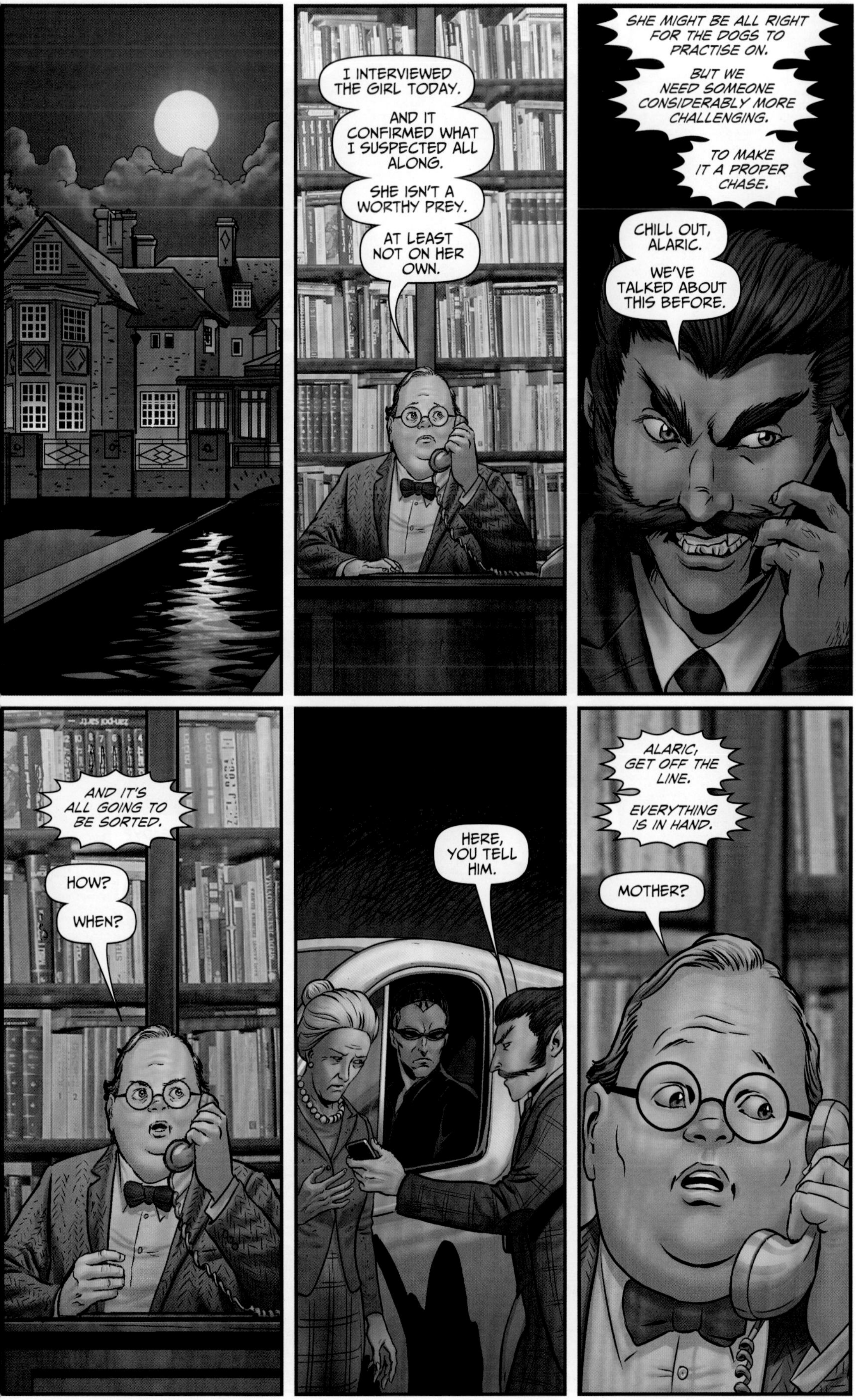
I INTERVIEWED THE GIRL TODAY.
AND IT CONFIRMED WHAT I SUSPECTED ALL ALONG.
SHE ISN'T A WORTHY PREY.
AT LEAST NOT ON HER OWN.
SHE MIGHT BE ALL RIGHT FOR THE DOGS TO PRACTISE ON.
BUT WE NEED SOMEONE CONSIDERABLY MORE CHALLENGING.
TO MAKE IT A PROPER CHASE.
CHILL OUT, ALARIC.
WE'VE TALKED ABOUT THIS BEFORE.
AND IT'S ALL GOING TO BE SORTED.
HOW?
WHEN?
HERE, YOU TELL HIM.
ALARIC, GET OFF THE LINE.
EVERYTHING IS IN HAND.
MOTHER?

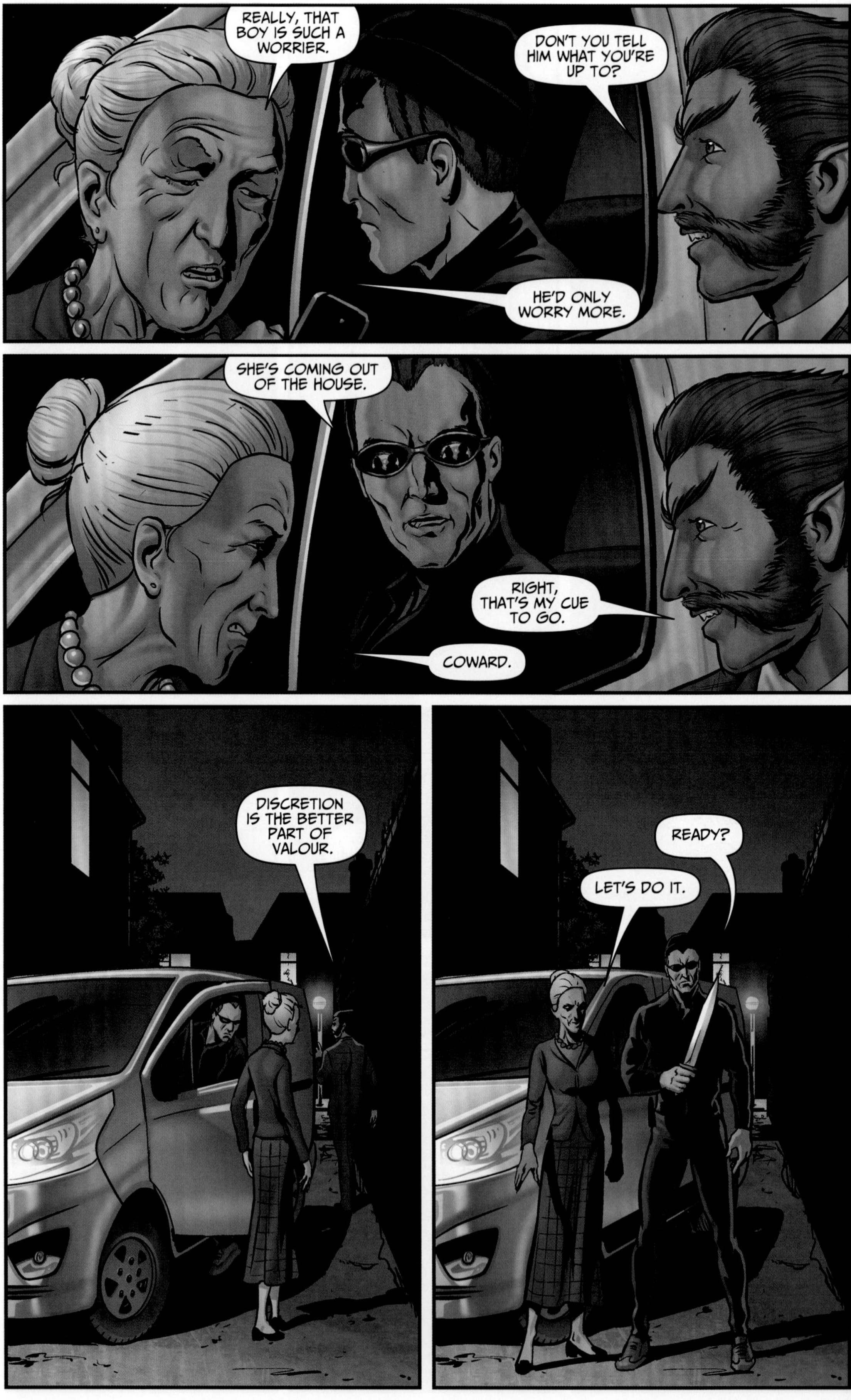
REALLY, THAT BOY IS SUCH A WORRIER.
DON'T YOU TELL HIM WHAT YOU'RE UP TO?
HE'D ONLY WORRY MORE.
SHE'S COMING OUT OF THE HOUSE.
RIGHT, THAT'S MY CUE TO GO.
COWARD.
DISCRETION IS THE BETTER PART OF VALOUR.
READY?
LET'S DO IT.

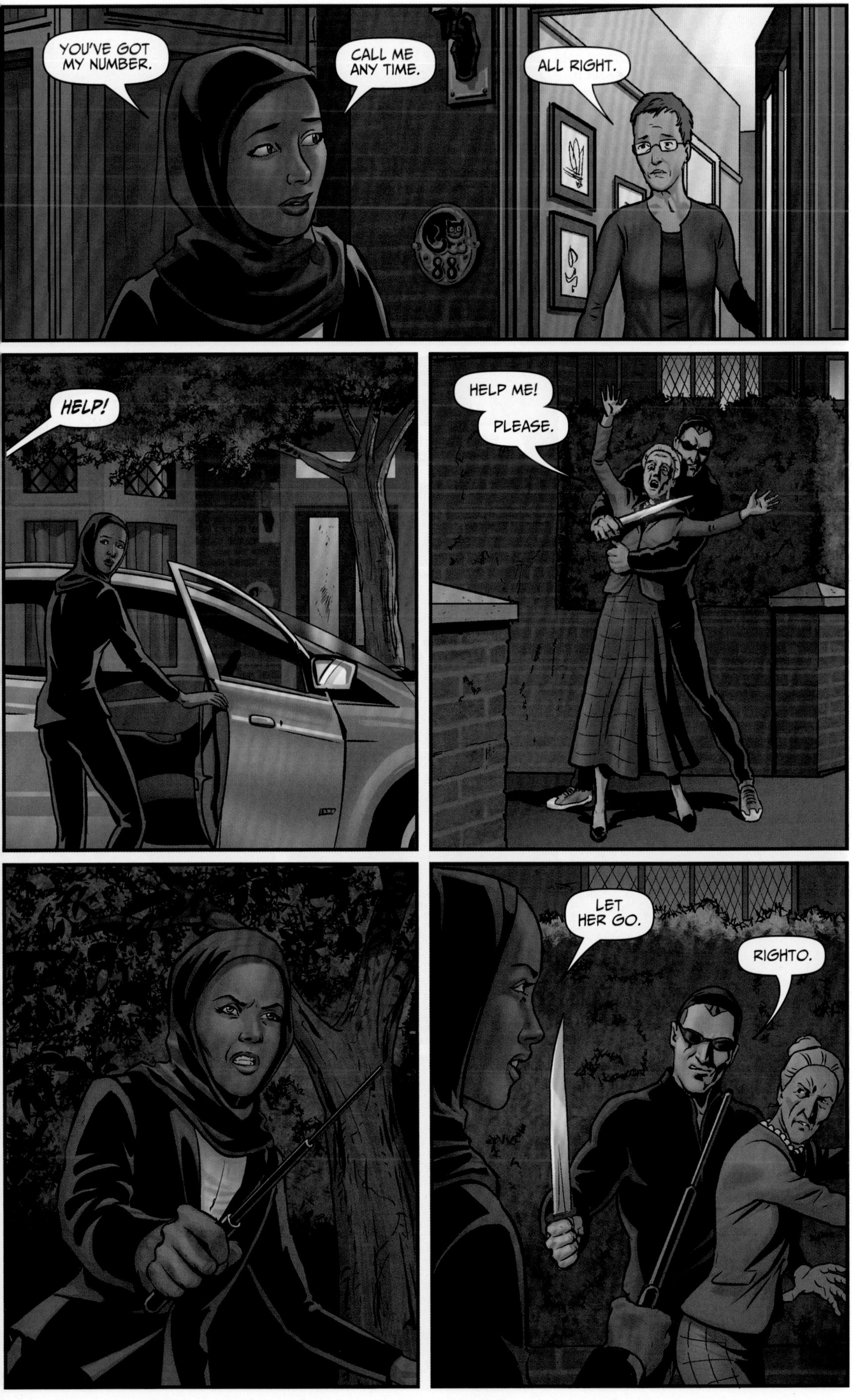
YOU'VE GOT MY NUMBER.
CALL ME ANY TIME.
ALL RIGHT.
HELP!
HELP ME!
PLEASE.
LET HER GO.
RIGHTO.

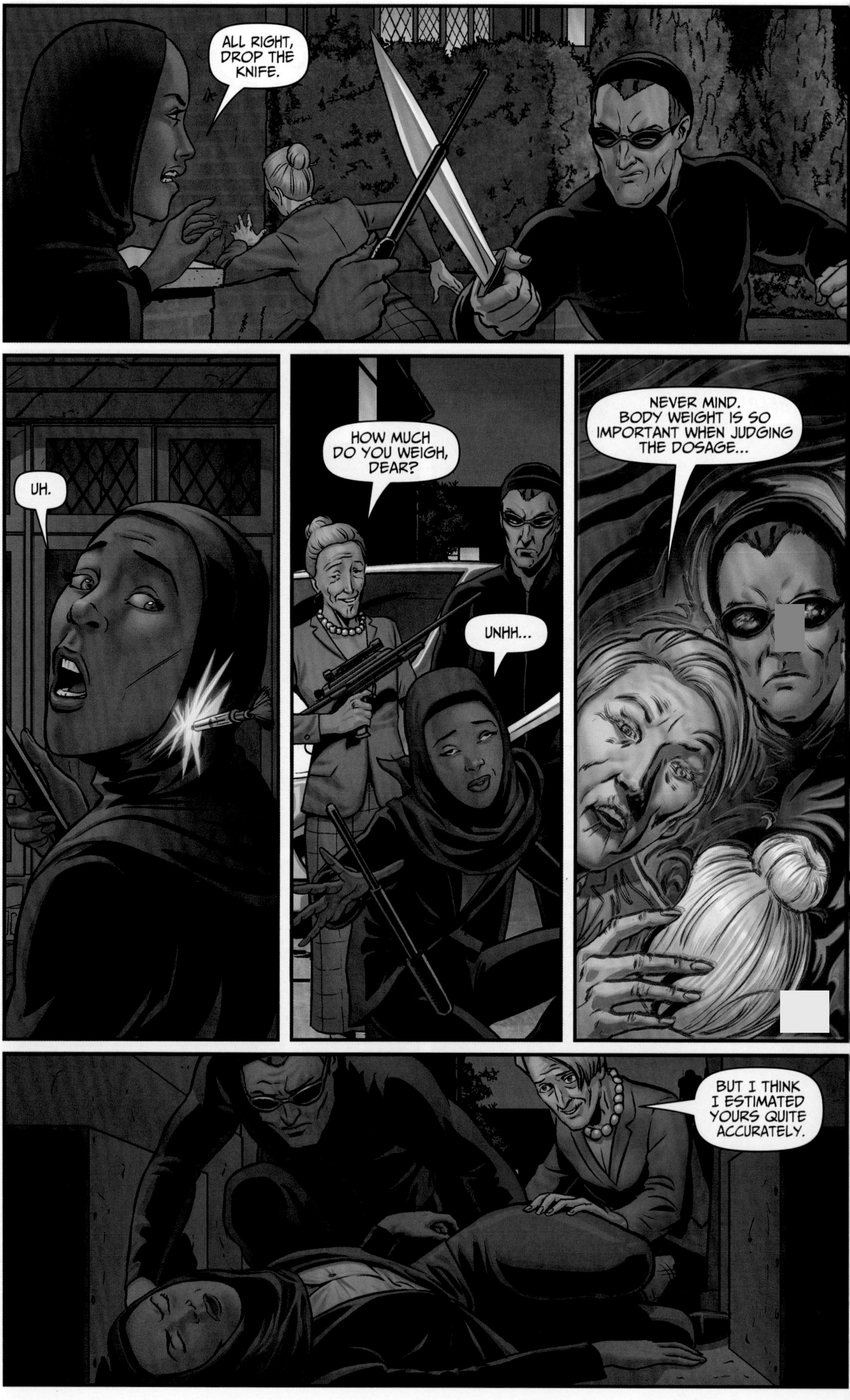
ALL RIGHT, DROP THE KNIFE.
UH.
HOW MUCH DO YOU WEIGH, DEAR?
UNHH...
NEVER MIND. BODY WEIGHT IS SO IMPORTANT WHEN JUDGING THE DOSAGE...
BUT I THINK I ESTIMATED YOURS QUITE ACCURATELY.

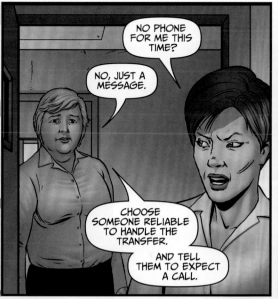

NO PHONE FOR ME THIS TIME?

NO, JUST A MESSAGE.

CHOOSE SOMEONE RELIABLE TO HANDLE THE TRANSFER.

AND TELL THEM TO EXPECT A CALL.

ARE YOU MAD?

I WON'T HELP YOU.

I AM NOT GOING TO ALLOW YOU TO MAKE A FOOL OF ME AGAIN.

THIS IS NOT ABOUT YOU.

IT IS ABOUT OUR DAUGHTER.

AND BESIDES, YOU DON'T HAVE TO DO ANYTHING.

JUST TELL THE MAN WHO DROVE US TO OUR WEDDING TO EXPECT A CALL.

TELEPHONE

Beverley Brook Walk

OY, MAXIM!

WHAT'S THE MATTER?

WEREN'T YOU EXPECTING A CALL?

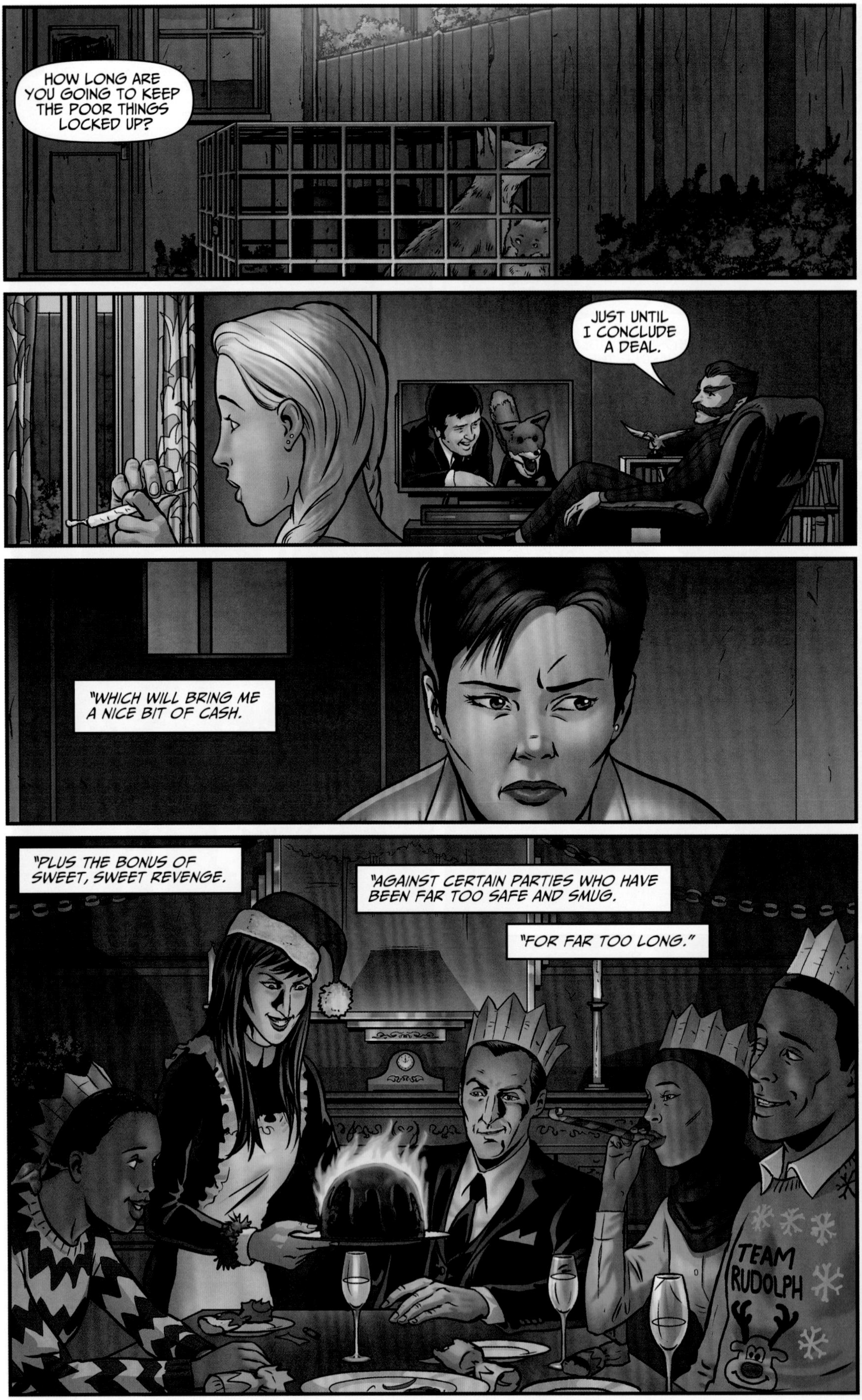
HOW LONG ARE YOU GOING TO KEEP THE POOR THINGS LOCKED UP?
JUST UNTIL I CONCLUDE A DEAL.
"WHICH WILL BRING ME A NICE BIT OF CASH.
"PLUS THE BONUS OF SWEET, SWEET REVENGE.
"AGAINST CERTAIN PARTIES WHO HAVE BEEN FAR TOO SAFE AND SMUG.
"FOR FAR TOO LONG."
TEAM RUDOLPH

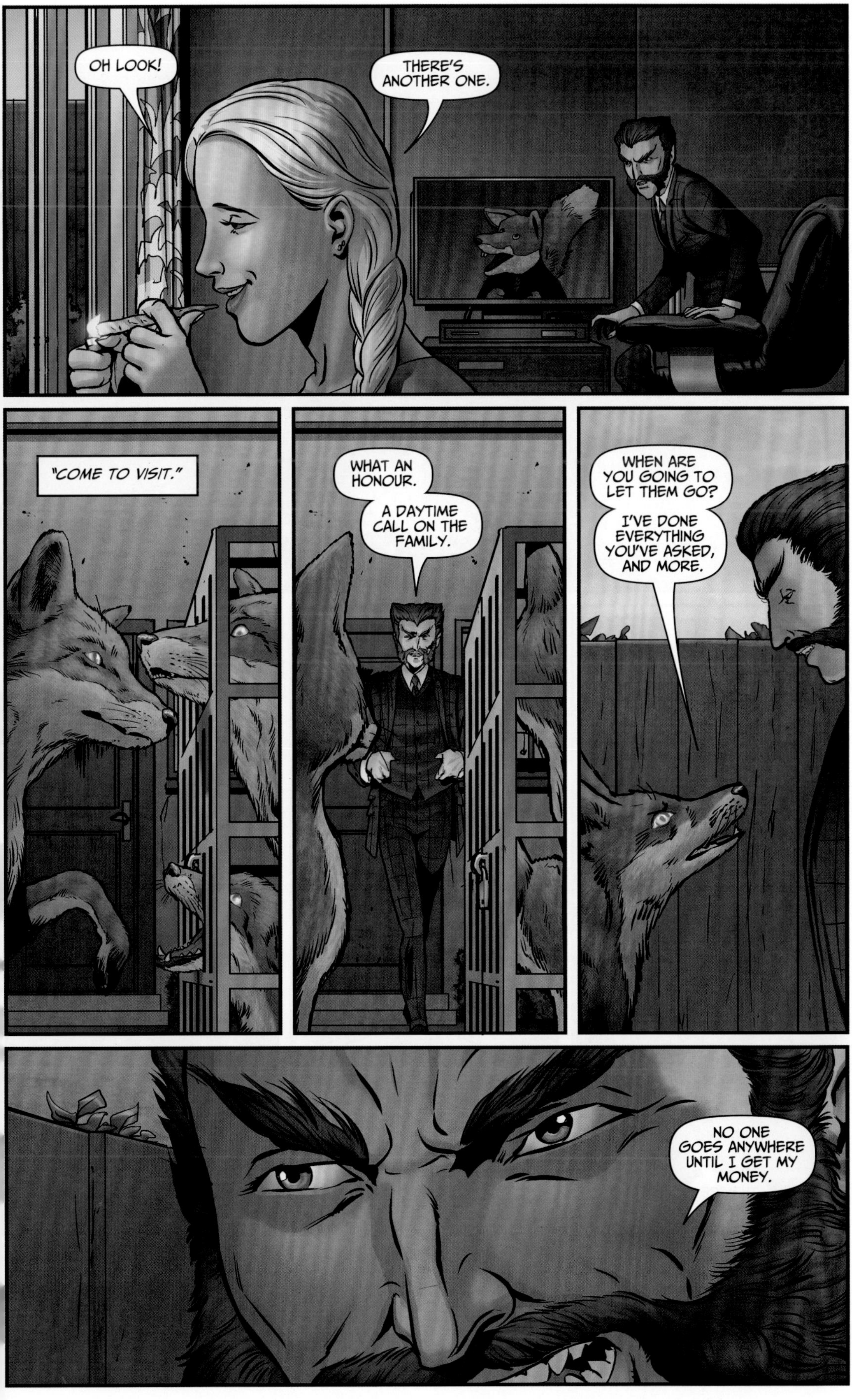
OH LOOK!
THERE'S ANOTHER ONE.
"COME TO VISIT."
WHAT AN HONOUR.
A DAYTIME CALL ON THE FAMILY.
WHEN ARE YOU GOING TO LET THEM GO?
I'VE DONE EVERYTHING YOU'VE ASKED, AND MORE.
NO ONE GOES ANYWHERE UNTIL I GET MY MONEY.

I TOLD YOU SHE'D BE HERE.

ARE YOU ADMIRING THE FLOWERS?

THEY'RE NICE.

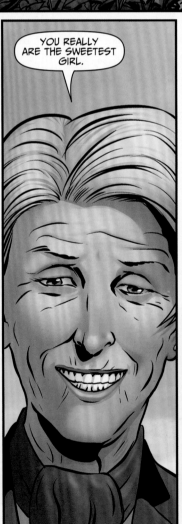

YOU REALLY ARE THE SWEETEST GIRL.

"BUT NOW YOU NEED TO GO BACK TO YOUR ROOM."

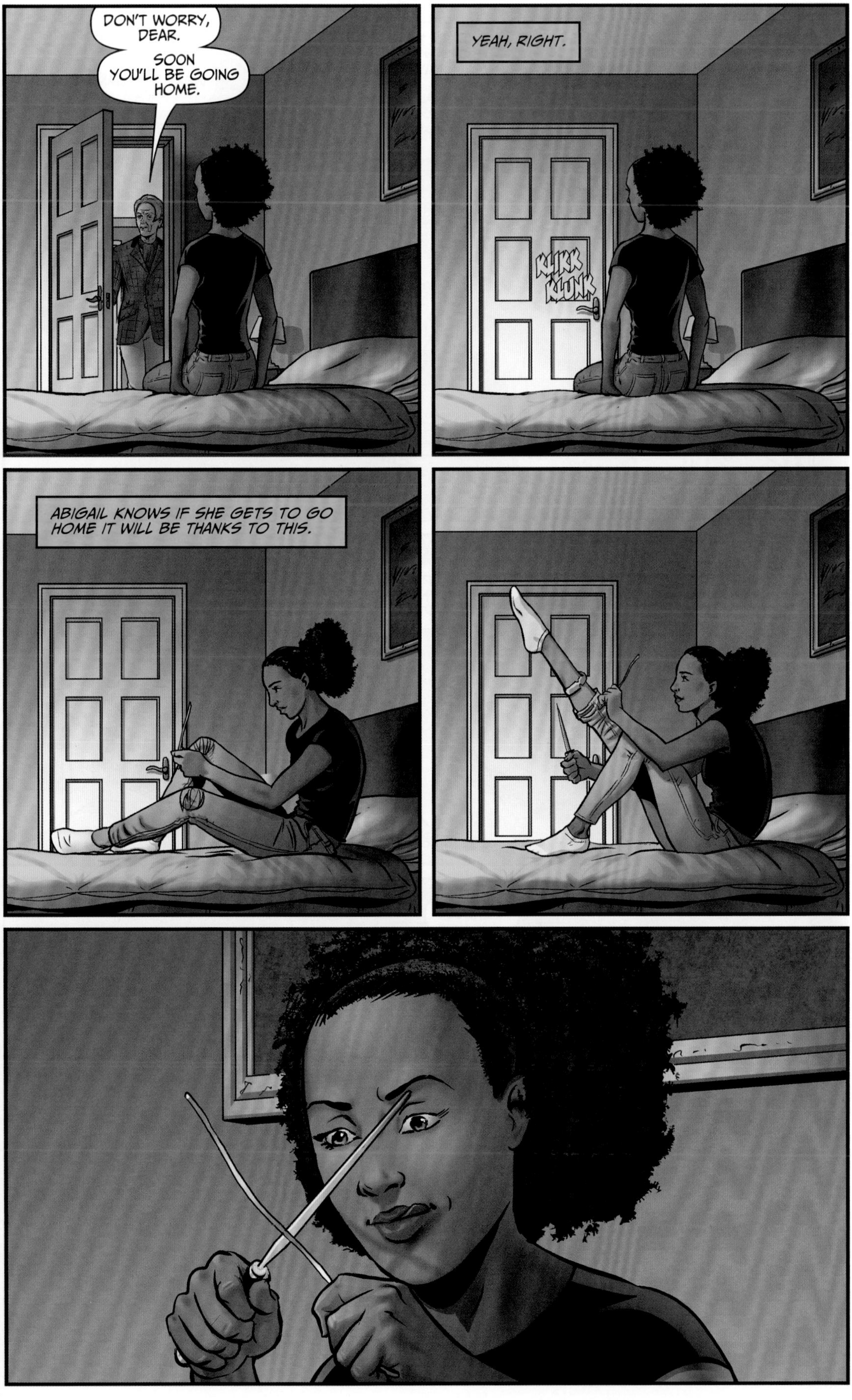
DON'T WORRY, DEAR.
SOON YOU'LL BE GOING HOME.
YEAH, RIGHT.
KLIKK KLUNK
ABIGAIL KNOWS IF SHE GETS TO GO HOME IT WILL BE THANKS TO THIS.

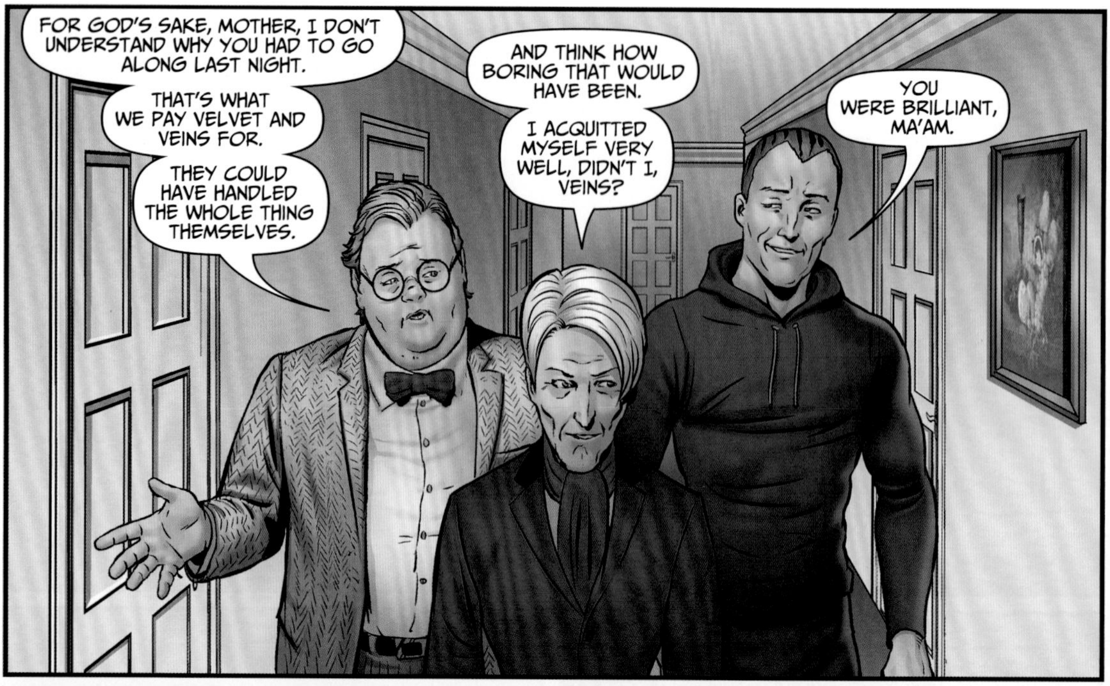
FOR GOD'S SAKE, MOTHER, I DON'T UNDERSTAND WHY YOU HAD TO GO ALONG LAST NIGHT.
THAT'S WHAT WE PAY VELVET AND VEINS FOR.
THEY COULD HAVE HANDLED THE WHOLE THING THEMSELVES.
AND THINK HOW BORING THAT WOULD HAVE BEEN.
I ACQUITTED MYSELF VERY WELL, DIDN'T I, VEINS?
YOU WERE BRILLIANT, MA'AM.

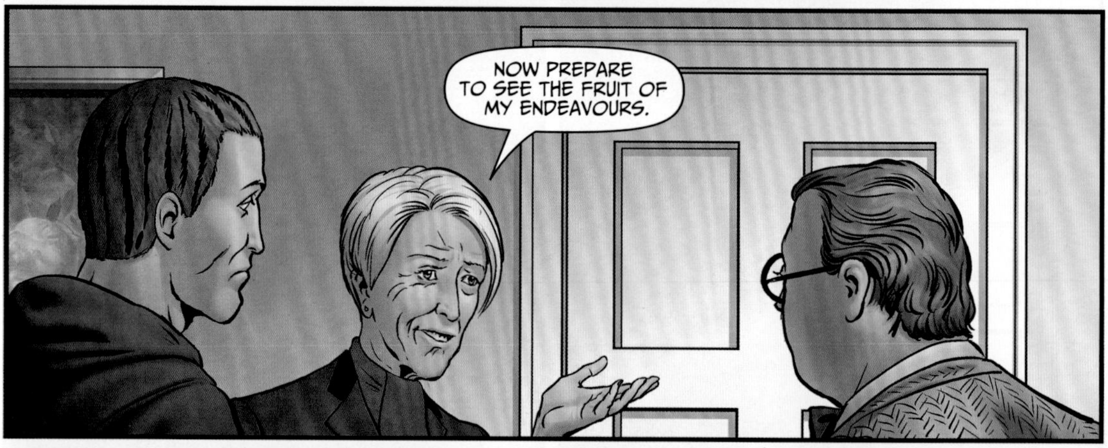
NOW PREPARE TO SEE THE FRUIT OF MY ENDEAVOURS.

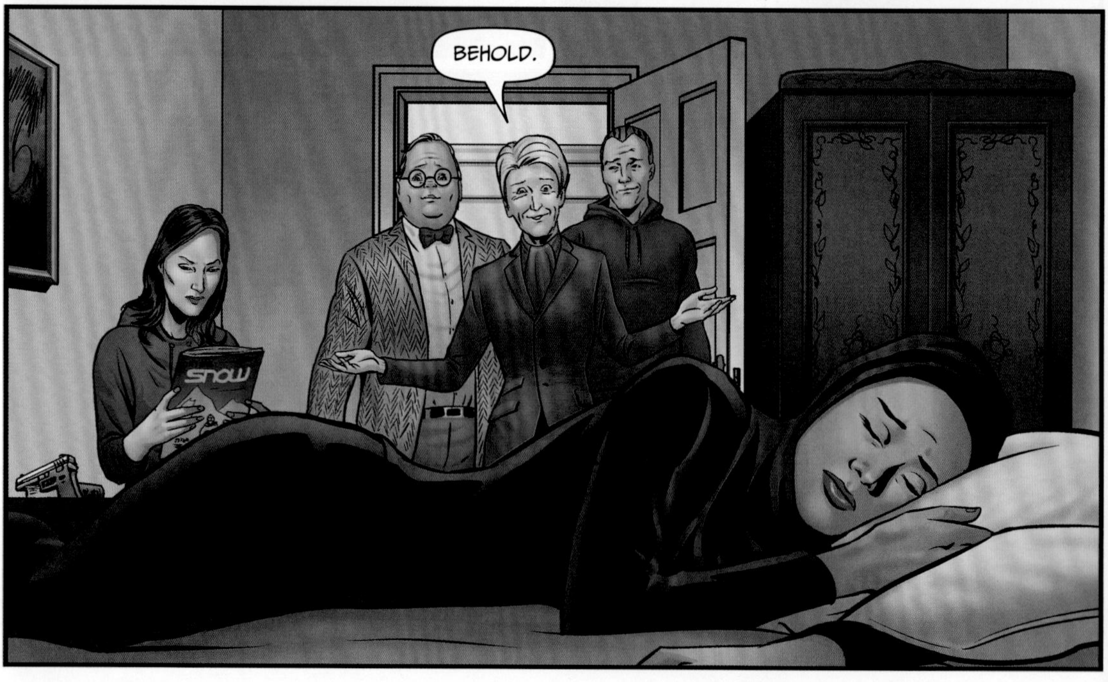
BEHOLD.
SNOW

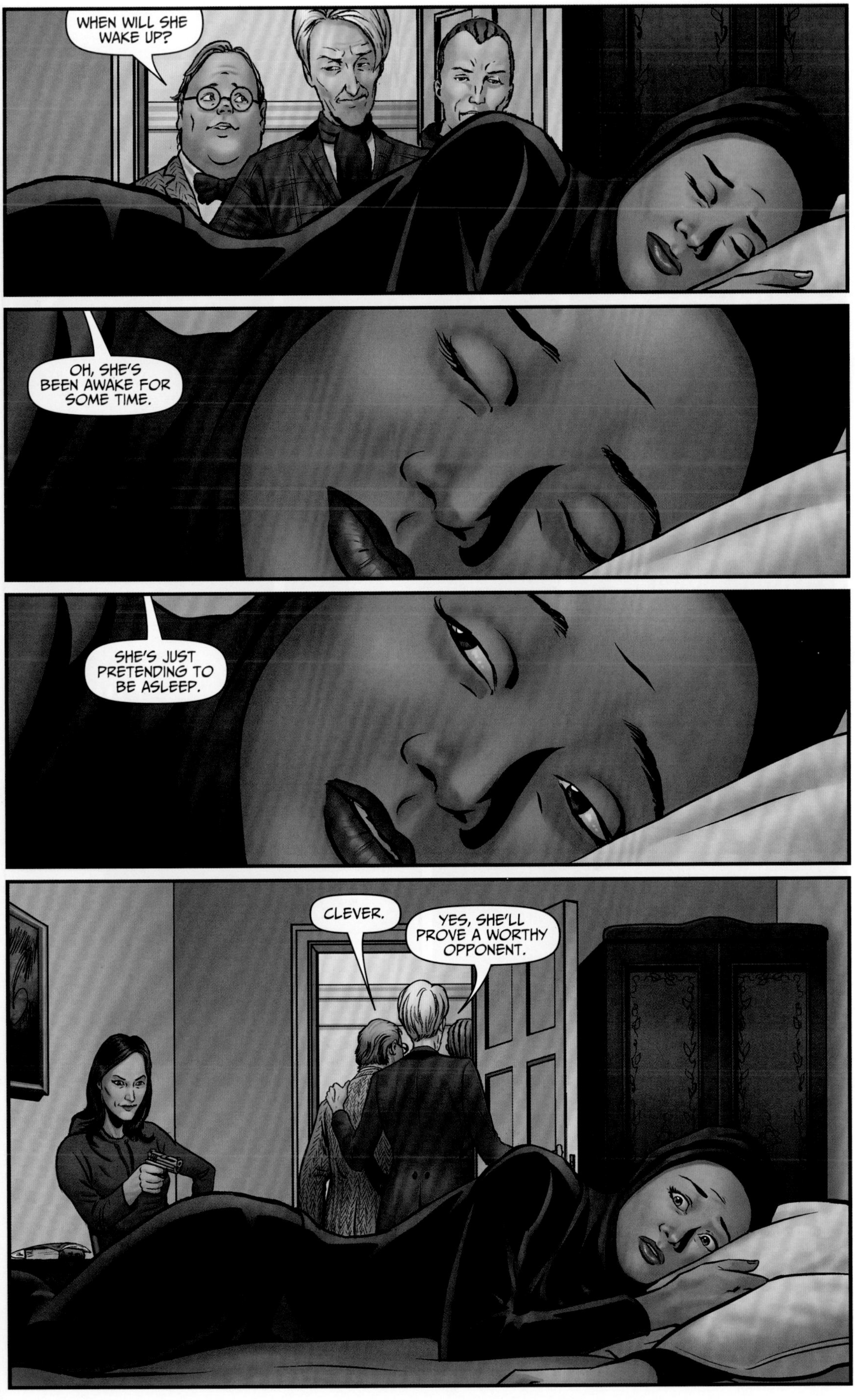
WHEN WILL SHE WAKE UP?
OH, SHE'S BEEN AWAKE FOR SOME TIME.
SHE'S JUST PRETENDING TO BE ASLEEP.
CLEVER.
YES, SHE'LL PROVE A WORTHY OPPONENT.

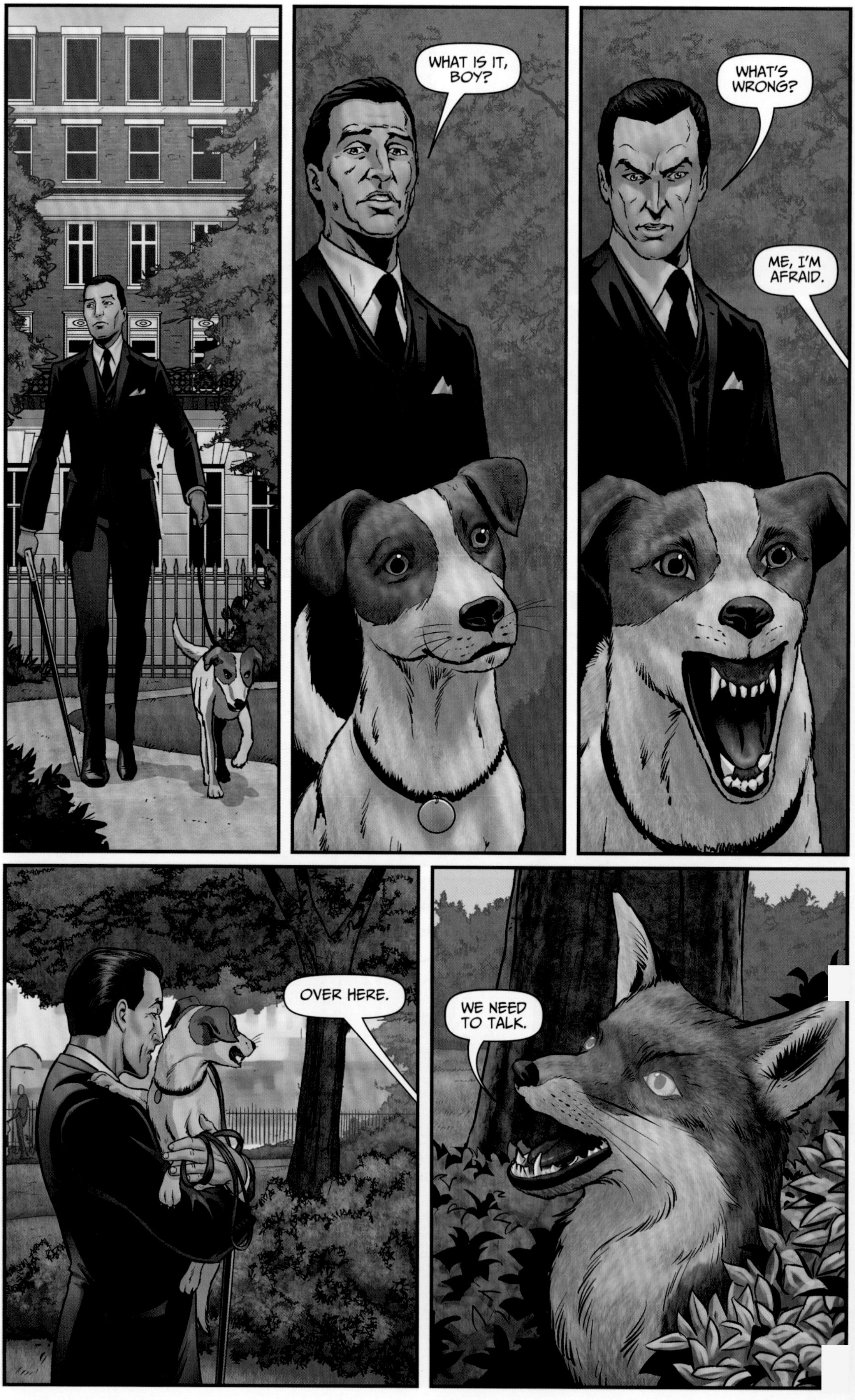
WHAT IS IT, BOY?
WHAT'S WRONG?
ME, I'M AFRAID.
OVER HERE.
WE NEED TO TALK.

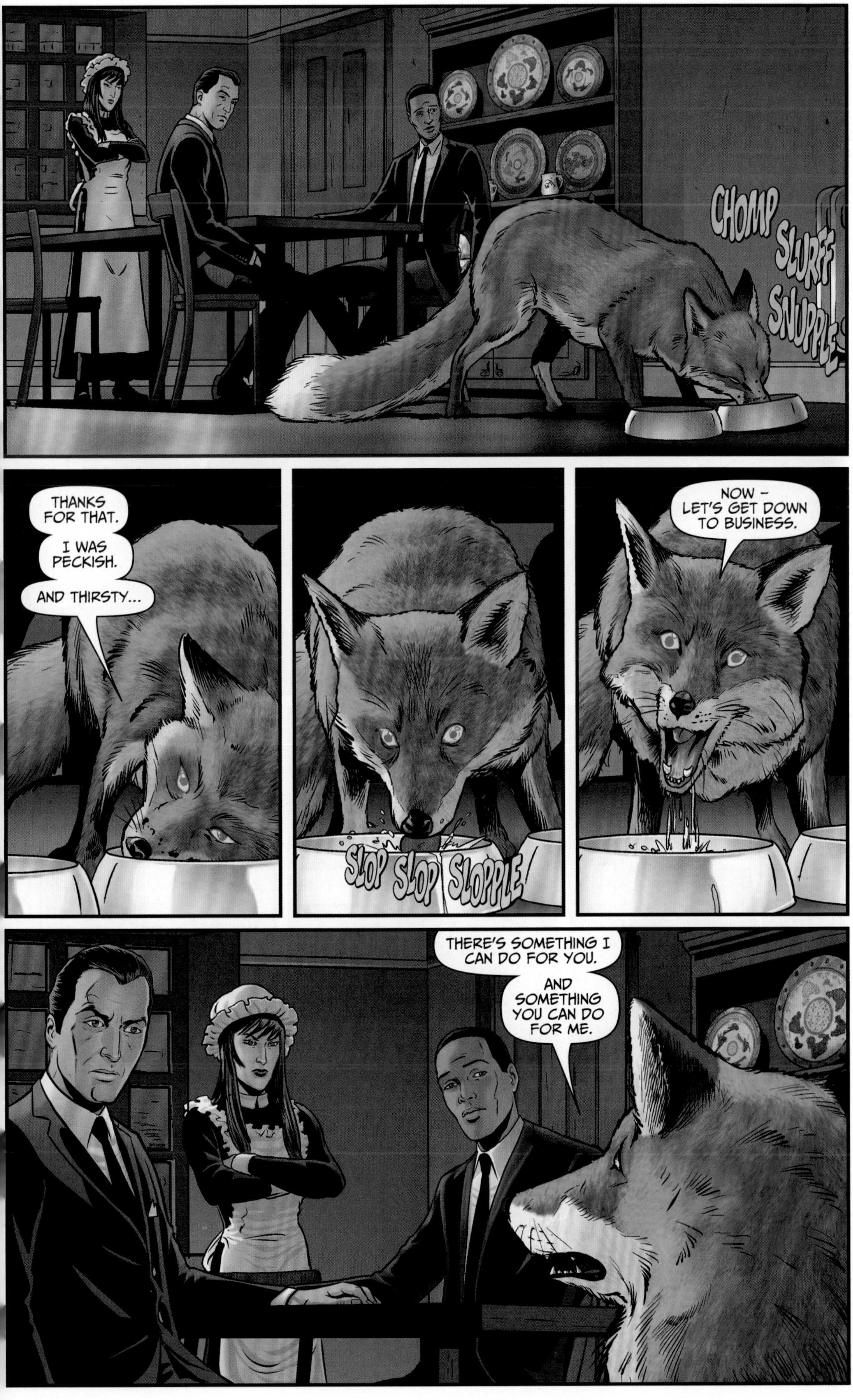
CHOMP
SLURFF
SNUPPLE
THANKS FOR THAT.
I WAS PECKISH.
AND THIRSTY...
SLOP SLOP SLOPPLE
NOW – LET'S GET DOWN TO BUSINESS.
THERE'S SOMETHING I CAN DO FOR YOU.
AND SOMETHING YOU CAN DO FOR ME.

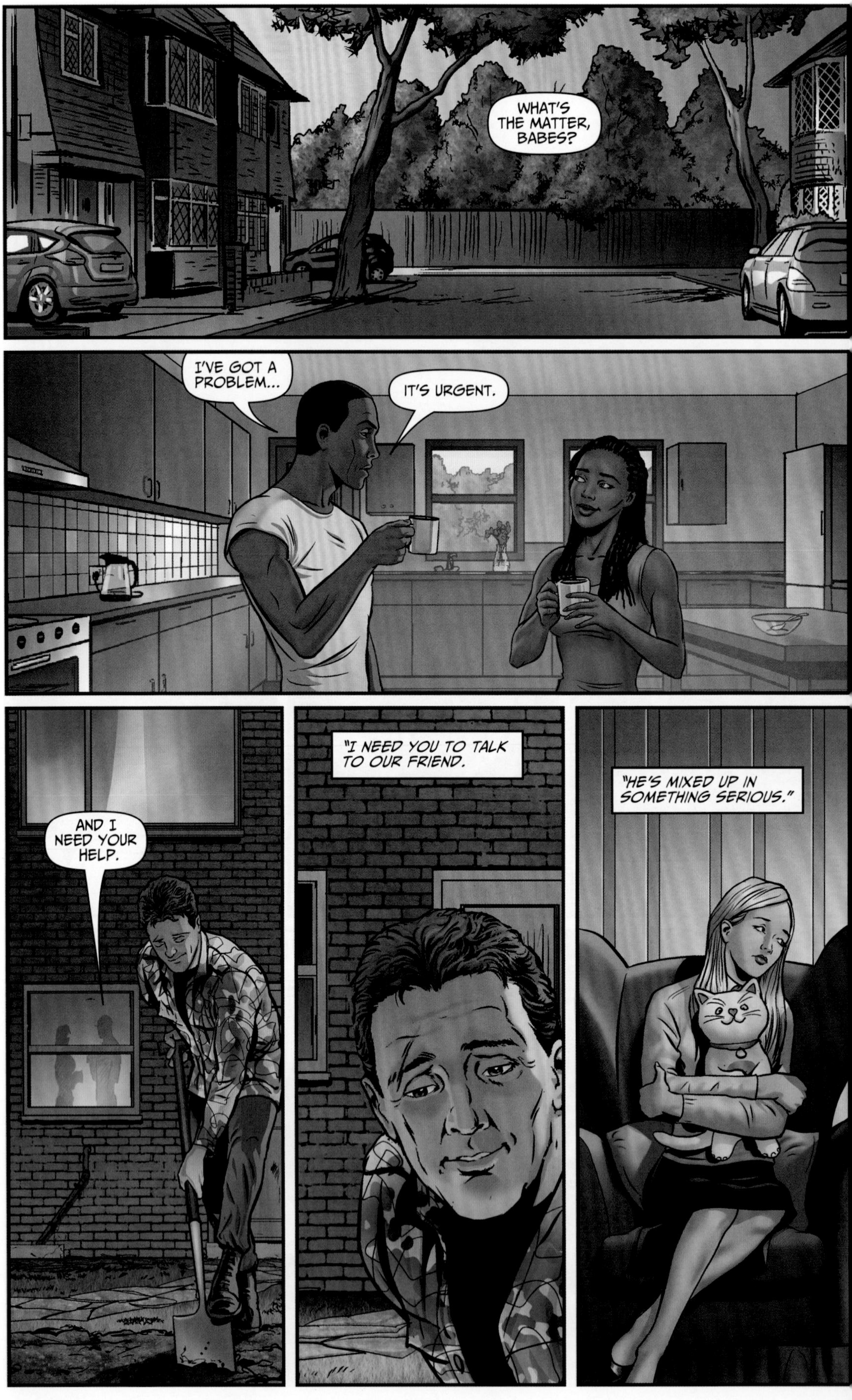
WHAT'S THE MATTER, BABES?
I'VE GOT A PROBLEM...
IT'S URGENT.
AND I NEED YOUR HELP.
"I NEED YOU TO TALK TO OUR FRIEND.
"HE'S MIXED UP IN SOMETHING SERIOUS."

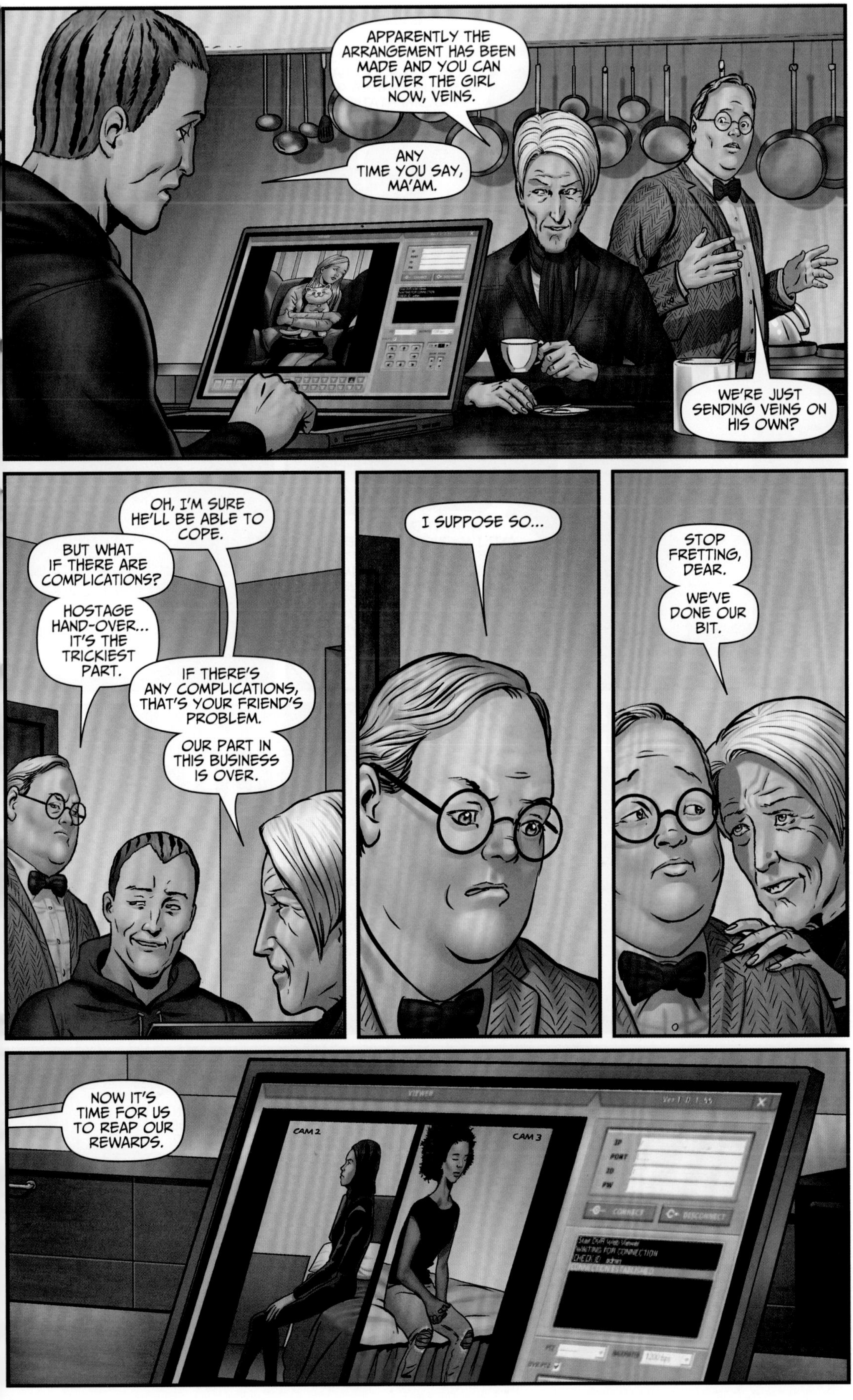
APPARENTLY THE ARRANGEMENT HAS BEEN MADE AND YOU CAN DELIVER THE GIRL NOW, VEINS.
ANY TIME YOU SAY, MA'AM.
WE'RE JUST SENDING VEINS ON HIS OWN?
OH, I'M SURE HE'LL BE ABLE TO COPE.
BUT WHAT IF THERE ARE COMPLICATIONS?
HOSTAGE HAND-OVER... IT'S THE TRICKIEST PART.
IF THERE'S ANY COMPLICATIONS, THAT'S YOUR FRIEND'S PROBLEM.
OUR PART IN THIS BUSINESS IS OVER.
I SUPPOSE SO...
STOP FRETTING, DEAR.
WE'VE DONE OUR BIT.
NOW IT'S TIME FOR US TO REAP OUR REWARDS.
CAM 2
CAM 3
CONNECT
DISCONNECT

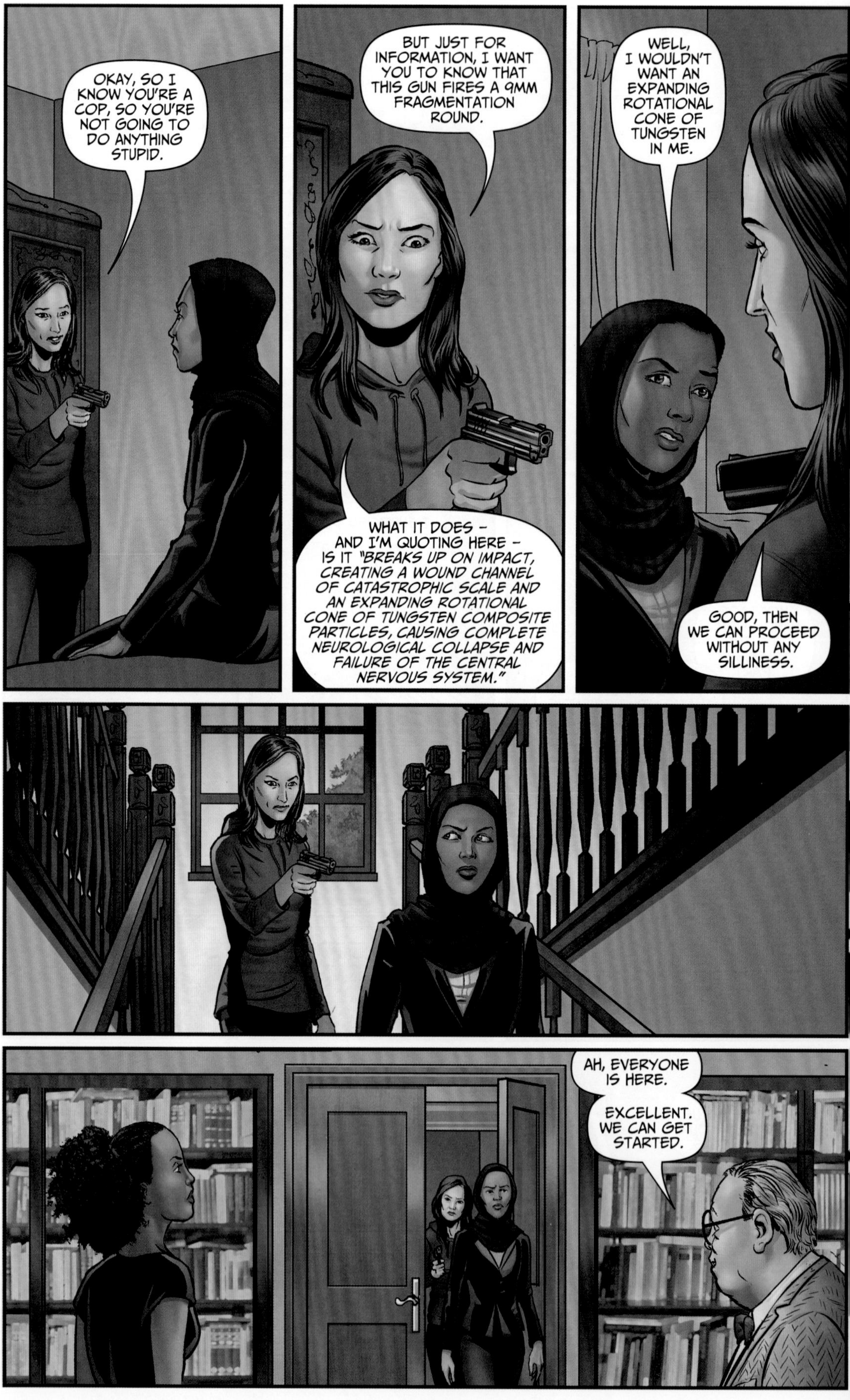

OKAY, SO I KNOW YOU'RE A COP, SO YOU'RE NOT GOING TO DO ANYTHING STUPID.
BUT JUST FOR INFORMATION, I WANT YOU TO KNOW THAT THIS GUN FIRES A 9MM FRAGMENTATION ROUND.
WHAT IT DOES – AND I'M QUOTING HERE – IS IT "BREAKS UP ON IMPACT, CREATING A WOUND CHANNEL OF CATASTROPHIC SCALE AND AN EXPANDING ROTATIONAL CONE OF TUNGSTEN COMPOSITE PARTICLES, CAUSING COMPLETE NEUROLOGICAL COLLAPSE AND FAILURE OF THE CENTRAL NERVOUS SYSTEM."
WELL, I WOULDN'T WANT AN EXPANDING ROTATIONAL CONE OF TUNGSTEN IN ME.
GOOD, THEN WE CAN PROCEED WITHOUT ANY SILLINESS.
AH, EVERYONE IS HERE.
EXCELLENT. WE CAN GET STARTED.

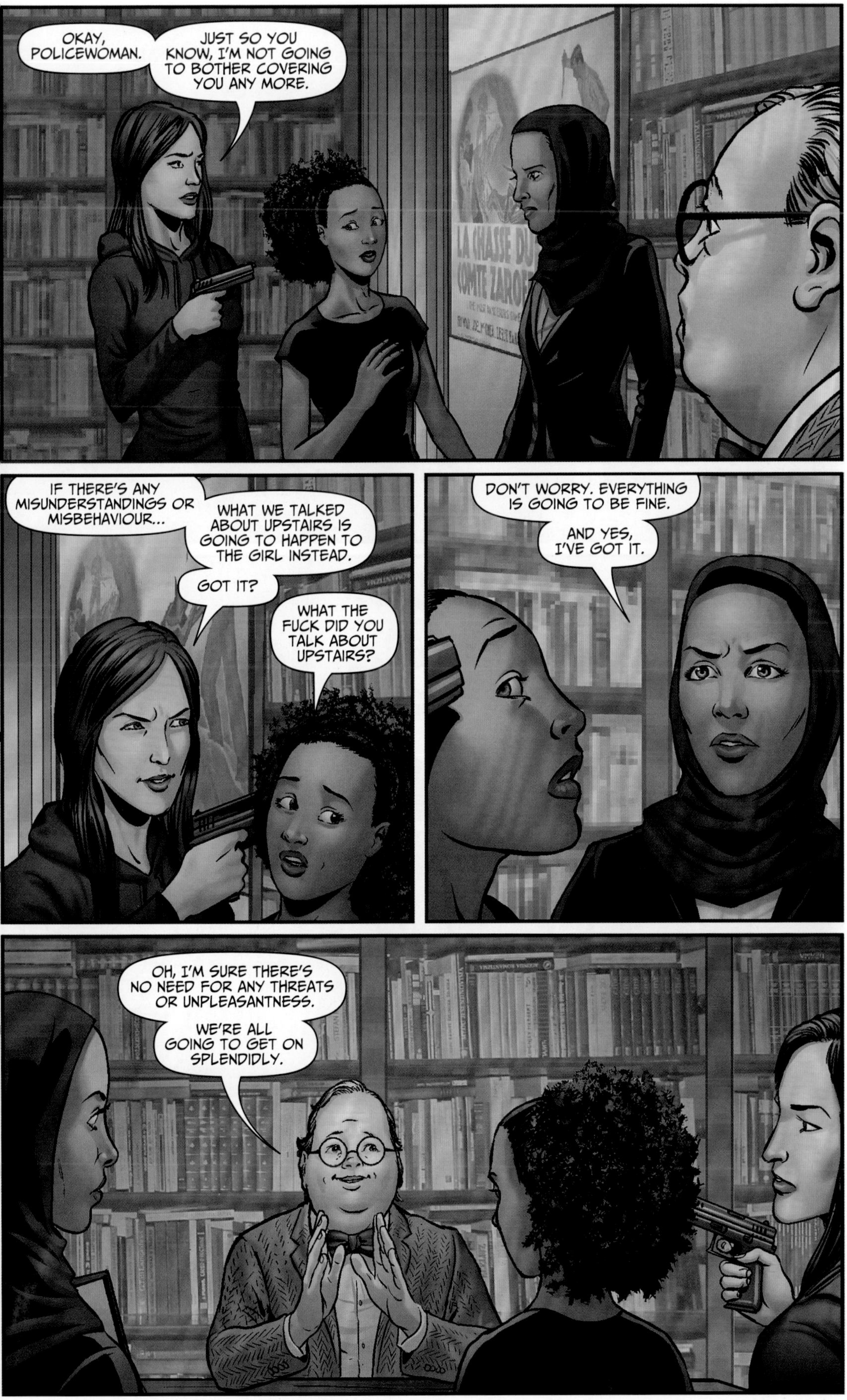

OKAY, POLICEWOMAN.
JUST SO YOU KNOW, I'M NOT GOING TO BOTHER COVERING YOU ANY MORE.
LA CHASSE DU
COMTE ZARO
IF THERE'S ANY MISUNDERSTANDINGS OR MISBEHAVIOUR...
WHAT WE TALKED ABOUT UPSTAIRS IS GOING TO HAPPEN TO THE GIRL INSTEAD.
GOT IT?
WHAT THE FUCK DID YOU TALK ABOUT UPSTAIRS?
DON'T WORRY. EVERYTHING IS GOING TO BE FINE.
AND YES, I'VE GOT IT.
OH, I'M SURE THERE'S NO NEED FOR ANY THREATS OR UNPLEASANTNESS.
WE'RE ALL GOING TO GET ON SPLENDIDLY.

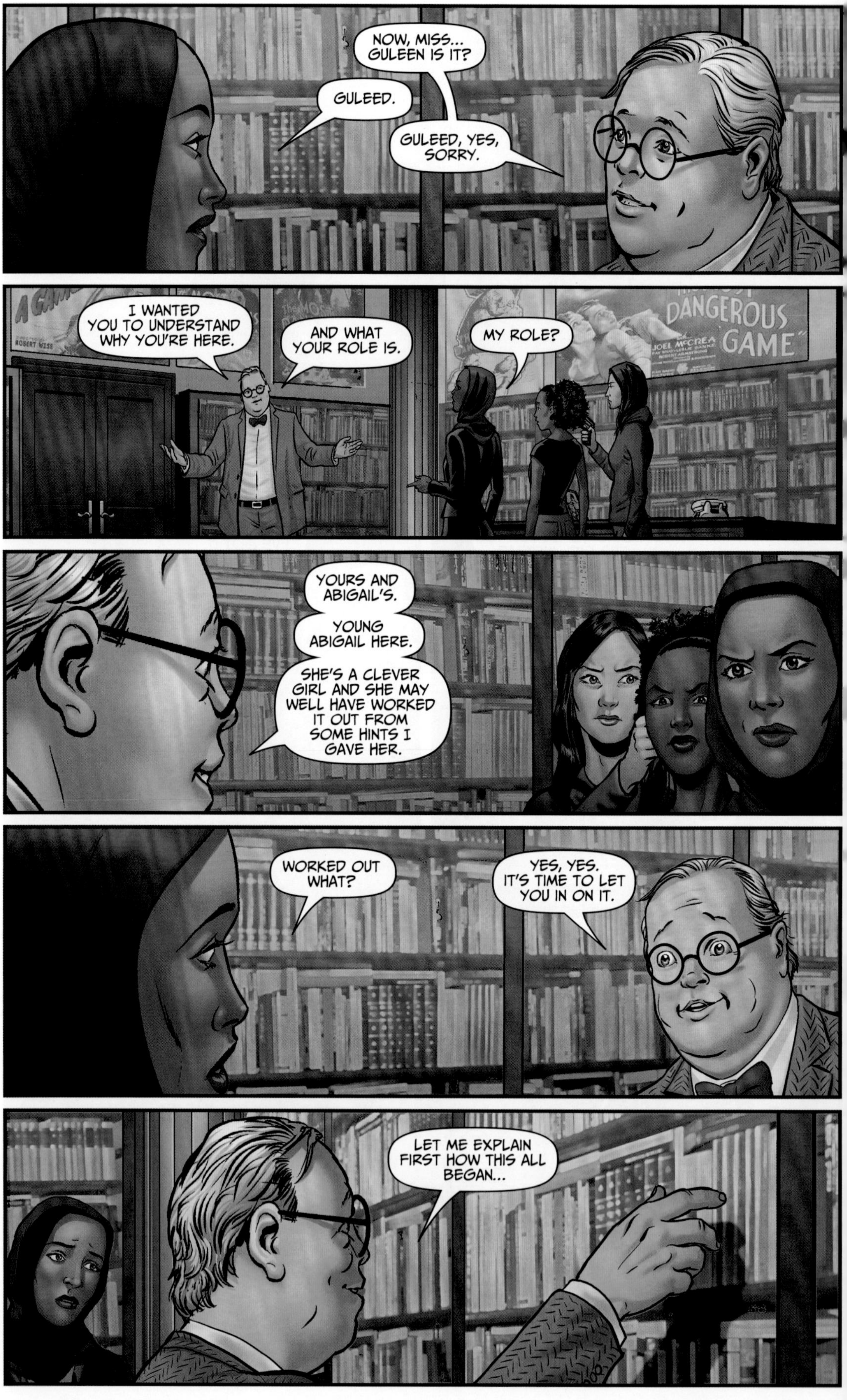
NOW, MISS... GULEEN IS IT?
GULEED.
GULEED, YES, SORRY.
A GAME
ROBERT WISE
THE MOST DANGEROUS GAME
JOEL McCREA
I WANTED YOU TO UNDERSTAND WHY YOU'RE HERE.
AND WHAT YOUR ROLE IS.
MY ROLE?
YOURS AND ABIGAIL'S.
YOUNG ABIGAIL HERE.
SHE'S A CLEVER GIRL AND SHE MAY WELL HAVE WORKED IT OUT FROM SOME HINTS I GAVE HER.
WORKED OUT WHAT?
YES, YES. IT'S TIME TO LET YOU IN ON IT.
LET ME EXPLAIN FIRST HOW THIS ALL BEGAN...

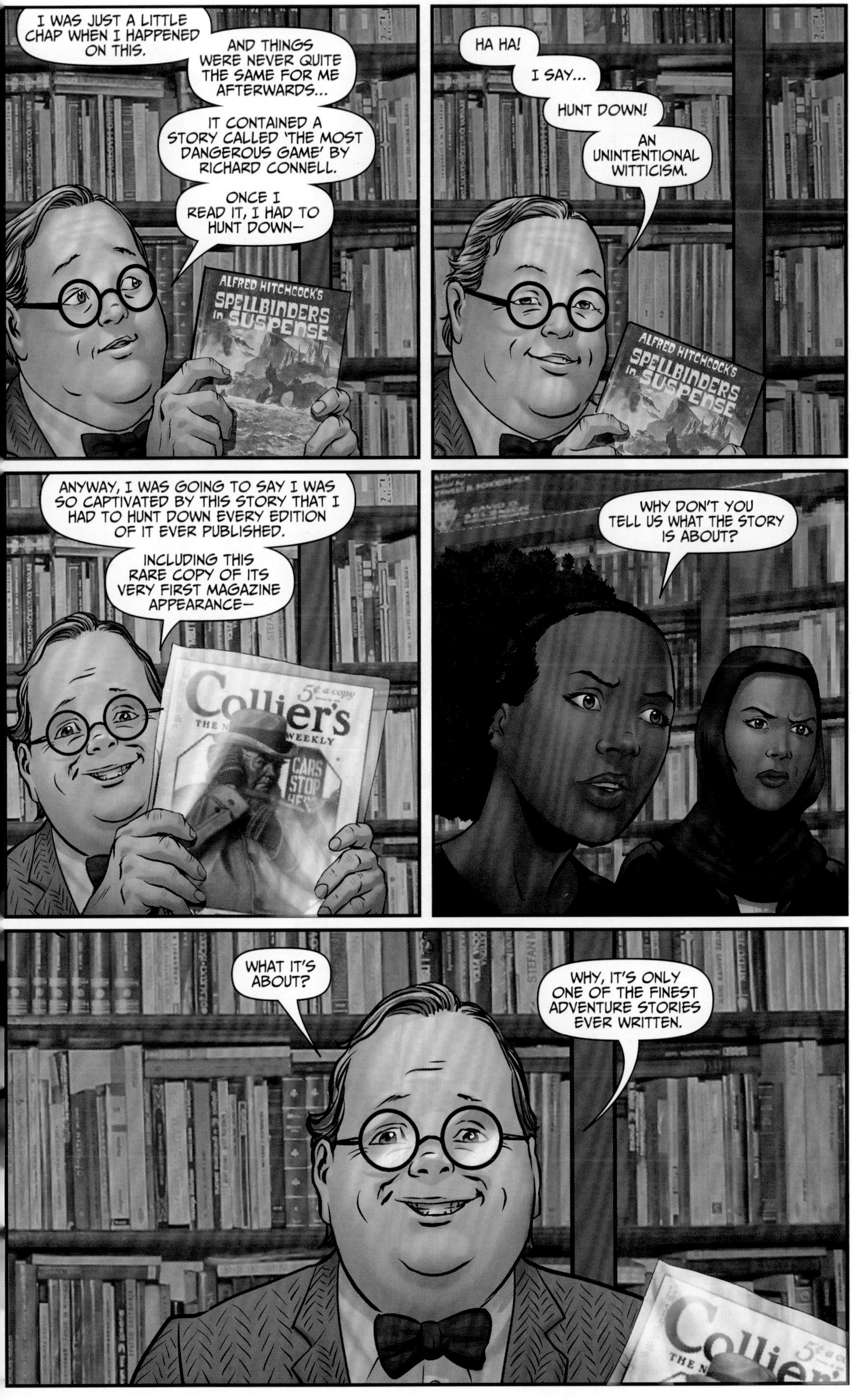

I WAS JUST A LITTLE CHAP WHEN I HAPPENED ON THIS.
AND THINGS WERE NEVER QUITE THE SAME FOR ME AFTERWARDS...
IT CONTAINED A STORY CALLED 'THE MOST DANGEROUS GAME' BY RICHARD CONNELL.
ONCE I READ IT, I HAD TO HUNT DOWN–
ALFRED HITCHCOCK'S SPELLBINDERS in SUSPENSE
HA HA!
I SAY...
HUNT DOWN!
AN UNINTENTIONAL WITTICISM.
ALFRED HITCHCOCK'S SPELLBINDERS in SUSPENSE
ANYWAY, I WAS GOING TO SAY I WAS SO CAPTIVATED BY THIS STORY THAT I HAD TO HUNT DOWN EVERY EDITION OF IT EVER PUBLISHED.
INCLUDING THIS RARE COPY OF ITS VERY FIRST MAGAZINE APPEARANCE–
Collier's
5¢ a copy
WHY DON'T YOU TELL US WHAT THE STORY IS ABOUT?
WHAT IT'S ABOUT?
WHY, IT'S ONLY ONE OF THE FINEST ADVENTURE STORIES EVER WRITTEN.

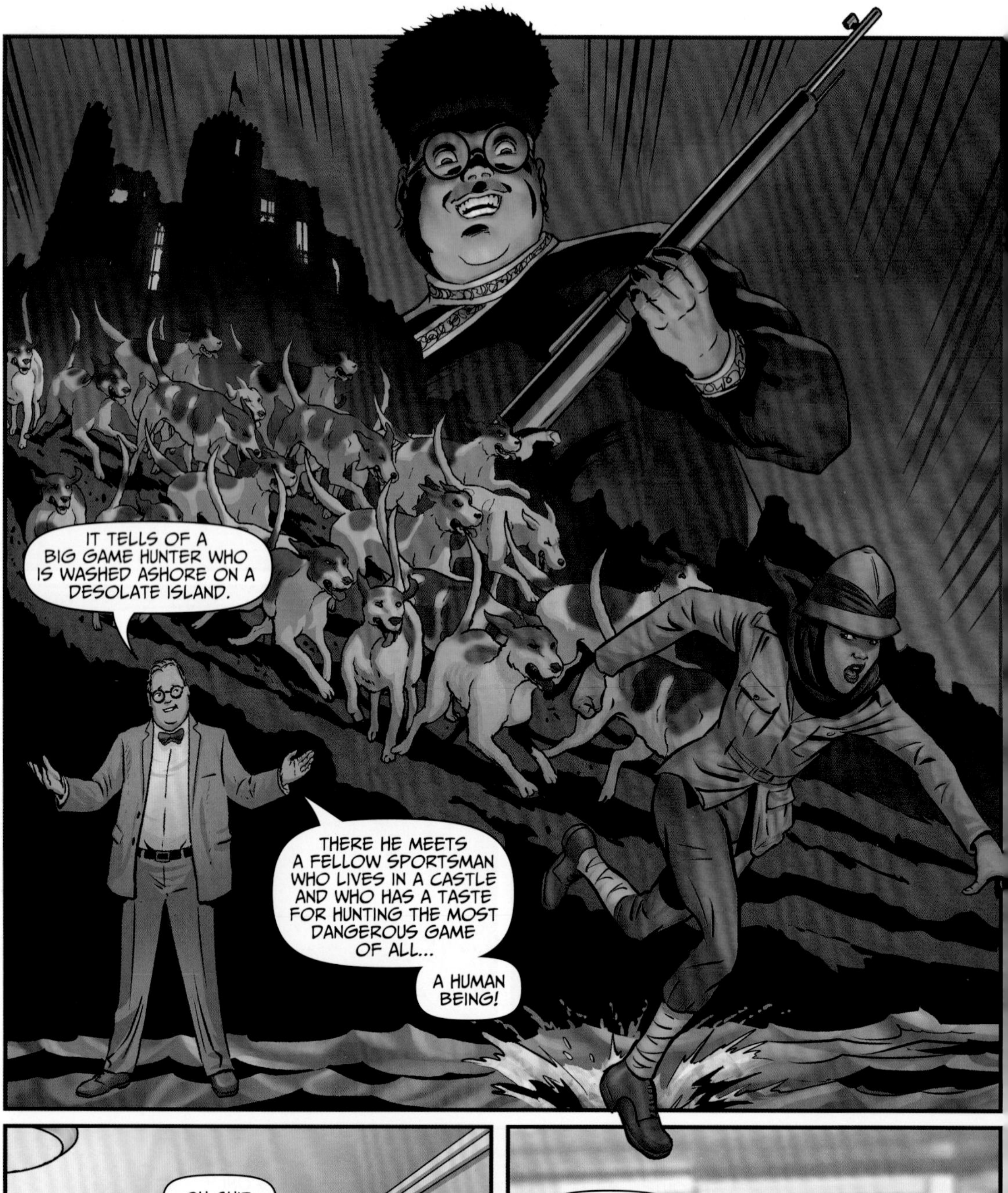
IT TELLS OF A BIG GAME HUNTER WHO IS WASHED ASHORE ON A DESOLATE ISLAND.
THERE HE MEETS A FELLOW SPORTSMAN WHO LIVES IN A CASTLE AND WHO HAS A TASTE FOR HUNTING THE MOST DANGEROUS GAME OF ALL...
A HUMAN BEING!

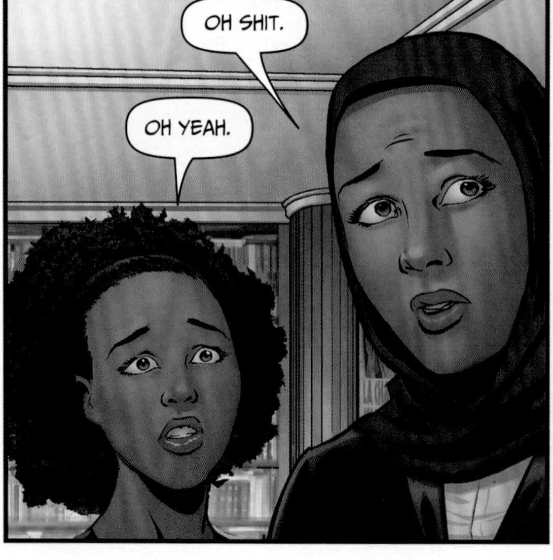
OH SHIT.
OH YEAH.

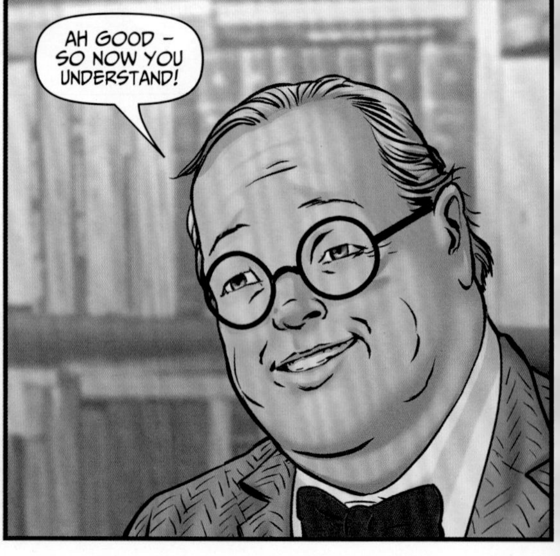
AH GOOD - SO NOW YOU UNDERSTAND!

IN THE STORY THE CHAP BEING HUNTED IS GIVEN A THREE HOUR HEAD START, SUITABLE CLOTHING, FOOD, AND OTHER USEFUL ITEMS.

NOW, *YOU* WILL BE PROVIDED WITH THIS MAP, SUITABLE CLOTHING, AND FOOD.

BUT I'M AFRAID I CAN'T GIVE YOU THREE HOURS.

MY PROPERTY IS EXTENSIVE, BUT NOT QUITE THAT EXTENSIVE.

SO YOU CAN HAVE THIRTY MINUTES.

BEFORE WHAT?

BEFORE WE COME AFTER YOU, ON HORSEBACK WITH THE DOGS.

BUT HERE'S THE IMPORTANT THING – IF YOU MANAGE TO EVADE US, YOU WILL BE SENT HOME UNHARMED AND WITH A NICE LITTLE CASH BONUS.

AND IF WE *DON'T* MANAGE TO EVADE YOU?

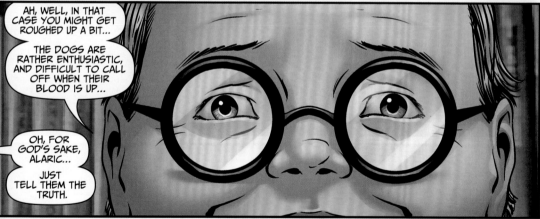

AH, WELL, IN THAT CASE YOU MIGHT GET ROUGHED UP A BIT...

THE DOGS ARE RATHER ENTHUSIASTIC, AND DIFFICULT TO CALL OFF WHEN THEIR BLOOD IS UP...

OH, FOR GOD'S SAKE, ALARIC...

JUST TELL THEM THE TRUTH.

IF WE CATCH YOU, YOU'LL BE KILLED.

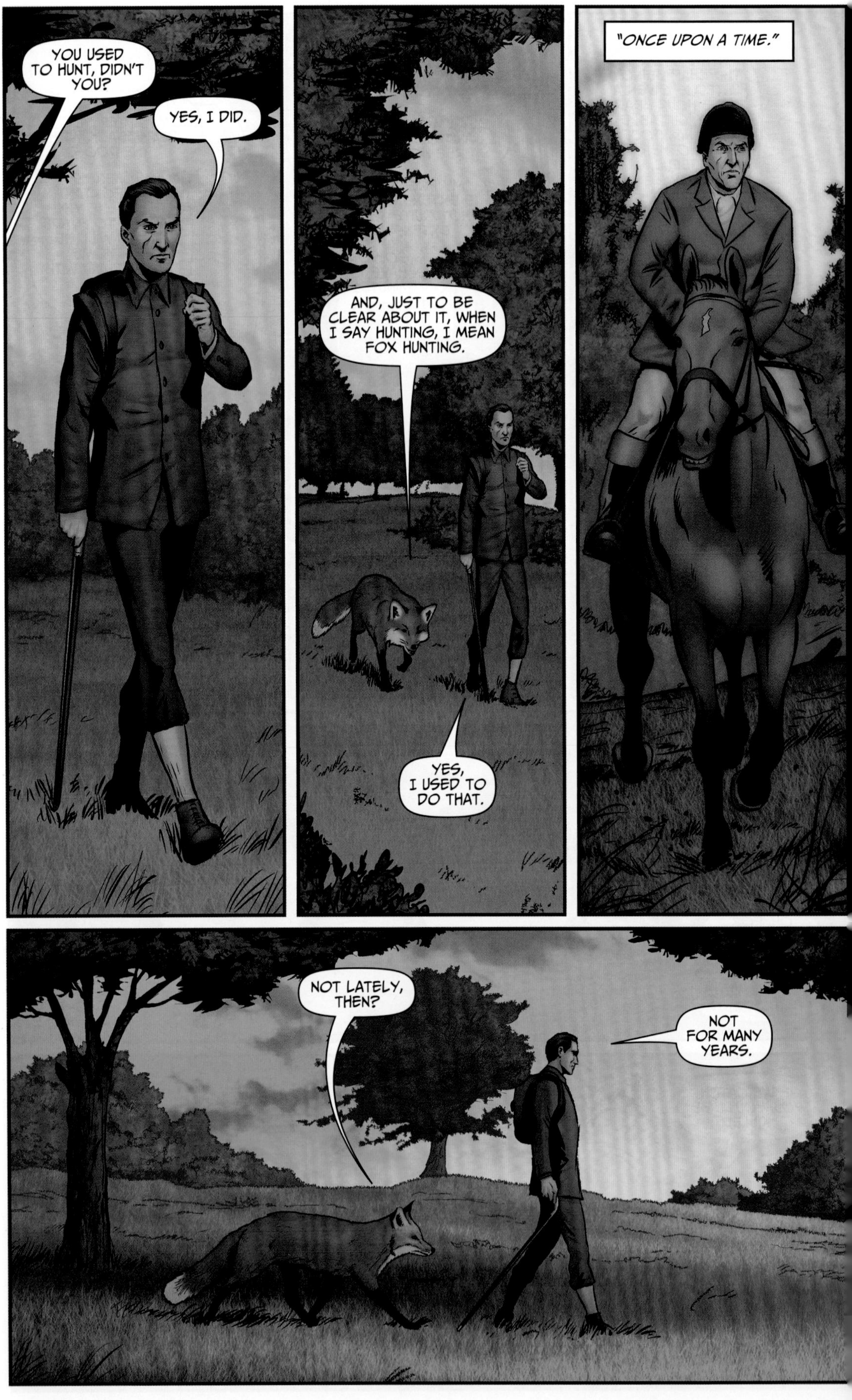
YOU USED TO HUNT, DIDN'T YOU?
YES, I DID.
AND, JUST TO BE CLEAR ABOUT IT, WHEN I SAY HUNTING, I MEAN FOX HUNTING.
YES, I USED TO DO THAT.
"ONCE UPON A TIME."
NOT LATELY, THEN?
NOT FOR MANY YEARS.

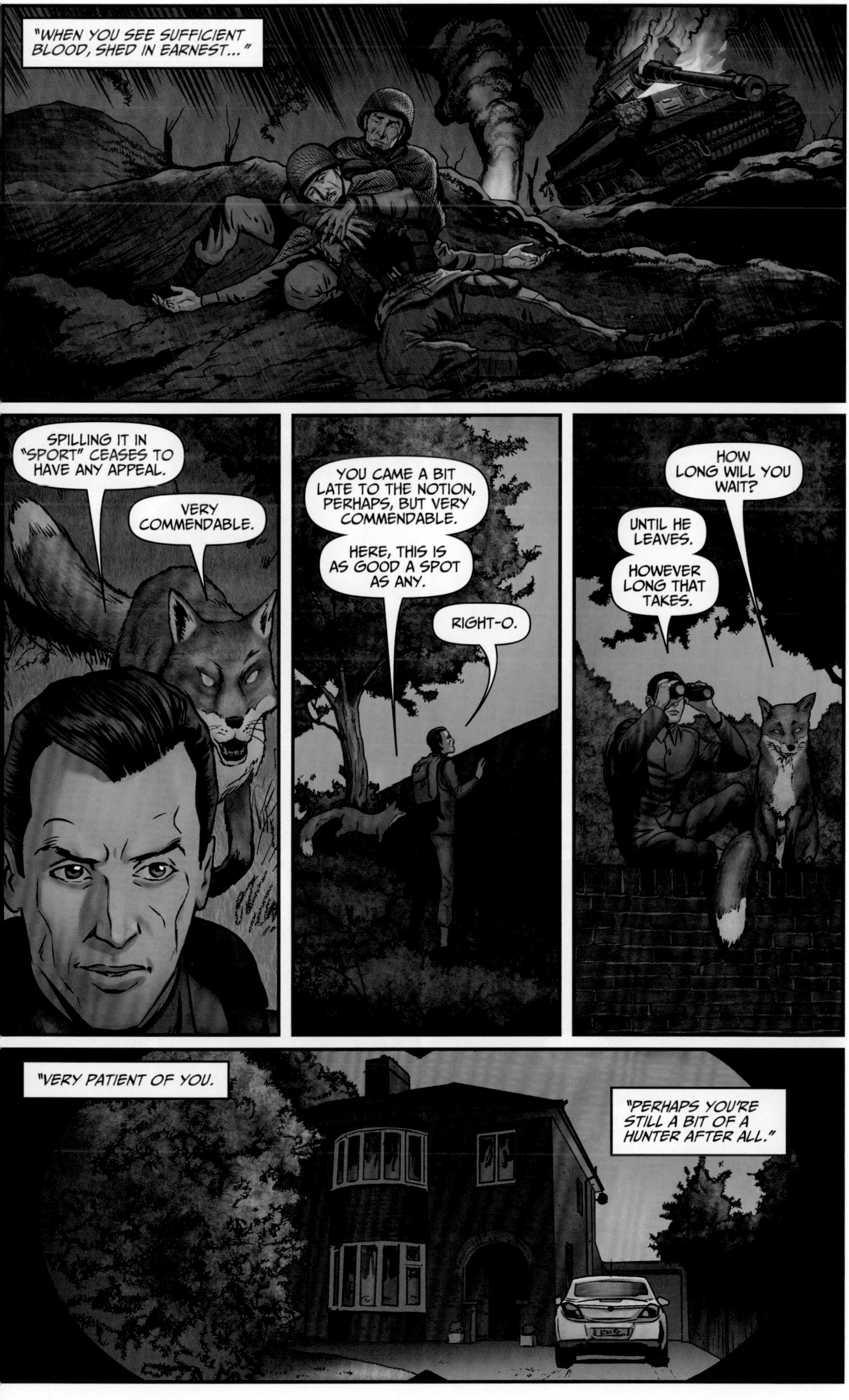
"WHEN YOU SEE SUFFICIENT BLOOD, SHED IN EARNEST..."
SPILLING IT IN "SPORT" CEASES TO HAVE ANY APPEAL.
VERY COMMENDABLE.
YOU CAME A BIT LATE TO THE NOTION, PERHAPS, BUT VERY COMMENDABLE.
HERE, THIS IS AS GOOD A SPOT AS ANY.
RIGHT-O.
HOW LONG WILL YOU WAIT?
UNTIL HE LEAVES.
HOWEVER LONG THAT TAKES.
"VERY PATIENT OF YOU.
"PERHAPS YOU'RE STILL A BIT OF A HUNTER AFTER ALL."

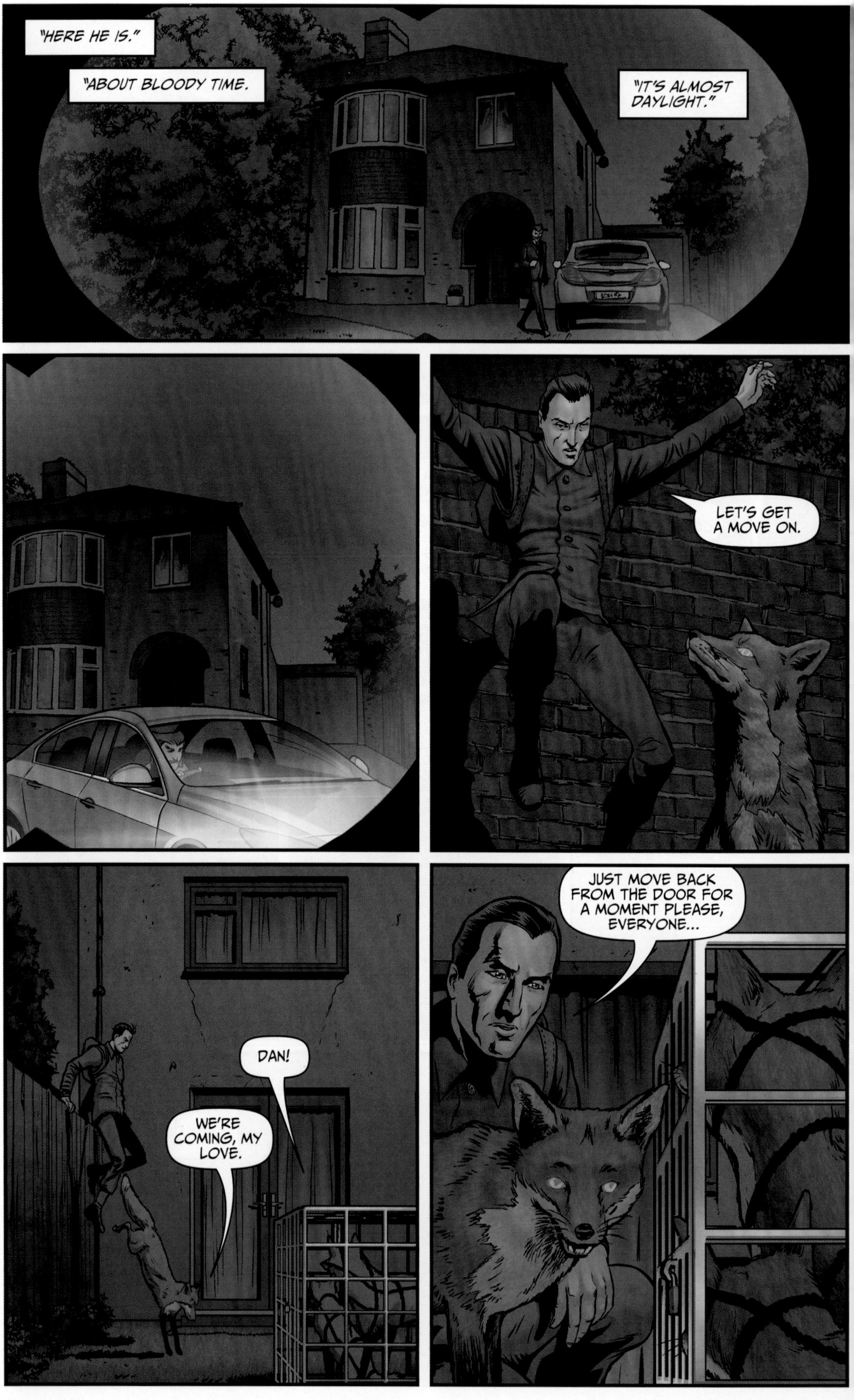
"HERE HE IS."
"ABOUT BLOODY TIME.
"IT'S ALMOST DAYLIGHT."
LET'S GET A MOVE ON.
DAN!
WE'RE COMING, MY LOVE.
JUST MOVE BACK FROM THE DOOR FOR A MOMENT PLEASE, EVERYONE...

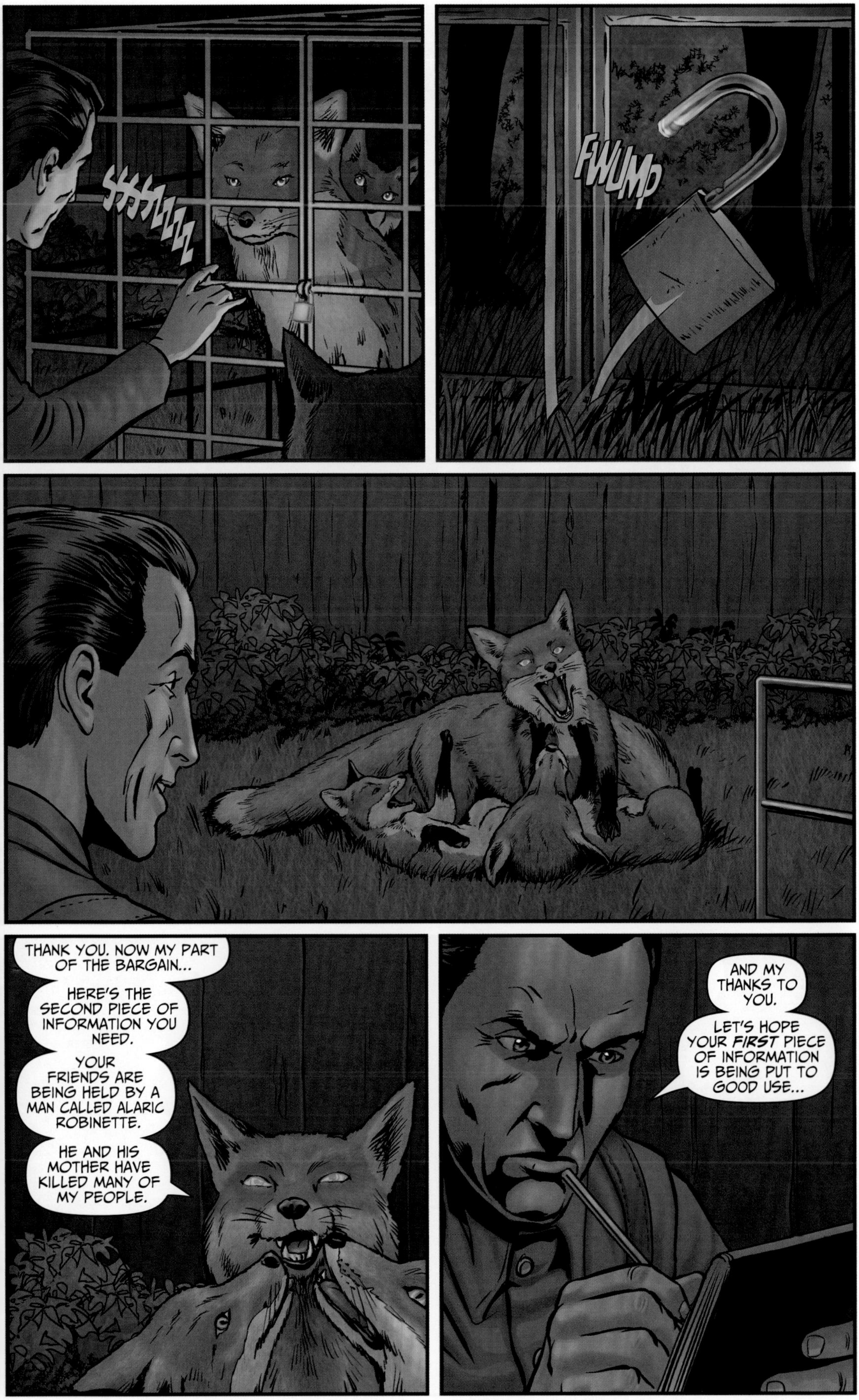
SSSSZZZZZ
FWUMP
THANK YOU. NOW MY PART OF THE BARGAIN...
HERE'S THE SECOND PIECE OF INFORMATION YOU NEED.
YOUR FRIENDS ARE BEING HELD BY A MAN CALLED ALARIC ROBINETTE.
HE AND HIS MOTHER HAVE KILLED MANY OF MY PEOPLE.
AND MY THANKS TO YOU.
LET'S HOPE YOUR *FIRST* PIECE OF INFORMATION IS BEING PUT TO GOOD USE...

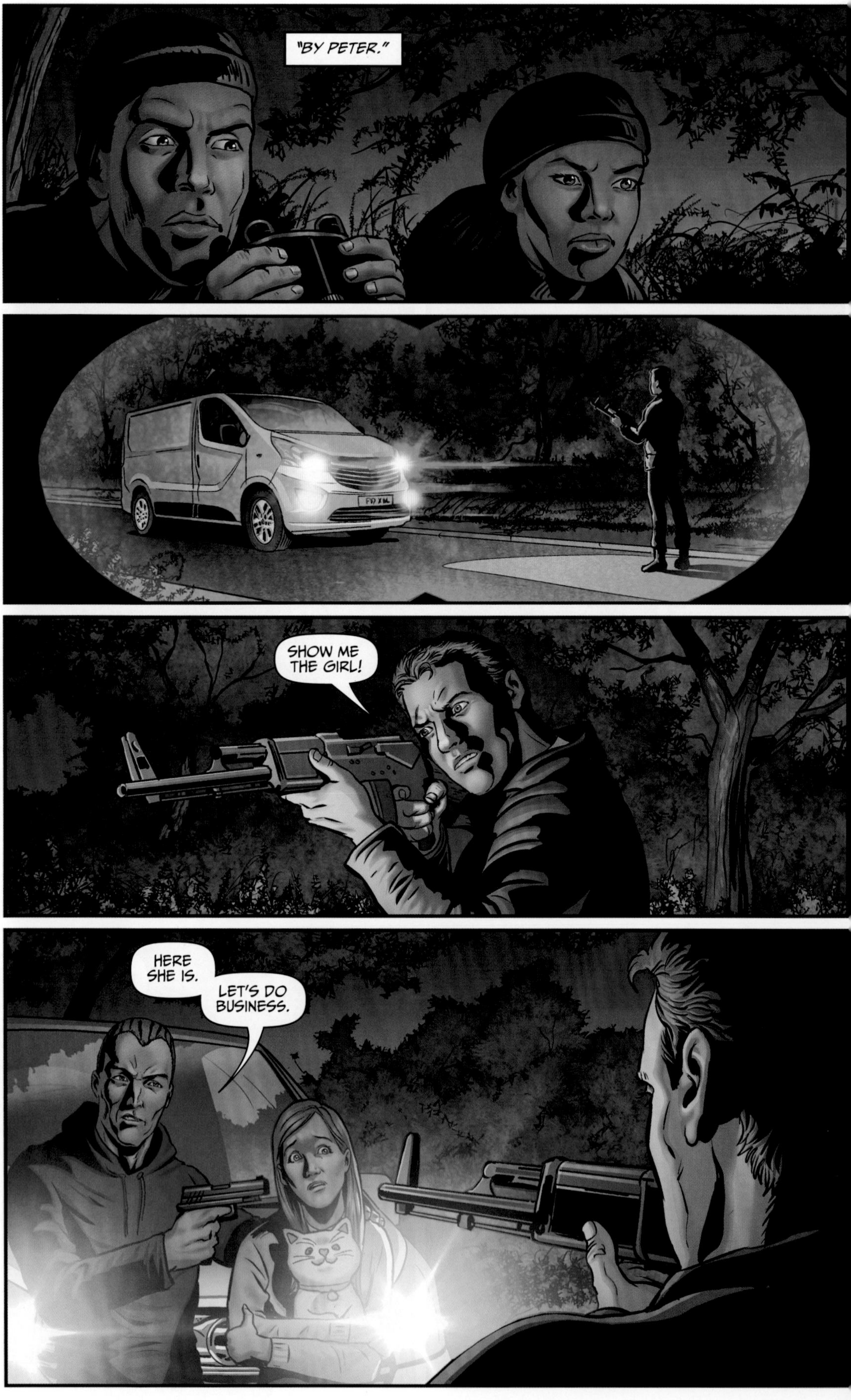
"BY PETER."
SHOW ME THE GIRL!
HERE SHE IS.
LET'S DO BUSINESS.

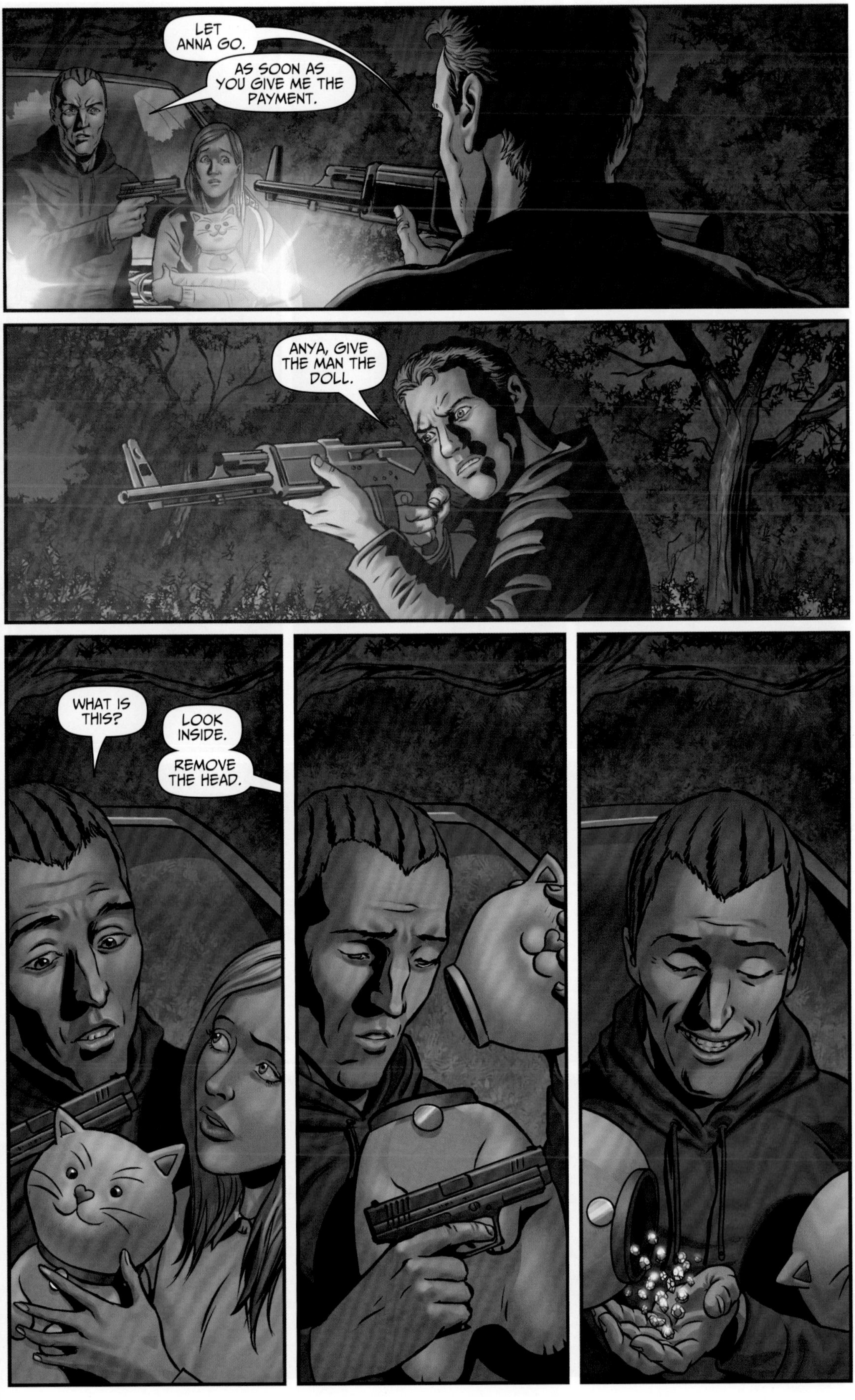
LET ANNA GO.
AS SOON AS YOU GIVE ME THE PAYMENT.
ANYA, GIVE THE MAN THE DOLL.
WHAT IS THIS?
LOOK INSIDE.
REMOVE THE HEAD.

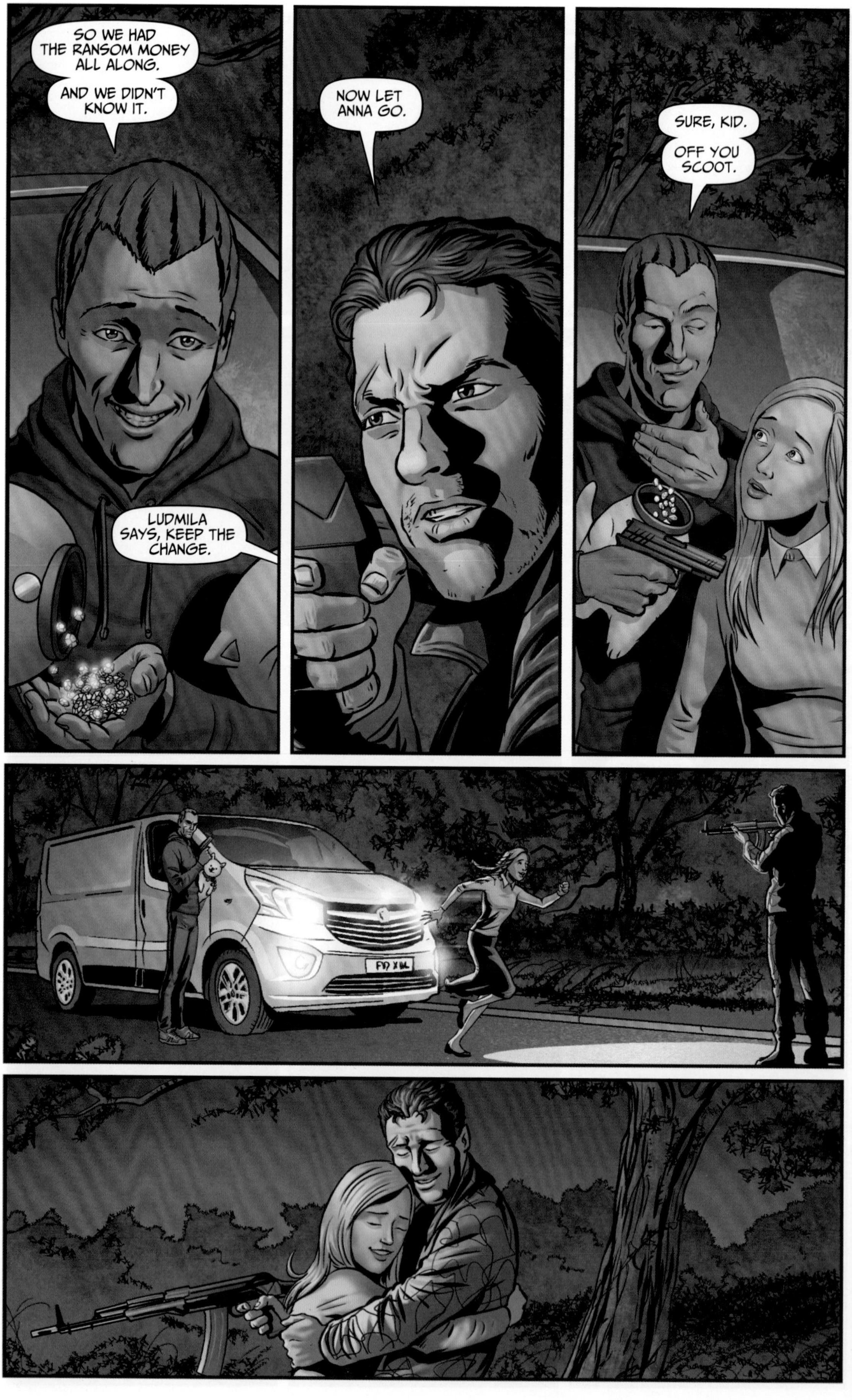
SO WE HAD THE RANSOM MONEY ALL ALONG.
AND WE DIDN'T KNOW IT.
LUDMILA SAYS, KEEP THE CHANGE.
NOW LET ANNA GO.
SURE, KID.
OFF YOU SCOOT.

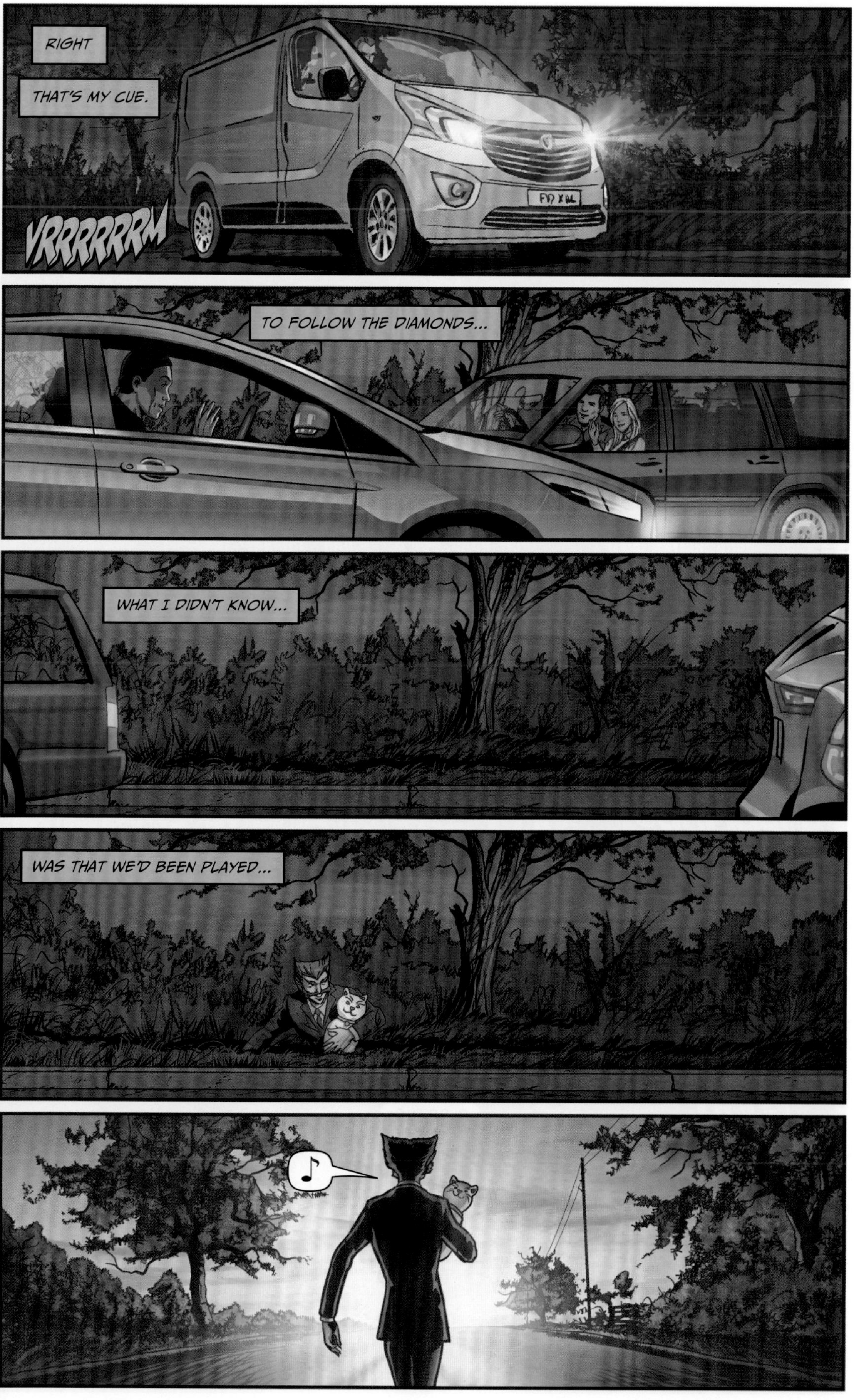
RIGHT
THAT'S MY CUE.
VRRRRRRM
TO FOLLOW THE DIAMONDS...
WHAT I DIDN'T KNOW...
WAS THAT WE'D BEEN PLAYED...
♪

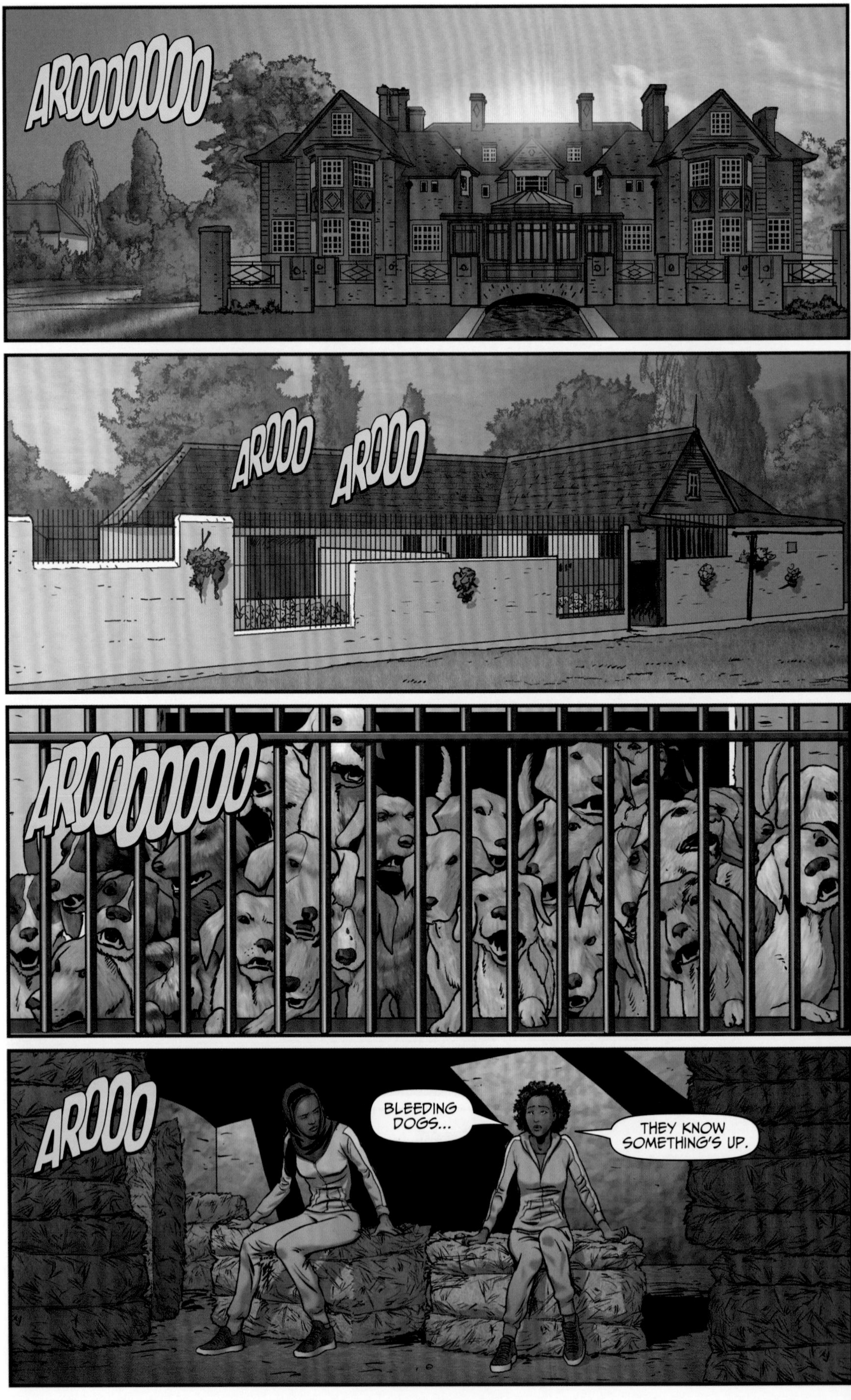
AROOOOOOO
AROOO AROOO
AROOOOOOOO
AROOO
BLEEDING DOGS...
THEY KNOW SOMETHING'S UP.

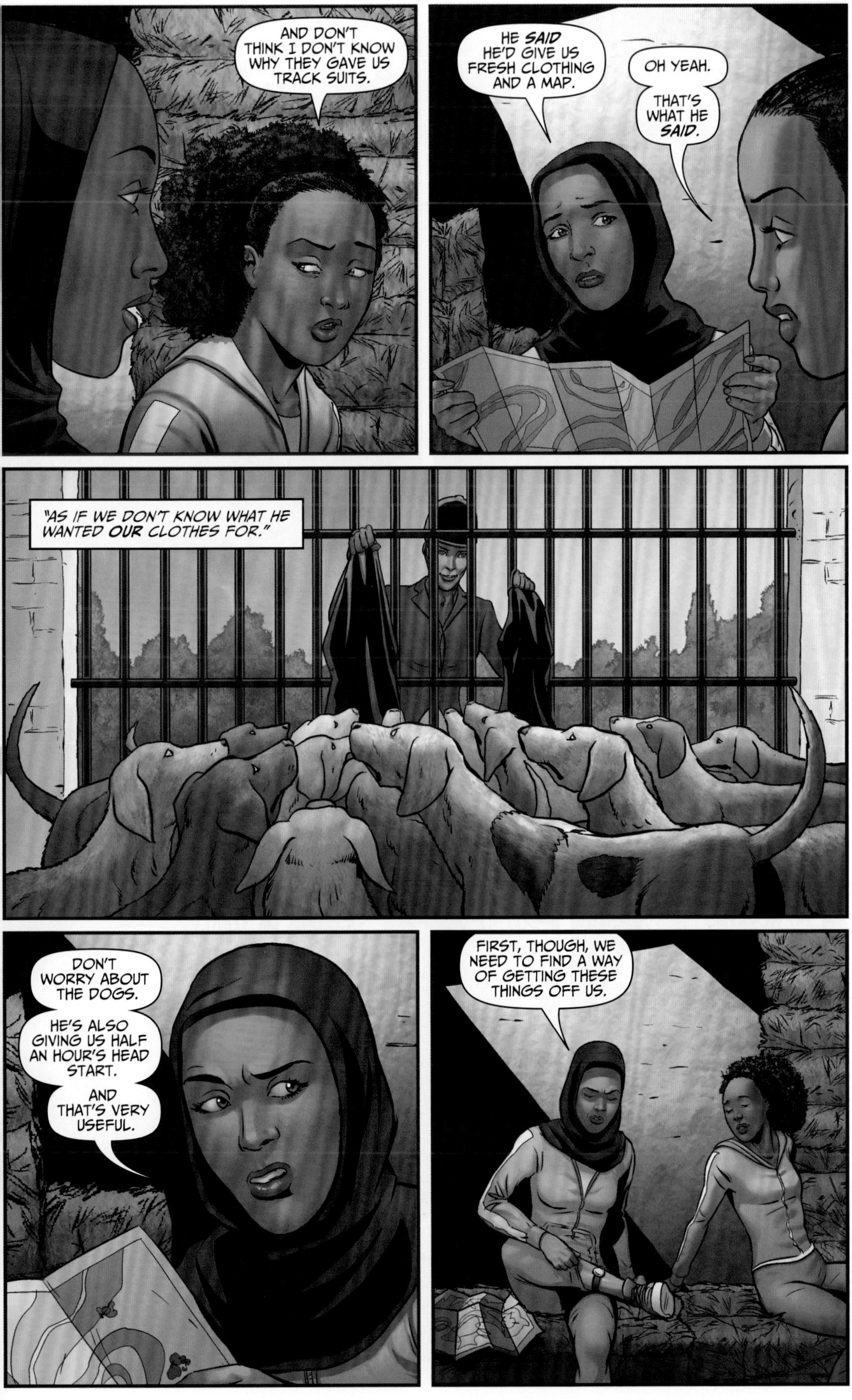
AND DON'T THINK I DON'T KNOW WHY THEY GAVE US TRACK SUITS.
HE SAID HE'D GIVE US FRESH CLOTHING AND A MAP.
OH YEAH.
THAT'S WHAT HE SAID.
"AS IF WE DON'T KNOW WHAT HE WANTED OUR CLOTHES FOR."
DON'T WORRY ABOUT THE DOGS.
HE'S ALSO GIVING US HALF AN HOUR'S HEAD START.
AND THAT'S VERY USEFUL.
FIRST, THOUGH, WE NEED TO FIND A WAY OF GETTING THESE THINGS OFF US.

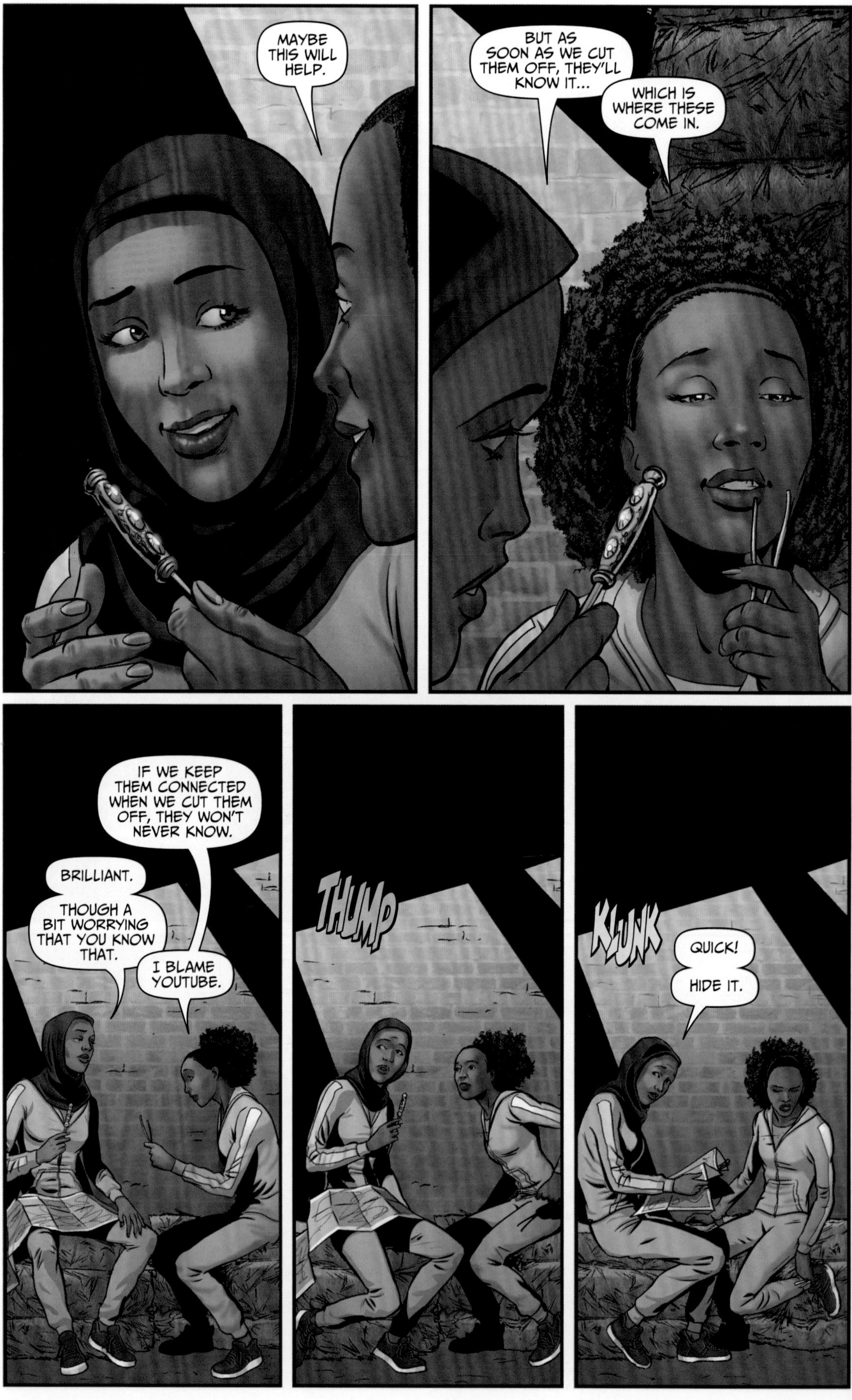
MAYBE THIS WILL HELP.
BUT AS SOON AS WE CUT THEM OFF, THEY'LL KNOW IT...
WHICH IS WHERE THESE COME IN.
IF WE KEEP THEM CONNECTED WHEN WE CUT THEM OFF, THEY WON'T NEVER KNOW.
BRILLIANT.
THOUGH A BIT WORRYING THAT YOU KNOW THAT.
I BLAME YOUTUBE.
THUMP
KLUNK
QUICK!
HIDE IT.

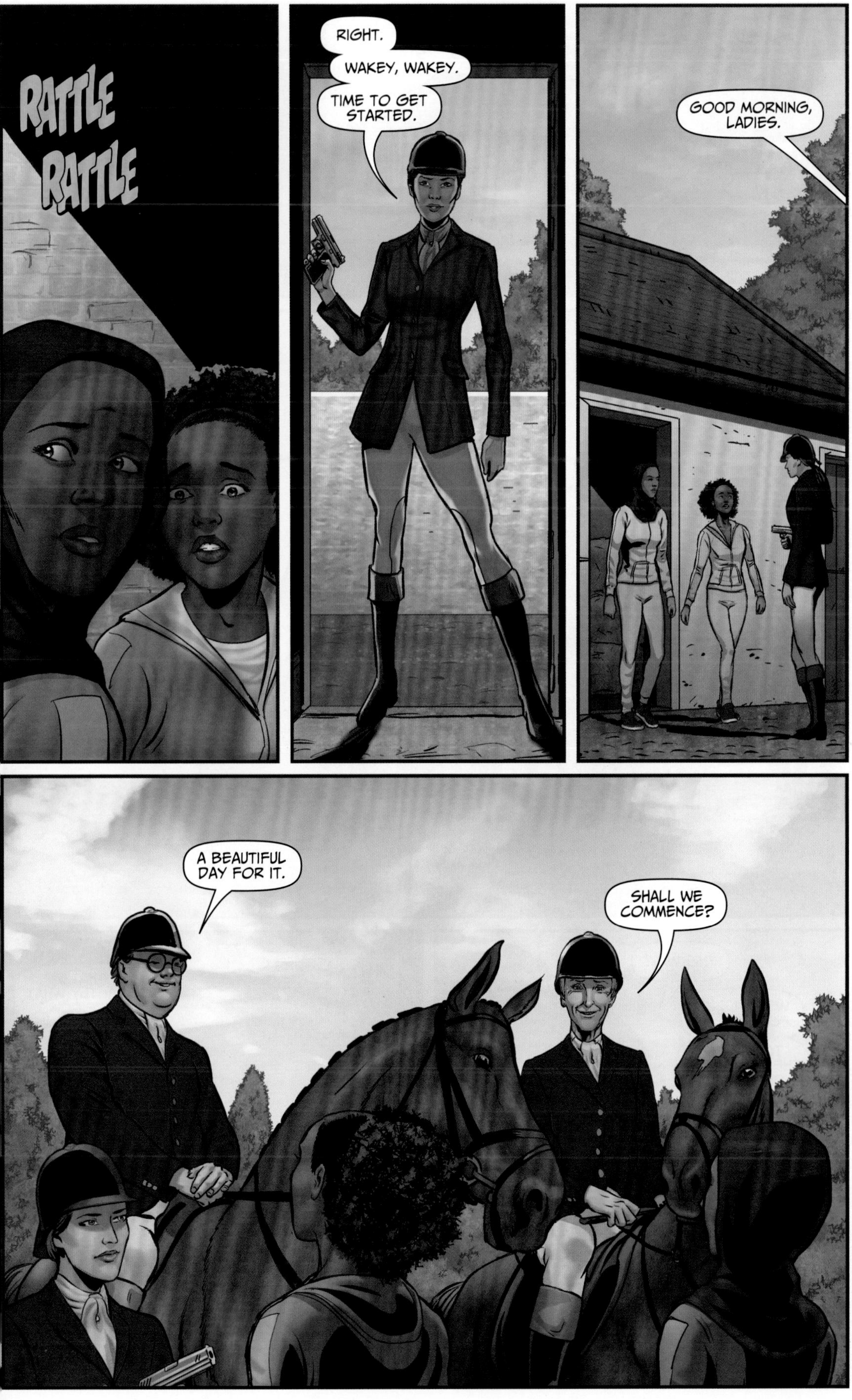
RATTLE RATTLE
RIGHT.
WAKEY, WAKEY.
TIME TO GET STARTED.
GOOD MORNING, LADIES.
A BEAUTIFUL DAY FOR IT.
SHALL WE COMMENCE?

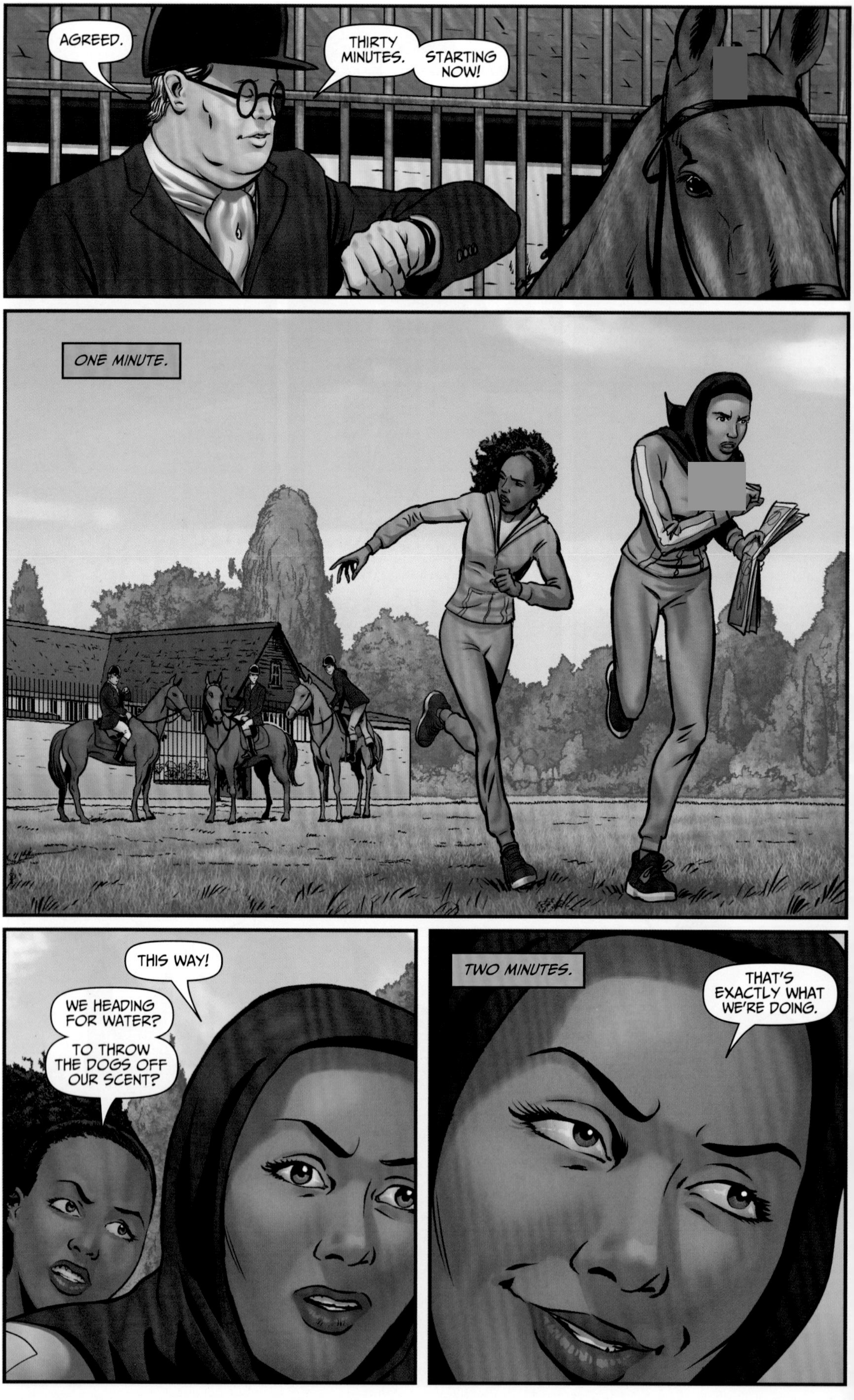
AGREED.
THIRTY MINUTES.
STARTING NOW!
ONE MINUTE.
THIS WAY!
WE HEADING FOR WATER?
TO THROW THE DOGS OFF OUR SCENT?
TWO MINUTES.
THAT'S EXACTLY WHAT WE'RE DOING.

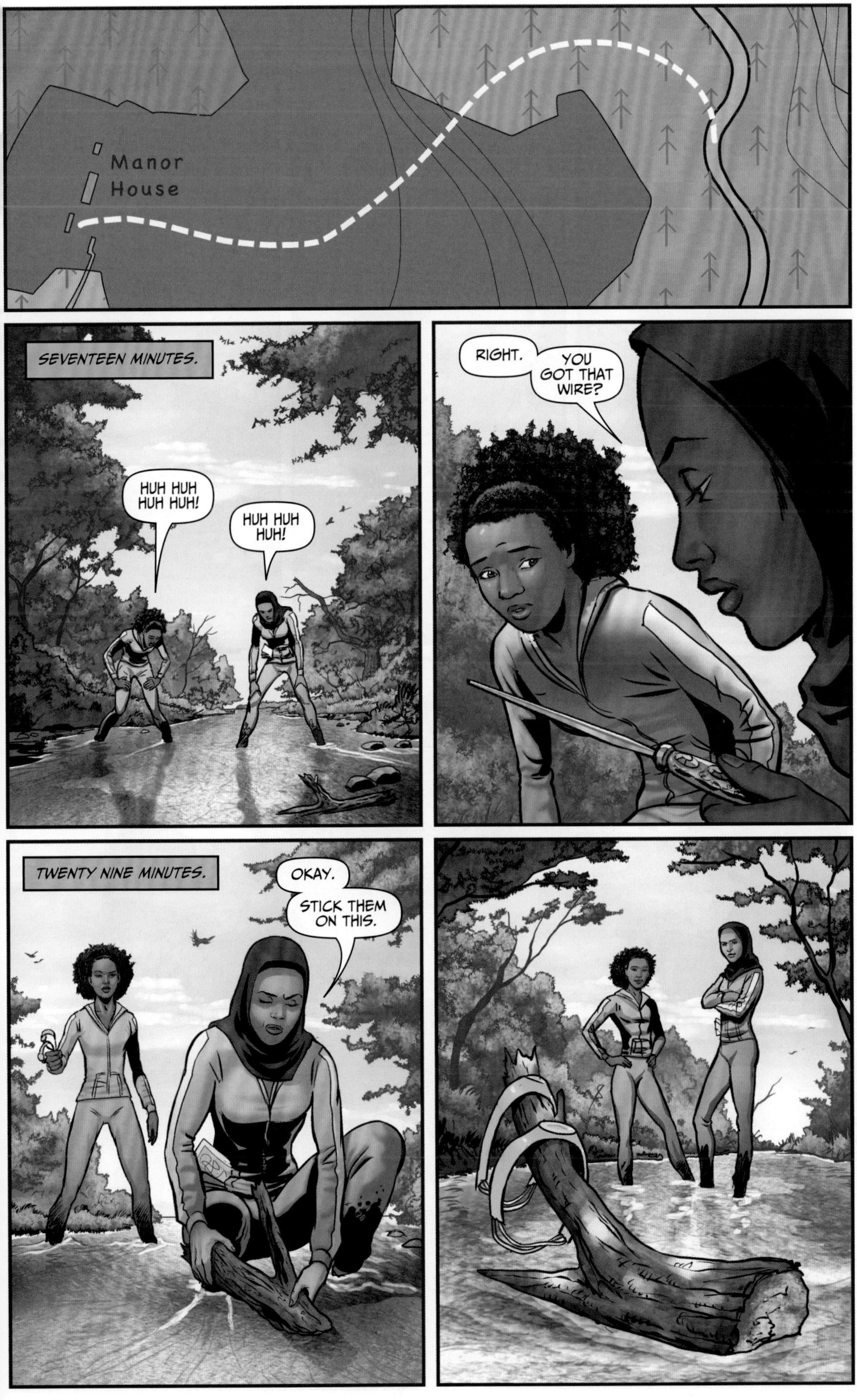
Manor
House
SEVENTEEN MINUTES.
HUH HUH
HUH HUH!
HUH HUH
HUH!
RIGHT.
YOU
GOT THAT
WIRE?
TWENTY NINE MINUTES.
OKAY.
STICK THEM
ON THIS.

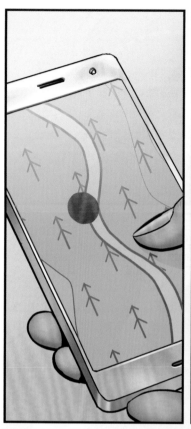

ALL RIGHT...

I MAKE THAT 32 MINUTES.

MORE THAN GENEROUS, I'D SAY.

TALLY HO!

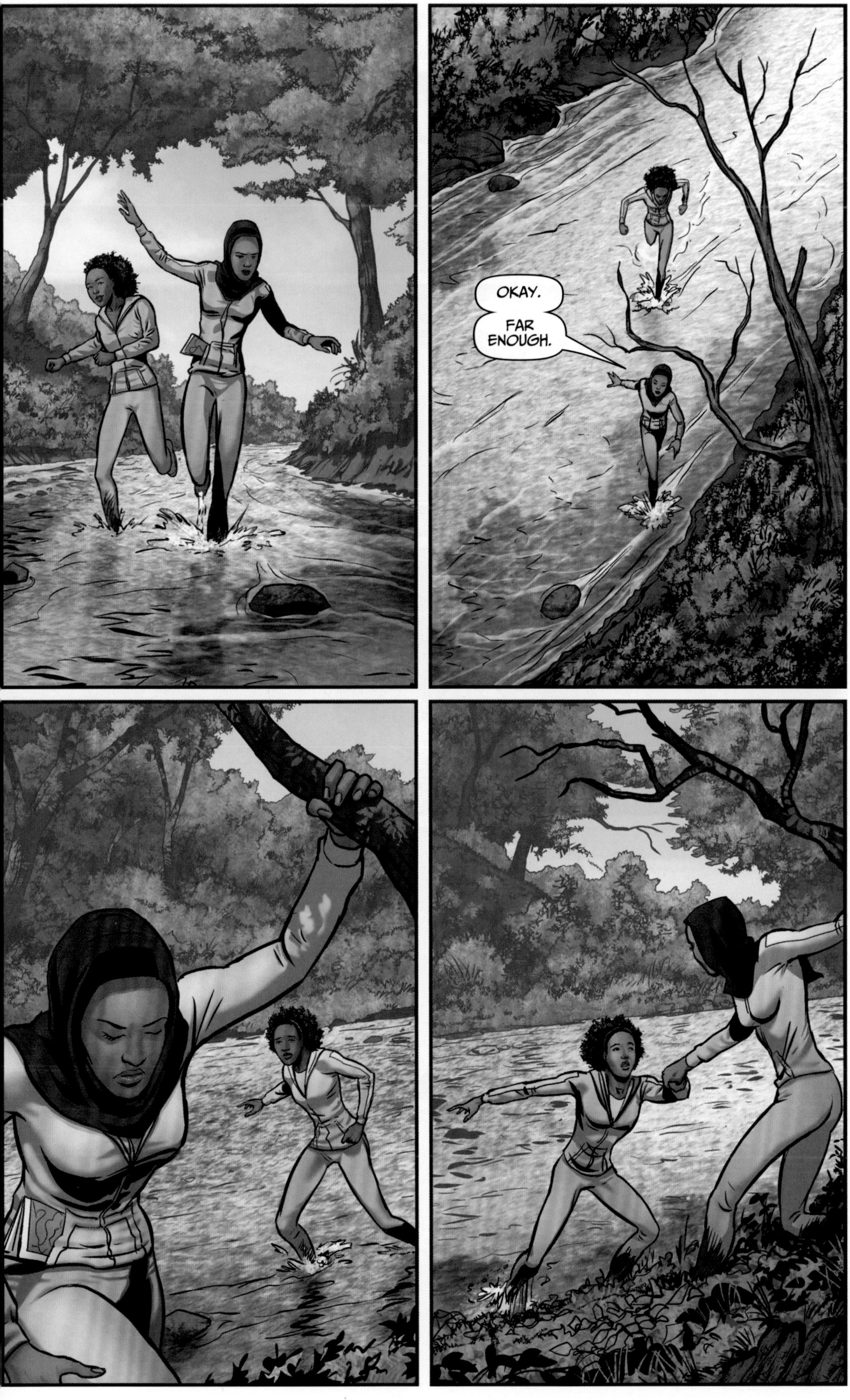
OKAY.
FAR ENOUGH.

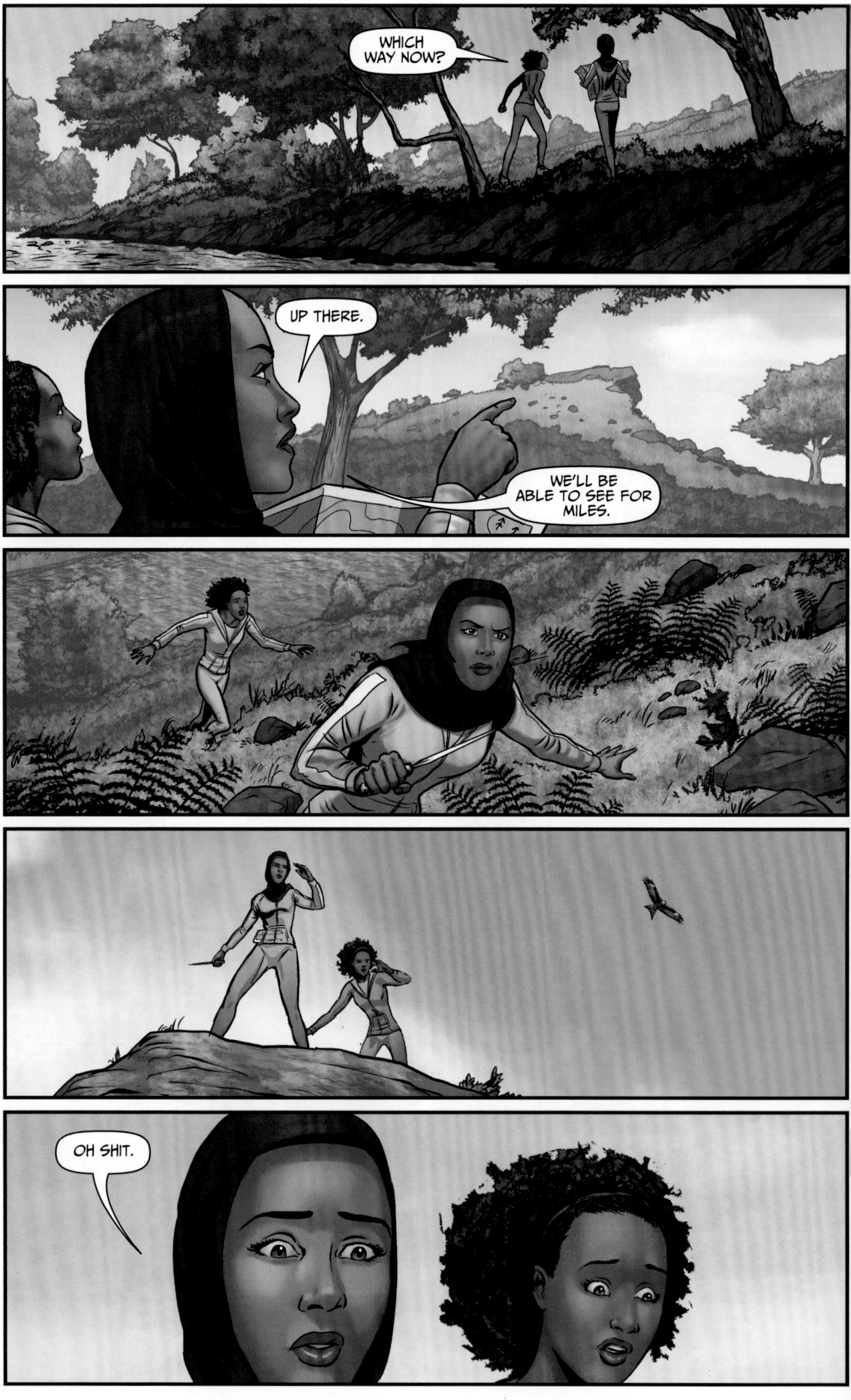
WHICH WAY NOW?
UP THERE.
WE'LL BE ABLE TO SEE FOR MILES.
OH SHIT.

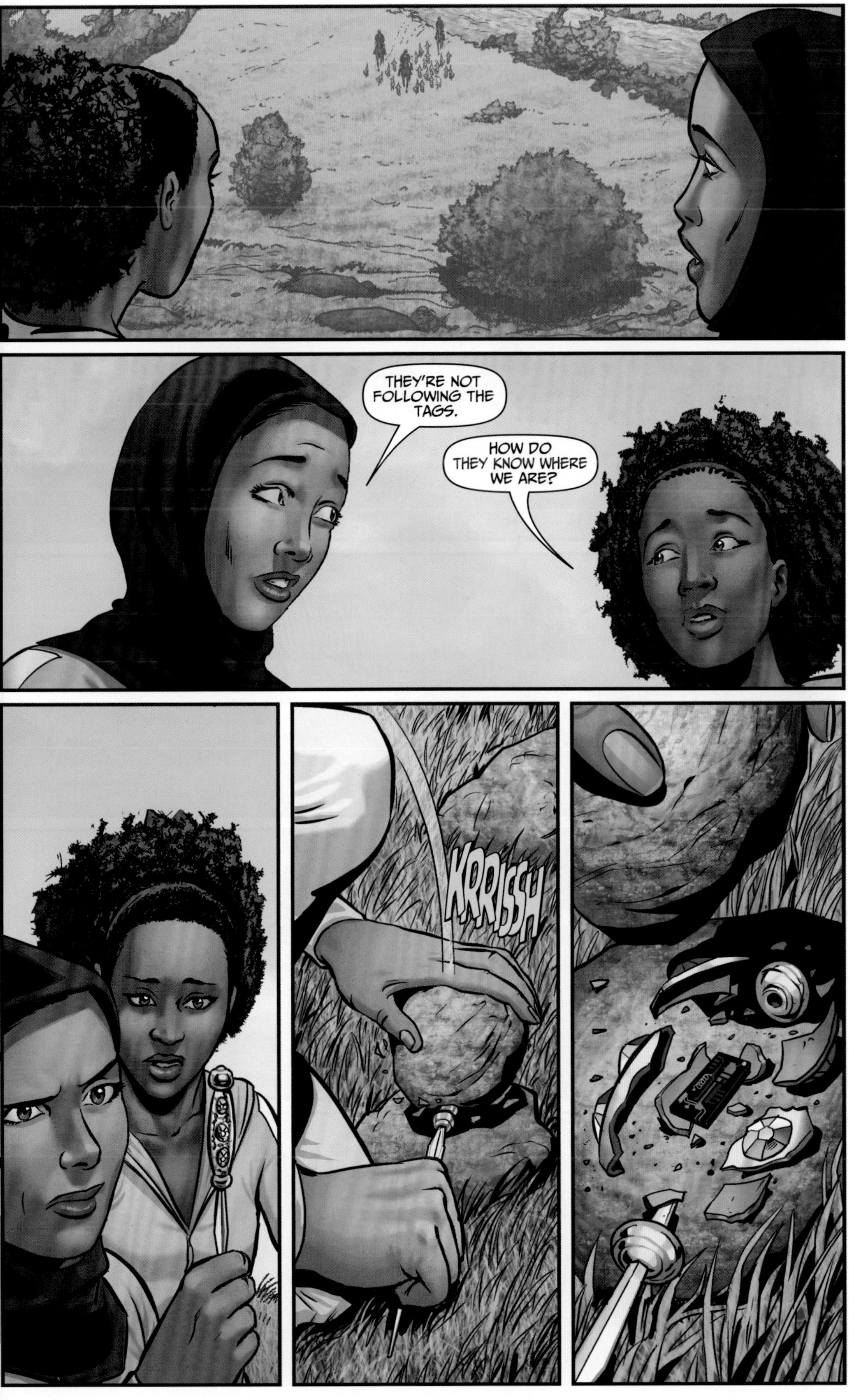
THEY'RE NOT FOLLOWING THE TAGS.
HOW DO THEY KNOW WHERE WE ARE?
KRRISSH

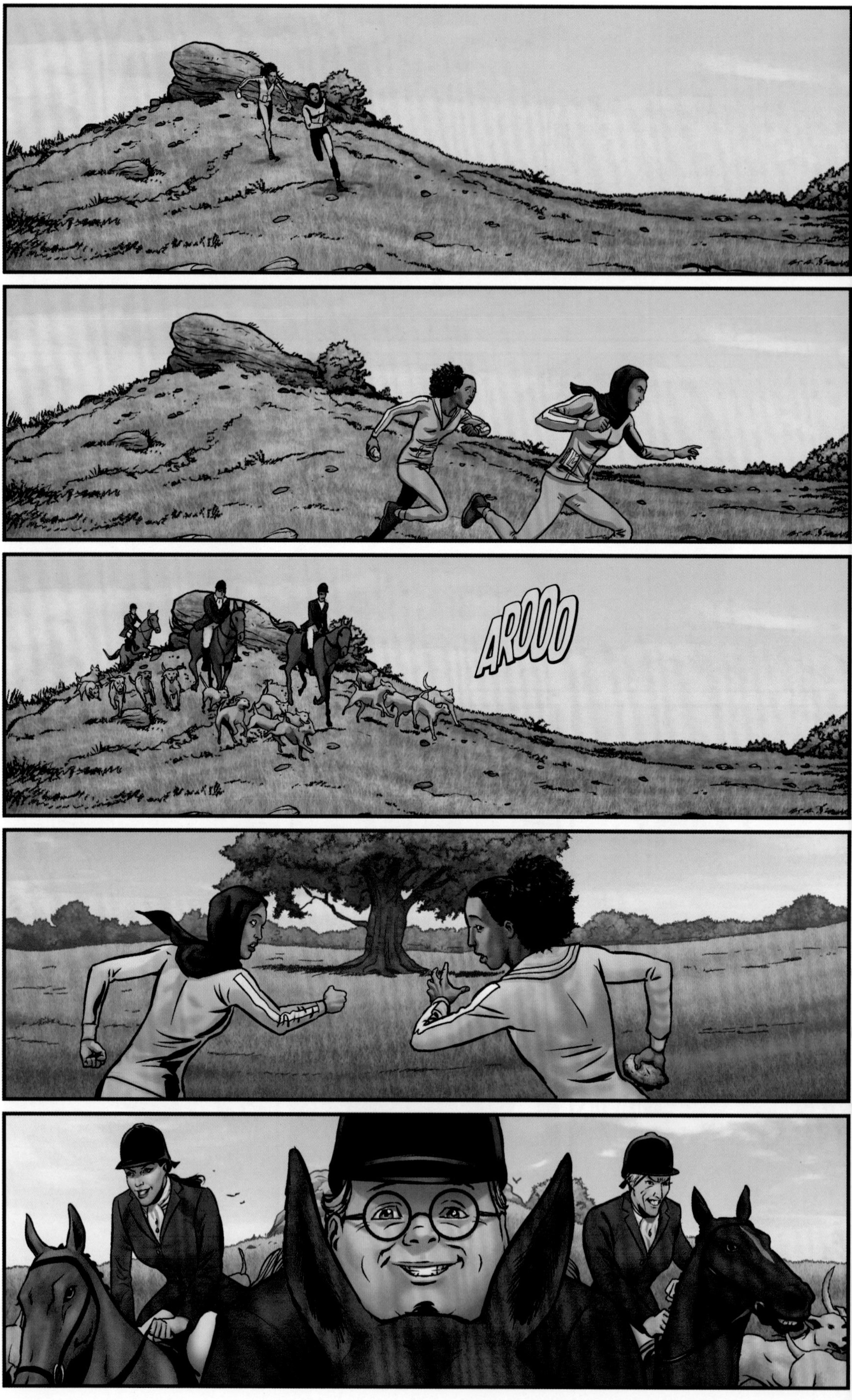
AROOO

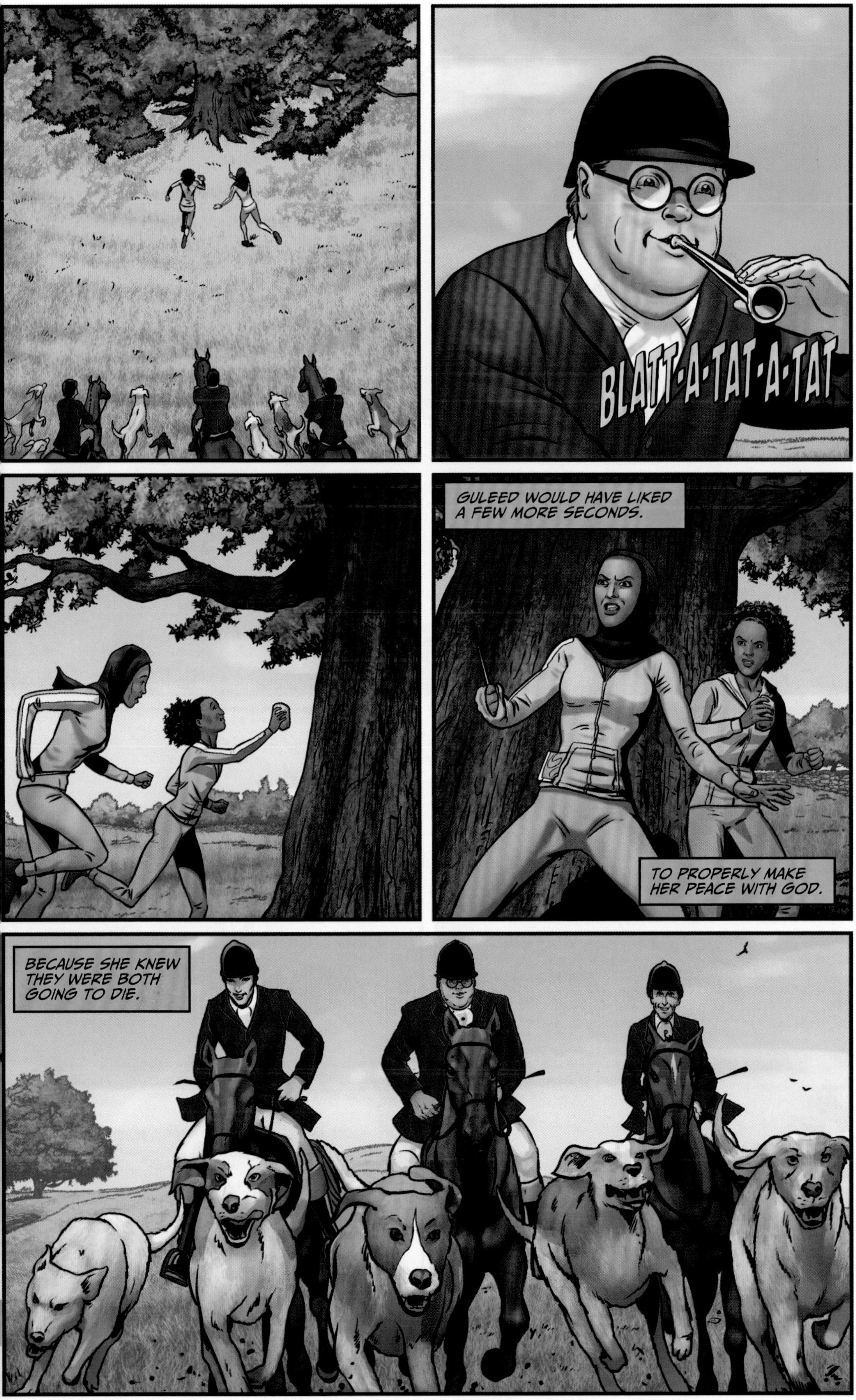
BLATT-A-TAT-A-TAT
GULEED WOULD HAVE LIKED A FEW MORE SECONDS.
TO PROPERLY MAKE HER PEACE WITH GOD.
BECAUSE SHE KNEW THEY WERE BOTH GOING TO DIE.

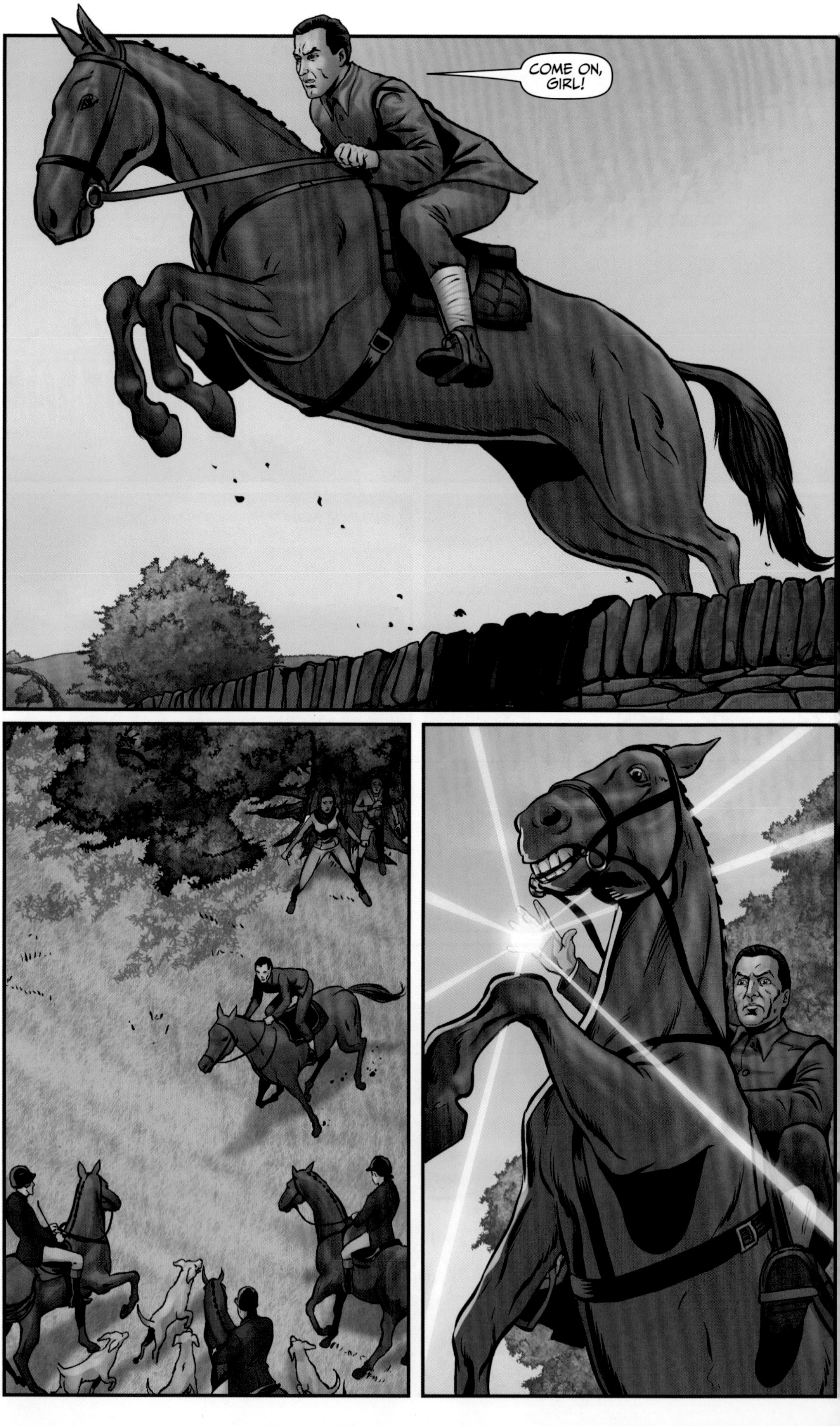
COME ON, GIRL!

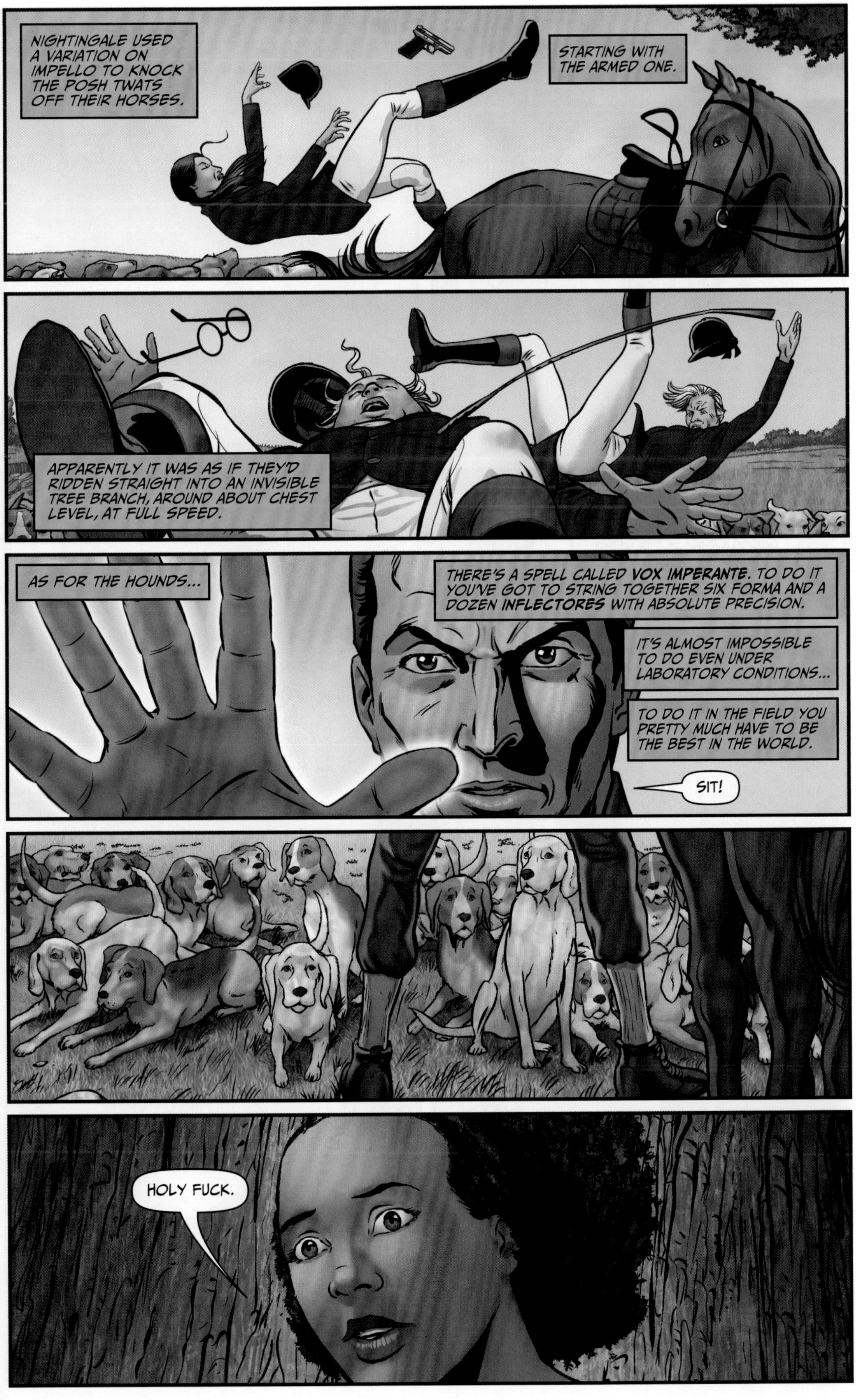
NIGHTINGALE USED A VARIATION ON IMPELLO TO KNOCK THE POSH TWATS OFF THEIR HORSES.
STARTING WITH THE ARMED ONE.
APPARENTLY IT WAS AS IF THEY'D RIDDEN STRAIGHT INTO AN INVISIBLE TREE BRANCH, AROUND ABOUT CHEST LEVEL, AT FULL SPEED.
AS FOR THE HOUNDS...
THERE'S A SPELL CALLED VOX IMPERANTE. TO DO IT YOU'VE GOT TO STRING TOGETHER SIX FORMA AND A DOZEN INFLECTORES WITH ABSOLUTE PRECISION.
IT'S ALMOST IMPOSSIBLE TO DO EVEN UNDER LABORATORY CONDITIONS...
TO DO IT IN THE FIELD YOU PRETTY MUCH HAVE TO BE THE BEST IN THE WORLD.
SIT!
HOLY FUCK.

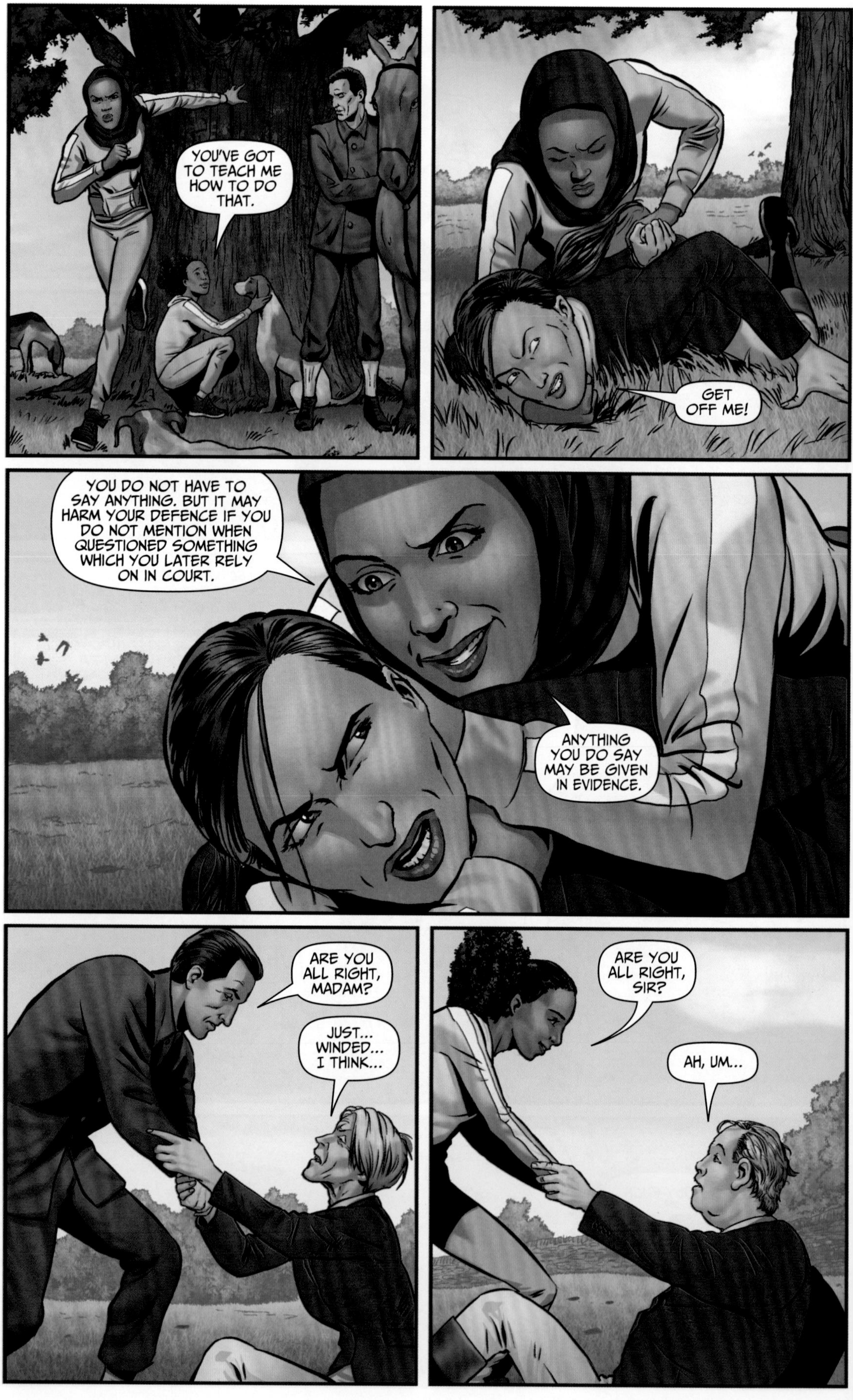

YOU'VE GOT TO TEACH ME HOW TO DO THAT.
GET OFF ME!
YOU DO NOT HAVE TO SAY ANYTHING. BUT IT MAY HARM YOUR DEFENCE IF YOU DO NOT MENTION WHEN QUESTIONED SOMETHING WHICH YOU LATER RELY ON IN COURT.
ANYTHING YOU DO SAY MAY BE GIVEN IN EVIDENCE.
ARE YOU ALL RIGHT, MADAM?
JUST... WINDED... I THINK...
ARE YOU ALL RIGHT, SIR?
AH, UM...

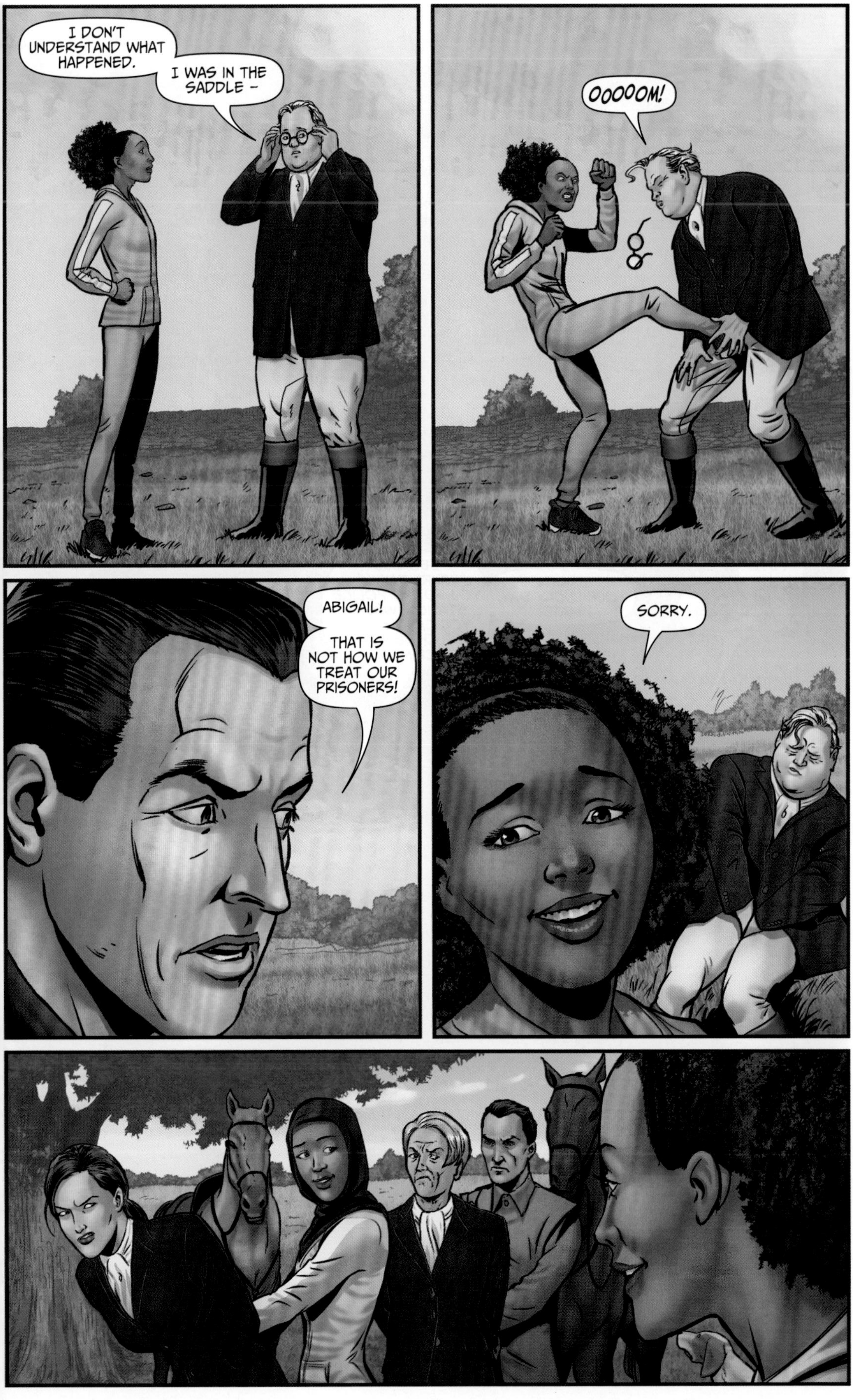
I DON'T UNDERSTAND WHAT HAPPENED.
I WAS IN THE SADDLE –
OOOOOM!
ABIGAIL!
THAT IS NOT HOW WE TREAT OUR PRISONERS!
SORRY.

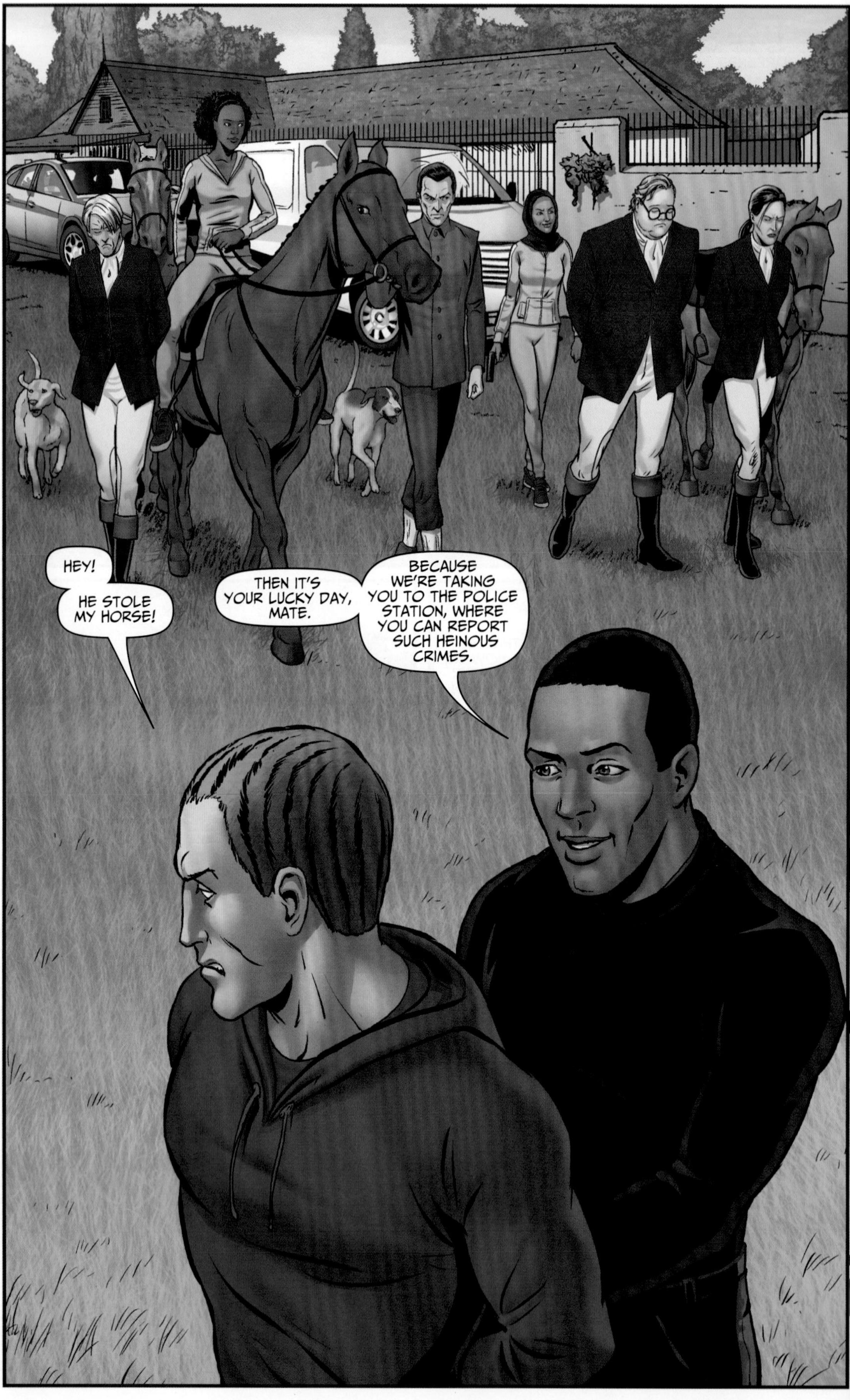
HEY!
HE STOLE MY HORSE!
THEN IT'S YOUR LUCKY DAY, MATE.
BECAUSE WE'RE TAKING YOU TO THE POLICE STATION, WHERE YOU CAN REPORT SUCH HEINOUS CRIMES.

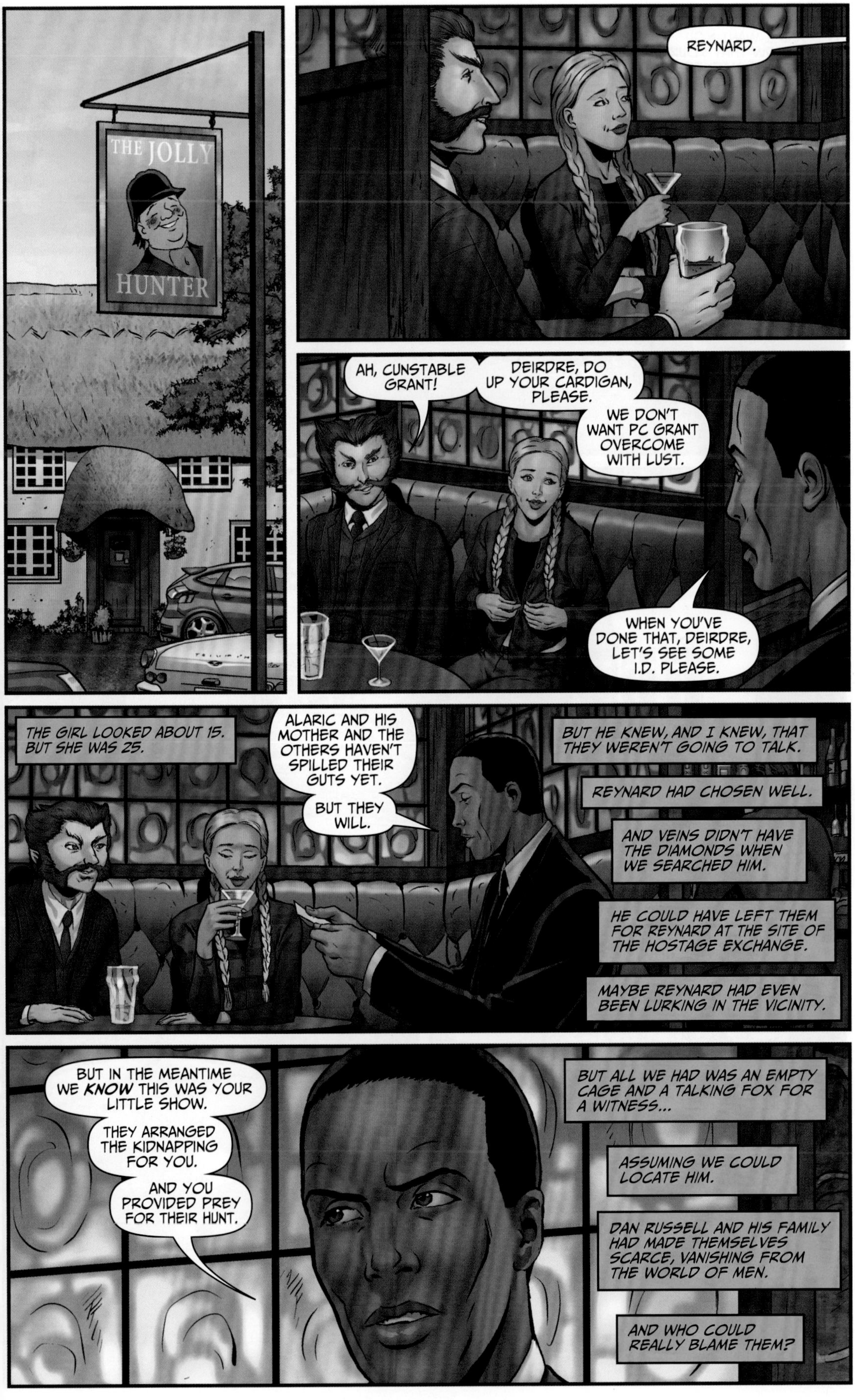
THE JOLLY HUNTER
REYNARD.
AH, CUNSTABLE GRANT!
DEIRDRE, DO UP YOUR CARDIGAN, PLEASE.
WE DON'T WANT PC GRANT OVERCOME WITH LUST.
WHEN YOU'VE DONE THAT, DEIRDRE, LET'S SEE SOME I.D. PLEASE.
THE GIRL LOOKED ABOUT 15. BUT SHE WAS 25.
ALARIC AND HIS MOTHER AND THE OTHERS HAVEN'T SPILLED THEIR GUTS YET.
BUT THEY WILL.
BUT HE KNEW, AND I KNEW, THAT THEY WEREN'T GOING TO TALK.
REYNARD HAD CHOSEN WELL.
AND VEINS DIDN'T HAVE THE DIAMONDS WHEN WE SEARCHED HIM.
HE COULD HAVE LEFT THEM FOR REYNARD AT THE SITE OF THE HOSTAGE EXCHANGE.
MAYBE REYNARD HAD EVEN BEEN LURKING IN THE VICINITY.
BUT IN THE MEANTIME WE KNOW THIS WAS YOUR LITTLE SHOW.
THEY ARRANGED THE KIDNAPPING FOR YOU.
AND YOU PROVIDED PREY FOR THEIR HUNT.
BUT ALL WE HAD WAS AN EMPTY CAGE AND A TALKING FOX FOR A WITNESS...
ASSUMING WE COULD LOCATE HIM.
DAN RUSSELL AND HIS FAMILY HAD MADE THEMSELVES SCARCE, VANISHING FROM THE WORLD OF MEN.
AND WHO COULD REALLY BLAME THEM?

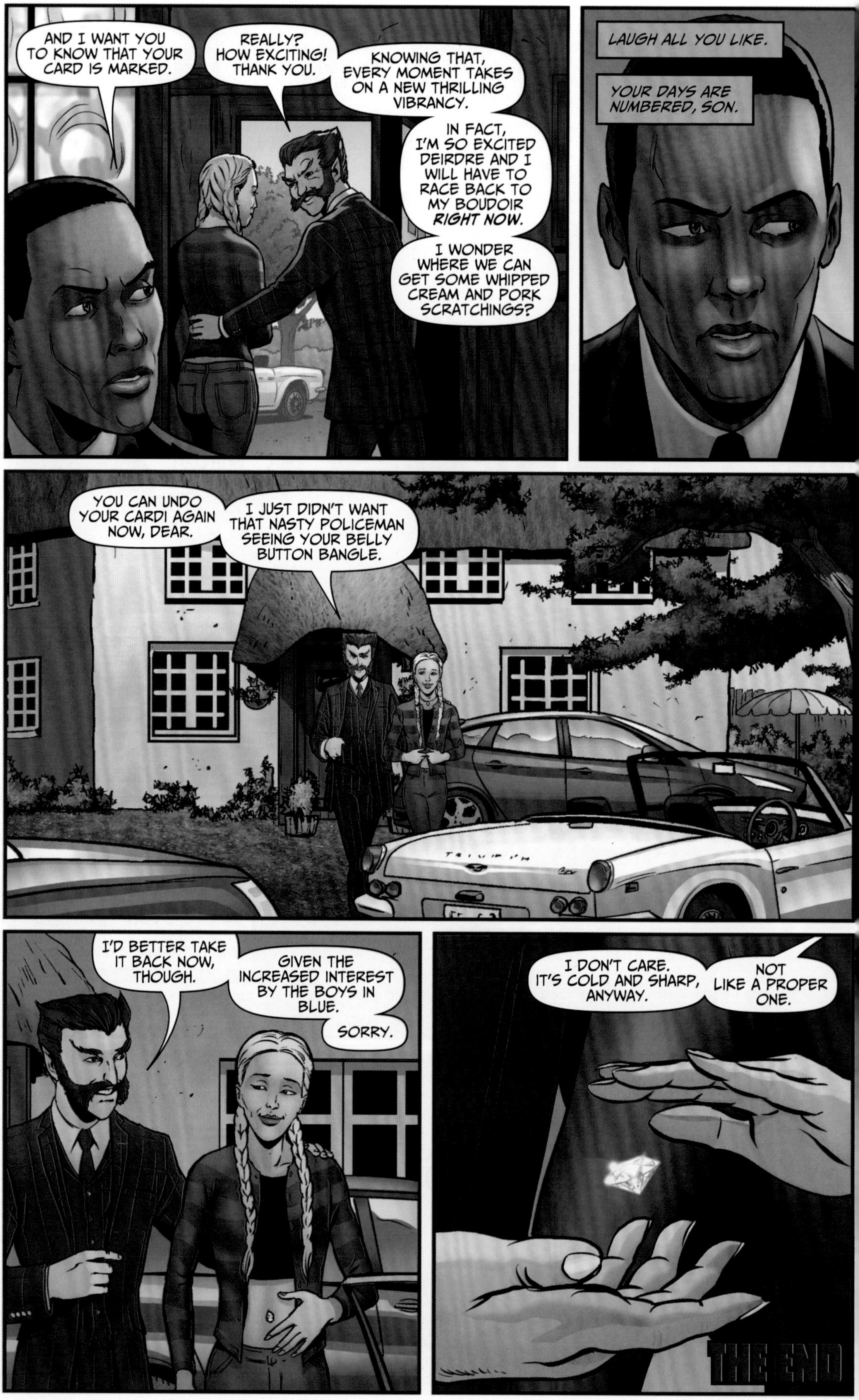
AND I WANT YOU TO KNOW THAT YOUR CARD IS MARKED.
REALLY? HOW EXCITING! THANK YOU.
KNOWING THAT, EVERY MOMENT TAKES ON A NEW THRILLING VIBRANCY.
IN FACT, I'M SO EXCITED DEIRDRE AND I WILL HAVE TO RACE BACK TO MY BOUDOIR *RIGHT NOW*.
I WONDER WHERE WE CAN GET SOME WHIPPED CREAM AND PORK SCRATCHINGS?
LAUGH ALL YOU LIKE.
YOUR DAYS ARE NUMBERED, SON.
YOU CAN UNDO YOUR CARDI AGAIN NOW, DEAR.
I JUST DIDN'T WANT THAT NASTY POLICEMAN SEEING YOUR BELLY BUTTON BANGLE.
I'D BETTER TAKE IT BACK NOW, THOUGH.
GIVEN THE INCREASED INTEREST BY THE BOYS IN BLUE.
SORRY.
I DON'T CARE. IT'S COLD AND SHARP, ANYWAY.
NOT LIKE A PROPER ONE.
THE END

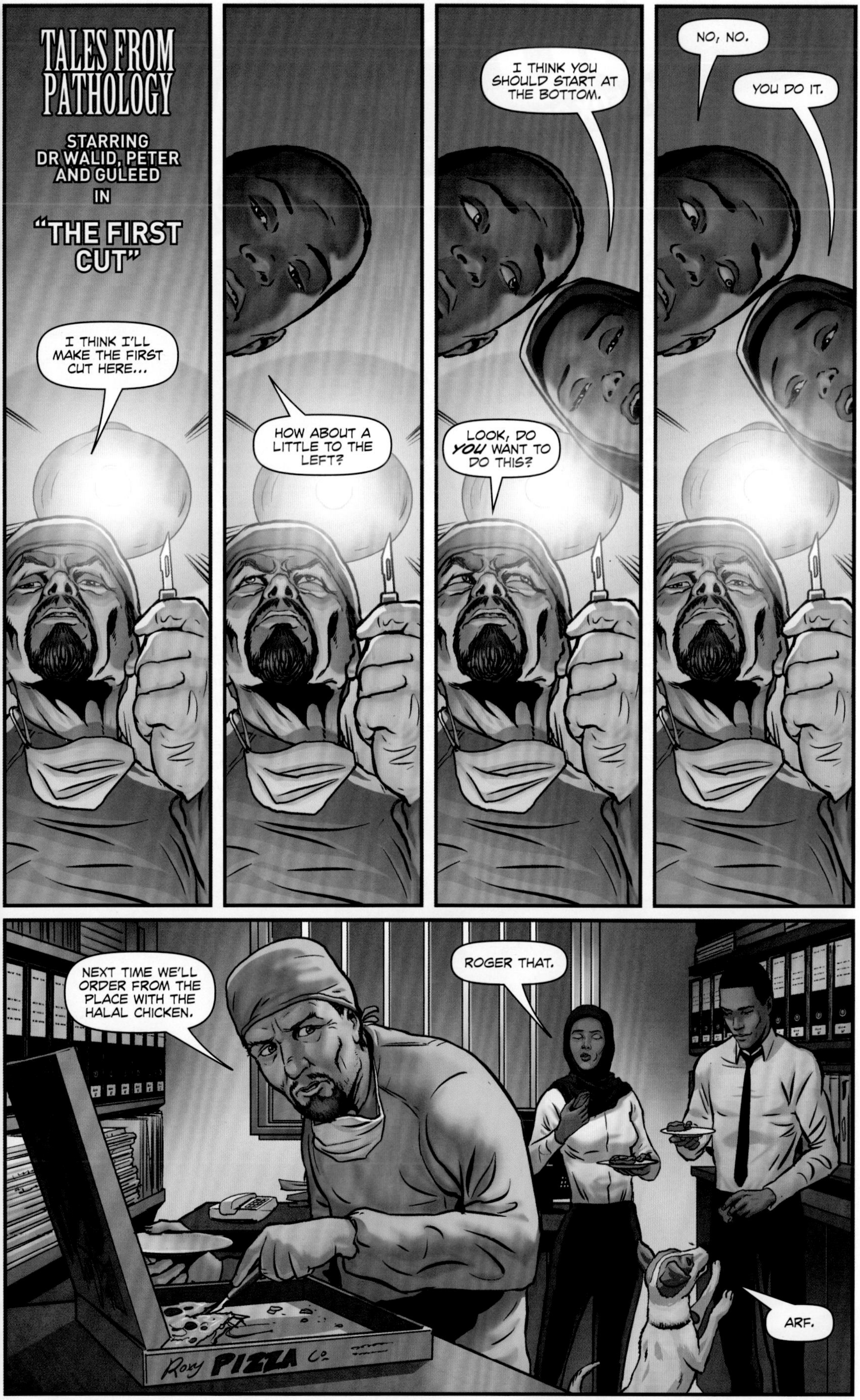
TALES FROM PATHOLOGY
STARRING DR WALID, PETER AND GULEED IN "THE FIRST CUT"
I THINK I'LL MAKE THE FIRST CUT HERE...
HOW ABOUT A LITTLE TO THE LEFT?
I THINK YOU SHOULD START AT THE BOTTOM.
LOOK, DO YOU WANT TO DO THIS?
NO, NO.
YOU DO IT.
NEXT TIME WE'LL ORDER FROM THE PLACE WITH THE HALAL CHICKEN.
ROGER THAT.
ARF.
Roxy PIZZA Co.

OUTFOXED

THE FOX OF FOLKLORE, MYTH, & CULTURE – PART ONE

It's an obscure scene in William Peter Blatty's novel *The Exorcist*. Father Damien Karras is engaging the young Regan MacNeil to divine whether she is suffering some psychological disorder or is actually, genuinely possessed. During some verbal jousting, Regan refers to Karras as 'foxy', reflecting how sad it was that Herod was not there to enjoy it. Pondering this later, Karras realises the pun is actually far cleverer than he first thought; after being warned of threats against him by King Herod, Jesus replies, "Go and tell that fox that I cast out devils" – clearly a reference to Karras' investigation into the possibilities of an exorcism.

However, Regan's use of the term 'foxy' pretty much sums up Western culture's view of the fox: as a creature of sublime cunning and dark intelligence. Few animals have such a broad, far-reaching presence in mythology and culture as the fox, in particular, the Red Fox (Latin name, *Vulpes vulpes*); this is perhaps reflected in the animal's broad geographical distribution. The red fox is the most widely ranging member of the Order *Carnivora* (which includes all members of the cat and dog families, as well as bears, hyenas and their relatives, and the mustelids – stoats, weasels, otters, and their relatives). The red fox lives throughout pretty much all of the Northern Hemisphere and as far south as North Africa. It has also now, thanks to a little help from its erstwhile nemesis, *Homo sapiens*, infiltrated Australia. The spread of the species can be, in part, attributed to its innate intelligence and a diet that willingly embraces omnivory – foxes will eat pretty much anything.

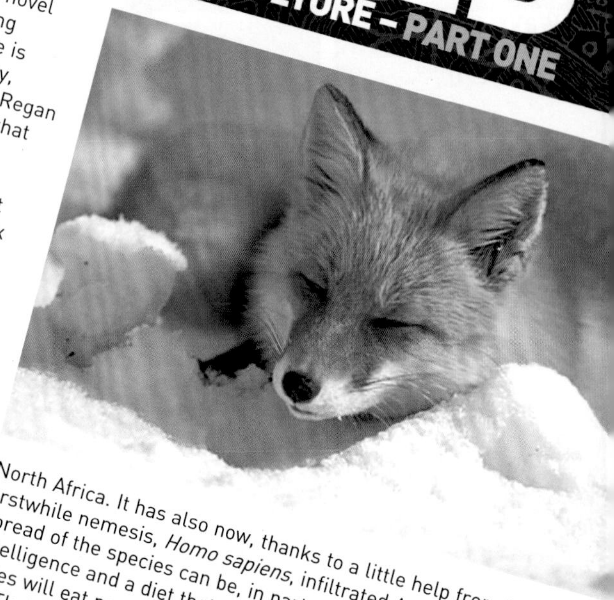

Their far-reaching presence and broad dietary church suggests the fox's relationship with humans probably goes back as long as the two co-existed; foxes may have scavenged around the camp sites and at the kills of

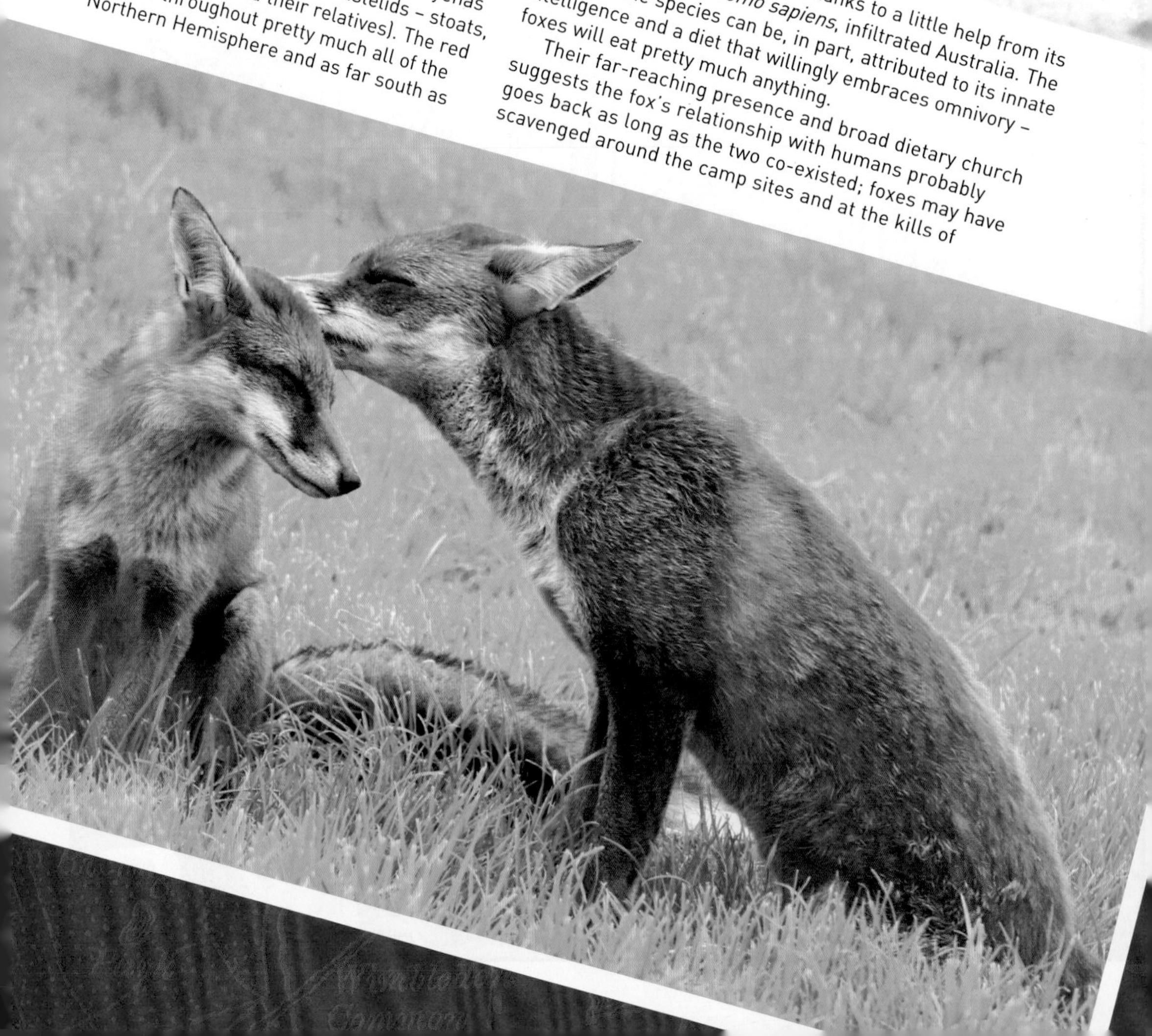

月百姿
むさしのゝ月

Tsukioka Yoshitoshi, *One Hundred Aspects of the Moon*

Early Man. But while the wolf fell to the pincer movement of domestication and ecological genocide, the fox has gone from strength to strength. London currently has one of the biggest populations of urban foxes in the world, where most city dwellers view them within the context of the second generalised notion of 'foxy' – that of something attractive. To be a 'fox' is to be sexy – just take 'Foxy Lady' by Jimi Hendrix as a fine example, used to great effect in *Wayne's World*

by Garth to elucidate on the finer points of his unrequited love through the medium of interpretative dance...

Certainly in Western culture and myth, the fox is a vessel of pure cunning and intrigue. However, its first entry into the West's cultural pantheon is less about games of mental intrigue and more about outright slaughter. The Teumessian fox, a vixen spawned by two serpents – snakes being another cadre of creatures

Depiction of the *kitsune* – Okada Gyokuzan,
Gyokuzan Gafu

not well treated in myth and legend – was
making life calamitous in the Greek city state
of Thebes. She was killing any young man who
ventured along the road to the city, apparently
with impunity, for it was said she was destined
never to be caught. The hero Amphitryon set
the famous hunting dog Laelaps on her, for it
was said that Laelaps was equally destined to
catch anything he hunted. Perhaps analogous
with the pursuit of woman by man (dog chasing
vixen), the two seemed ready to be locked into
an endless chase until Zeus interceded and
turned both canines to stone.

'Vixen' is also applied in the West as a
term for an attractive woman, an aspect in
which the Shinto spirit foxes of Japan would
often appear. *Kitsune* is the Japanese
word for fox, but it also applies to their
spirit cousins, who are shapeshifters that
can, almost as a direct affront to the
werewolves of lore, take on a human shape but
only after reaching a certain age – some stories
say a century, others just 50 years. They also
have as many as nine tails – the more tails, the
older, wiser, and more powerful the spirit fox.
Those *kitsune* who reach their ninth tail find
their fur turned white or gold, and become all-
seeing. Should they reach their millennium,
they ascend to the status of tenko, the
celestial fox who rises unto the heavens.

In this form, the *kitsune* seek to engage
with the human world; they often appear as
beautiful women with supernatural powers
that westerners would usually associate
with such night terrors as succubi.
However, the *kitsune* are a little more

Tamamo-no-Mae – Yoshitoshi, *New Forms of Thirty-Six Ghosts.*

philosophical in style, seeking not just base pleasures such
as sex and money but also wisdom and enlightenment;
they can also serve as messengers from the spirit world.
They are also often seen as spanning borders – between
the physical and the ethereal, between dark and light,
between conventional norms and more radical thought.
Not surprisingly, they fall into roughly two categories. The
zenko, or 'good foxes', usually associated with the Shinto
god Inari; Inari is a god often associated with food, in
particular rice, but is also known as the god that changed
gender, originally worshipped as female. This may explain
why some *kitsune* are associated with shapeshifting.

The yako are those *kitsune* trickier by nature, the
pranksters and the downright malevolent. Perhaps
the most famous of these is the Jewel Maiden, a
beautiful woman about whom little is

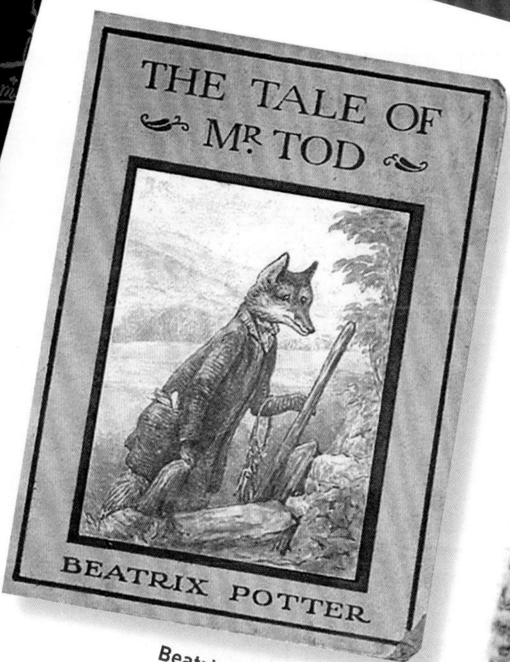
THE TALE OF
MR. TOD
BEATRIX POTTER

Beatrix Potter

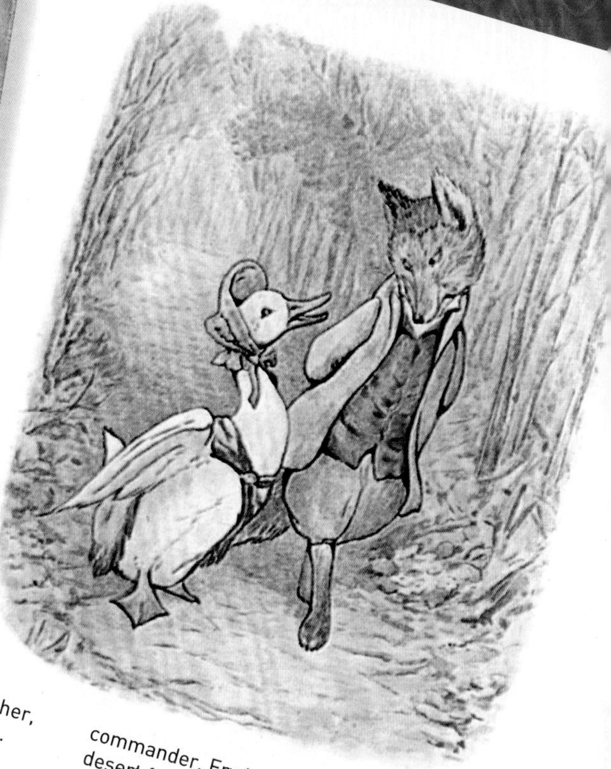

known. However, despite the mystery surrounding her, she becomes a favourite of the emperor Toba-no-in. On a dark and stormy night, the emperor is amazed when the woman is suffused with a brilliant light and he names her Tamamo-no-mae – the Jewel Maiden. However, soon after, the emperor and his son fall ill and, because she is believed responsible, the Jewel Maiden is driven out of the court, whereupon she reveals her true form as a nine-tailed fox and flees to the north east, the direction from which demonic influence is said to manifest itself. The Maiden finds herself pursued by two warriors, who finally corner and kill her. However, the *kitsune* assumes the form of a stone that exudes poison, killing anything that goes near it. The spirit in he stone was finally pacified a century later and noved to Nasuno, where it still resides.

Half a world away, foxes were really living up o their reputation as suave tricksters in Beatrix otter's green and pleasant England. In her ales, the appearance of a fox is usually a sure ign of vulpine malice aforethought. In *The ale of Jemima Puddle-Duck*, the eponymous eroine comes within a feather's breadth of eing roasted by a silver tongued fox, Mr. Tod pparently Tod was a regular Saxon term r a fox) who offers her shelter from the umans constantly taking her eggs. Tod himself the similarly eponymous heart *The Tale of Mr. Tod*, although on this ccasion, the gentlemanly, landed vulpine nds himself the victim of a dastardly, ieving badger's shenanigans.

Potter's foxes are very much the uintessential British view of the x until fairly recently; wily vermin ho, when they weren't breaking to your chicken coup, were being orn by the upper classes. Little onder that when British soldiers ere battling the Afrika Korps during e Second World War, the German commander, Erwin Rommel, was nicknamed 'the desert fox.' Not because he had very large ears and was predominantly nocturnal, like the actual desert fox, better known as the fennec fox (*Vulpes zerda*), but because he was regarded as a wily customer, intelligent and crafty, for whom the British had a fond, if grudging, regard. •

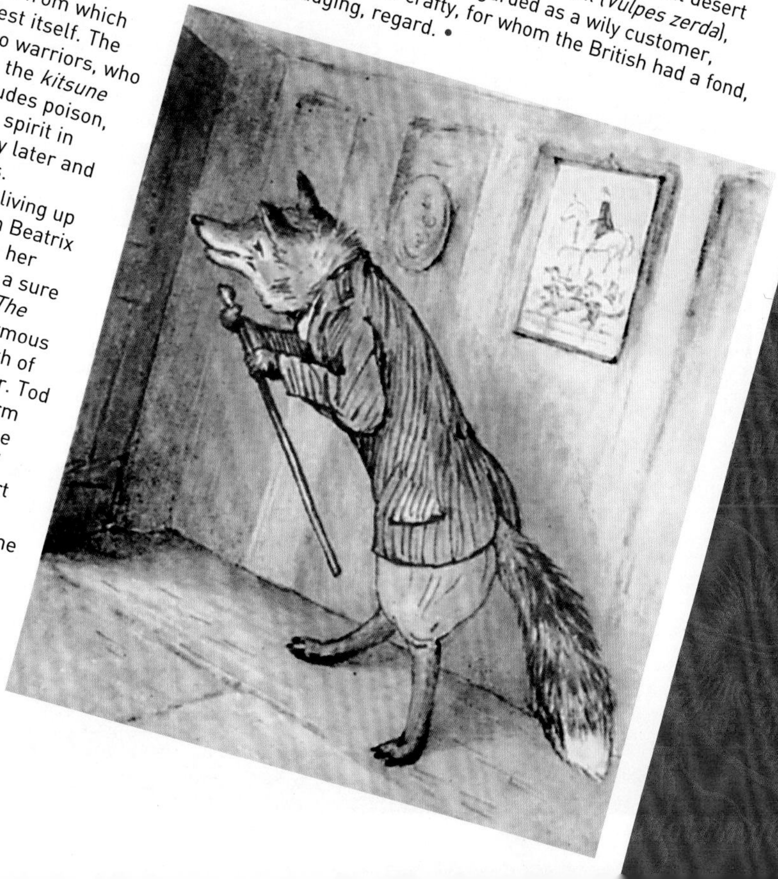

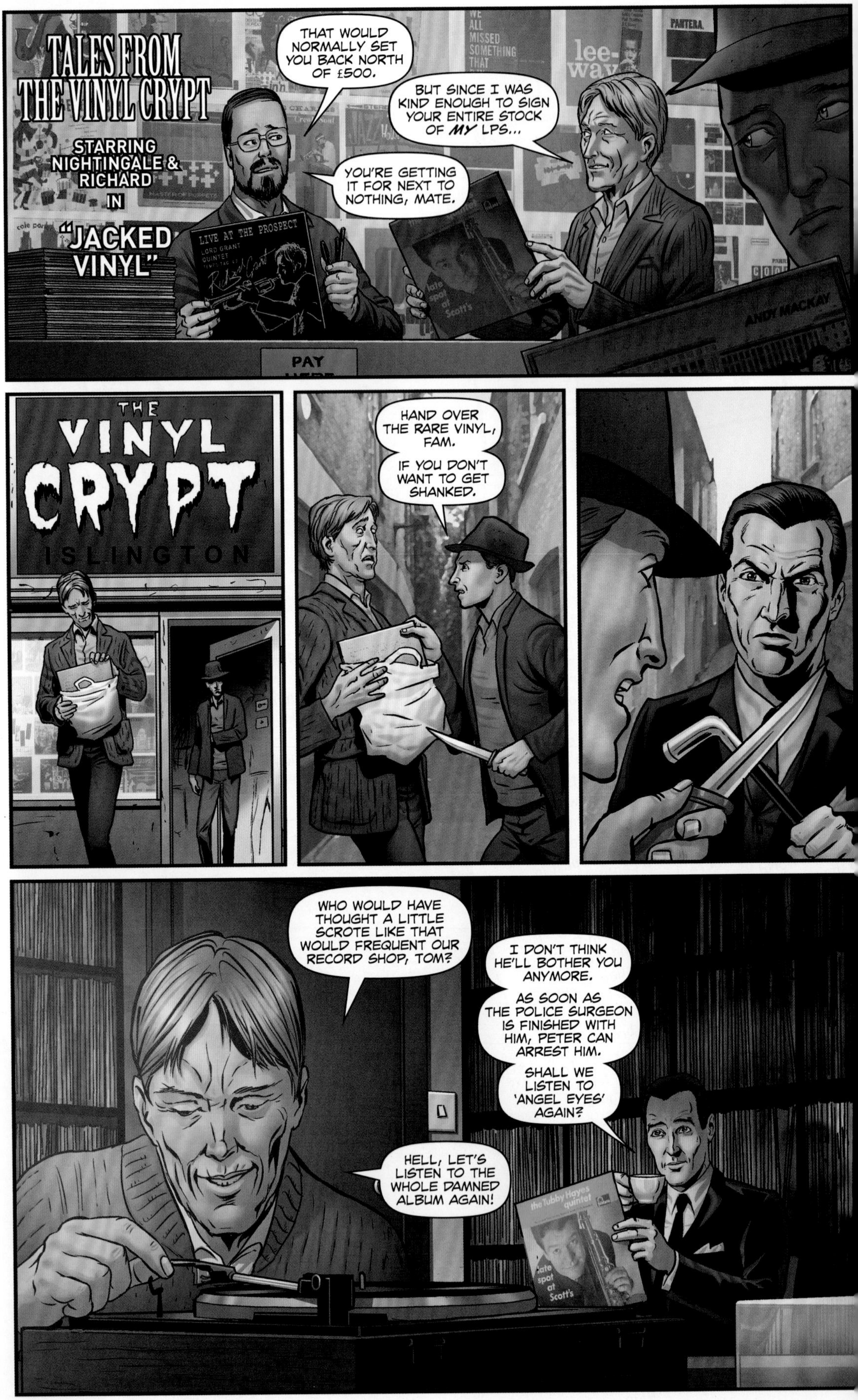

TALES FROM THE VINYL CRYPT
STARRING NIGHTINGALE & RICHARD IN "JACKED VINYL"
THAT WOULD NORMALLY SET YOU BACK NORTH OF £500.
BUT SINCE I WAS KIND ENOUGH TO SIGN YOUR ENTIRE STOCK OF *MY* LPS...
YOU'RE GETTING IT FOR NEXT TO NOTHING, MATE.
LIVE AT THE PROSPECT
PAY
THE VINYL CRYPT ISLINGTON
HAND OVER THE RARE VINYL, FAM.
IF YOU DON'T WANT TO GET SHANKED.
WHO WOULD HAVE THOUGHT A LITTLE SCROTE LIKE THAT WOULD FREQUENT OUR RECORD SHOP, TOM?
I DON'T THINK HE'LL BOTHER YOU ANYMORE.
AS SOON AS THE POLICE SURGEON IS FINISHED WITH HIM, PETER CAN ARREST HIM.
SHALL WE LISTEN TO 'ANGEL EYES' AGAIN?
HELL, LET'S LISTEN TO THE WHOLE DAMNED ALBUM AGAIN!
the Tubby Hayes quintet
late spot at Scott's

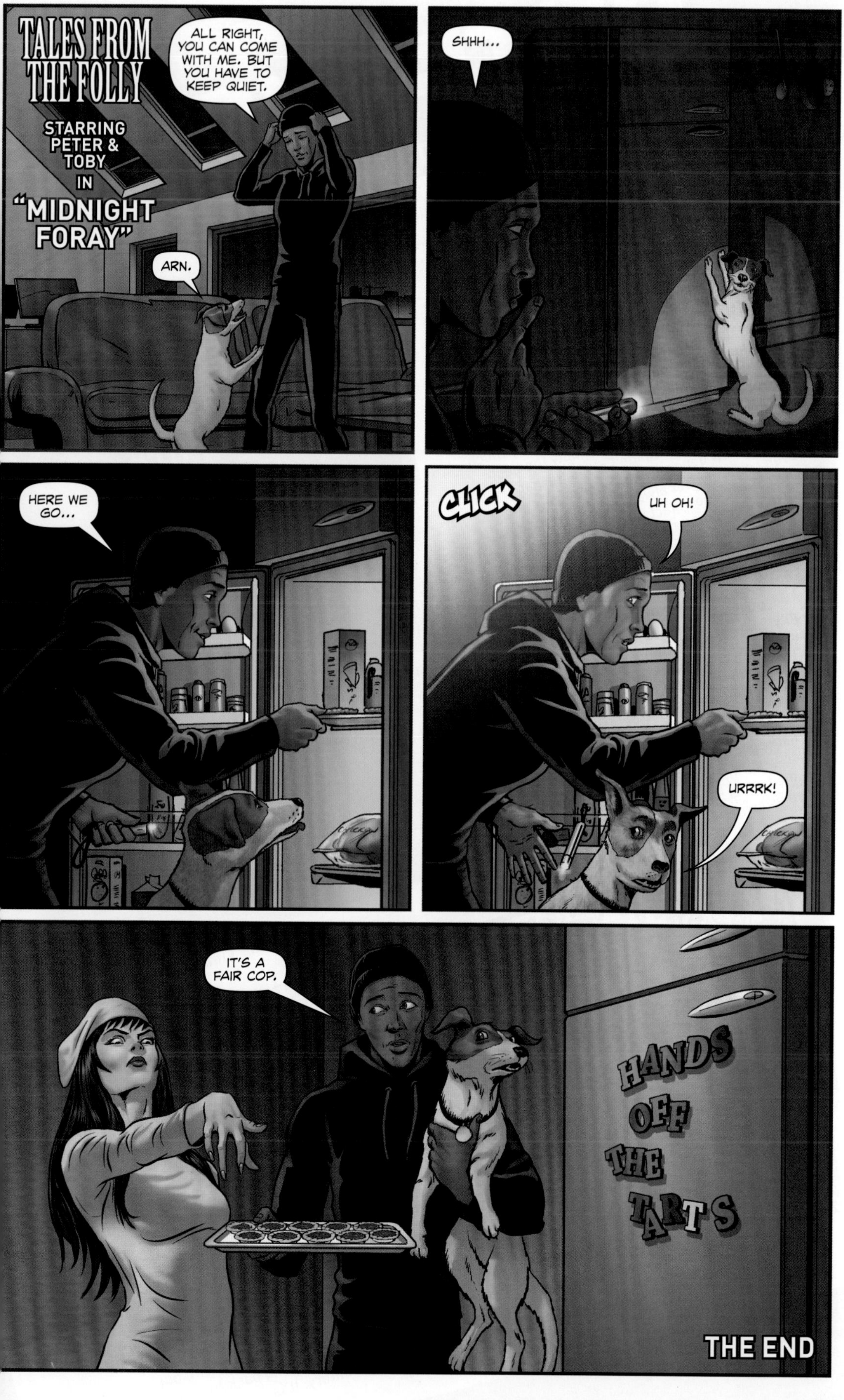
TALES FROM THE FOLLY
STARRING PETER & TOBY IN "MIDNIGHT FORAY"
ALL RIGHT, YOU CAN COME WITH ME. BUT YOU HAVE TO KEEP QUIET.
ARN.
SHHH...
HERE WE GO...
CLICK
UH OH!
URRRK!
IT'S A FAIR COP.
HANDS OFF THE TARTS
THE END

OUTFOXED

THE FOX OF FOLKLORE, MYTH, & CULTURE – PART TWO: REYNARD THE FOX

Long-time fans of *The Simpsons* may well be familiar with the concept of the trickster canid. Voiced by Johnny Cash no less, a coyote – nay, space coyote – leads Homer on an odyssey through a dreamscape induced by a Guatemalan insanity chilli on an ultimately successful quest for his soulmate. The coyote has long been part of Native American mythology and tradition, seen very much as a mischief-maker and thief (like a canine Prometheus, he is also said to have stolen fire from the gods).

It's interesting but perhaps not surprising, then, that in Europe, the coyote's not-so-close relative (coyotes are closer to dogs, foxes are very much a pack unto themselves, in the genus *Vulpes*) are also very much steeped in trickster mythology. Probably the best-known example of this vulpine Loki is Reynard.

Although now generally considered wily and sly, even cowardly, but always self-serving, the origins of his name in fact allude to a highly intelligent figure (not unlike the animal…); Reynard is actually derived from the original German version of the character, *Reginhard*, which roughly translates from Low German as *Reynke de Vos*, which is translated from Low German into 'Reginhard', which means 'mighty' and 'strong in counsel' – that is, wise, someone to be listened to.

The main thrust of the stories surrounding Reynard is the defeat of brute force by wit and intelligence. It's usually him talking himself out of trouble or manoeuvring more dull-witted adversaries into situations favourable for the fox. As such, while he may be seen as something of villain, he's also something of an anti-hero – little wonder Disney chose to portray Robin Hood as a fox.

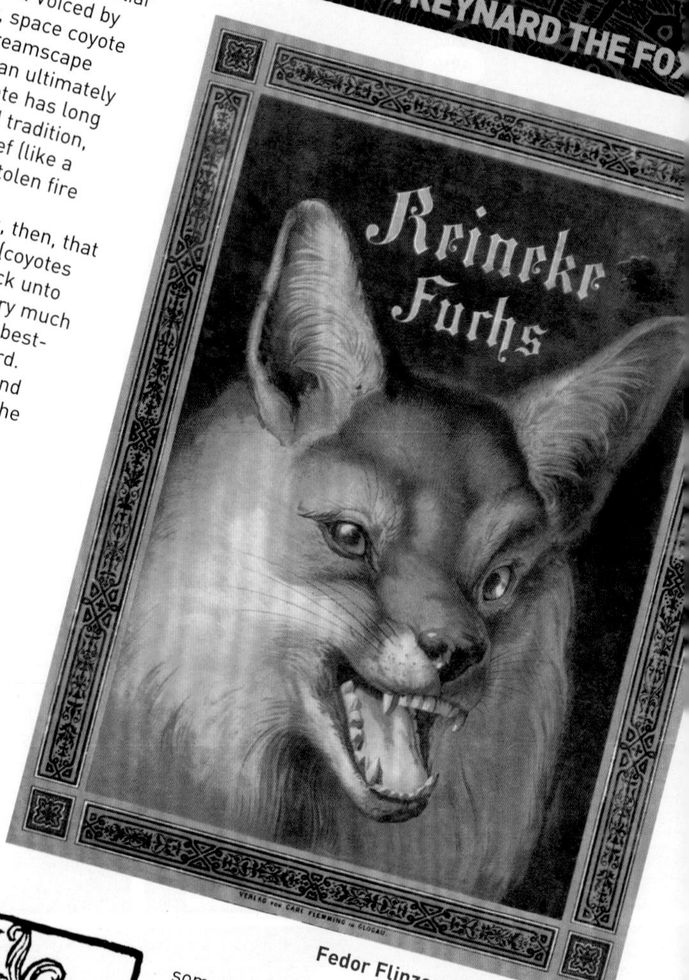

Reineke
Fuchs

Fedor Flinzer, *Reineke Fuchs*

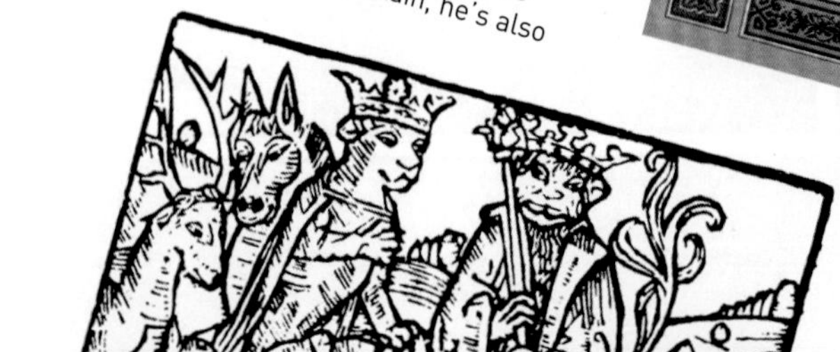

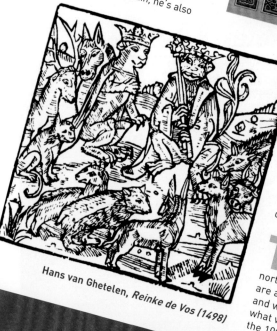

Hans van Ghetelen, *Reinke de Vos (1498)*

Reynard's principal adversaries in early medieval tales were usually anthropomorphic characters like him. Among them was Isengrim, a wolf of little brains, but big on greed and brute force. The bear, in the form of Bruin, was portrayed in a similar fashion. It's interesting to note that these two top predators were victims of such harsh propaganda while the fox seems to have been viewed almost fondly and with respect, despite its thieving ways.

THE EXTINCTION OF GOUPIL

Reynard is best known as a character in French literature, originating in the northerly region of Lorraine, but early stories are also known to have been written in Germany and what is now Dutch-speaking Belgium, but what was then Flanders, dating back to the 10th and 11th Century. It is

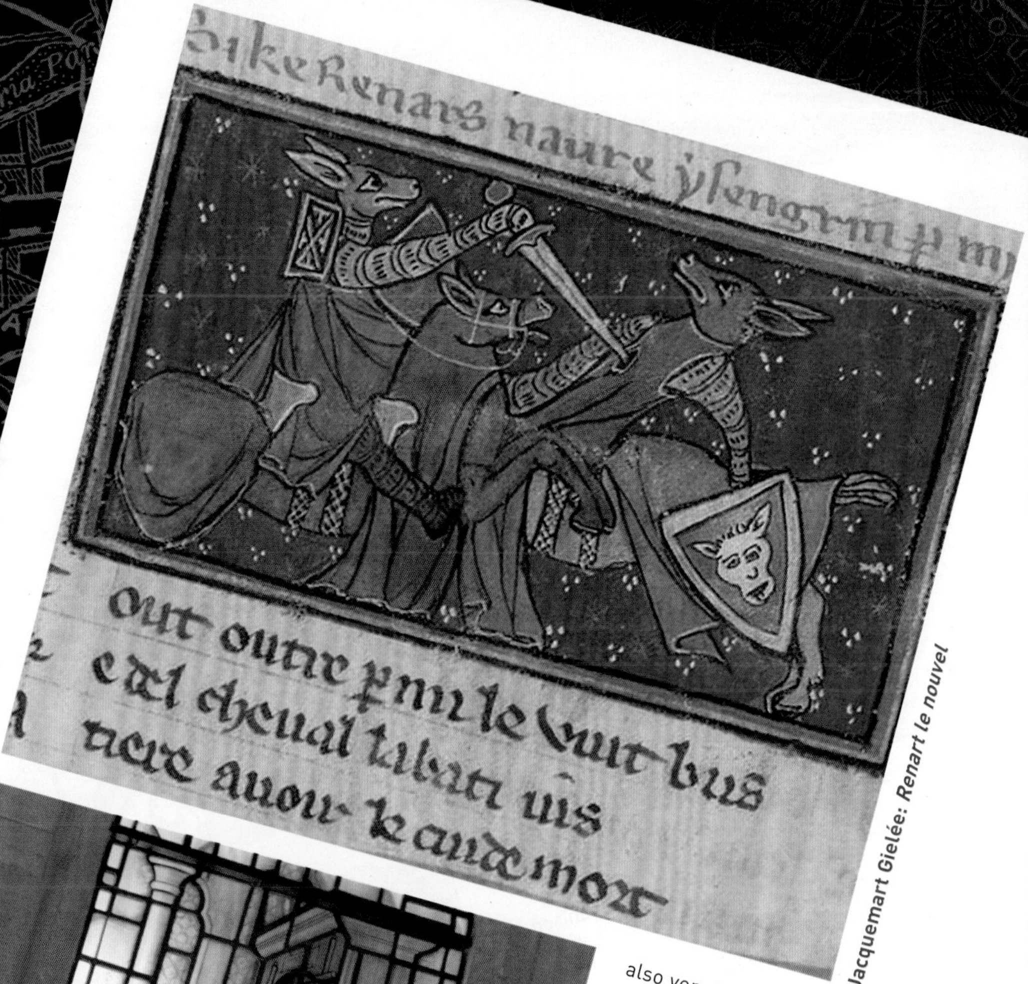

Jacquemart Gielée: *Renart le nouvel*

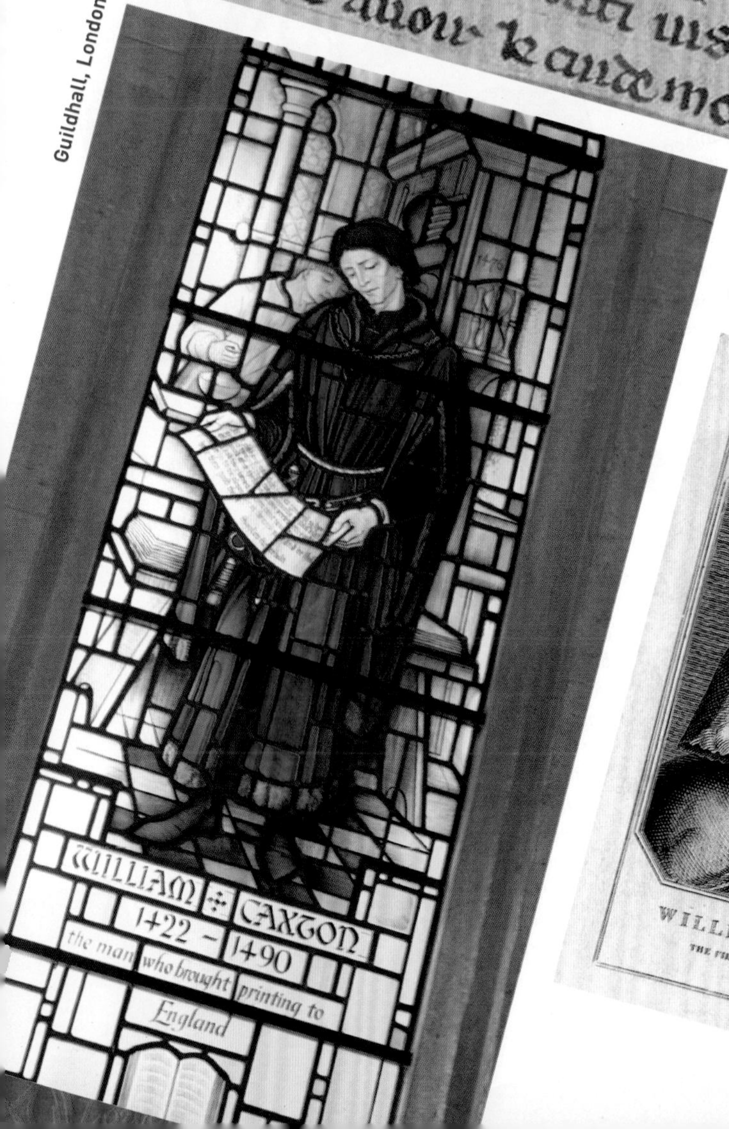
WILLIAM ✣ CAXTON
1422 – 1490
the man who brought printing to
England

Guildhall, London

also very likely that some of the story elements were lifted from Ancient Greece and Rome epics.

The stories themselves were written as poems, an approach that generated a

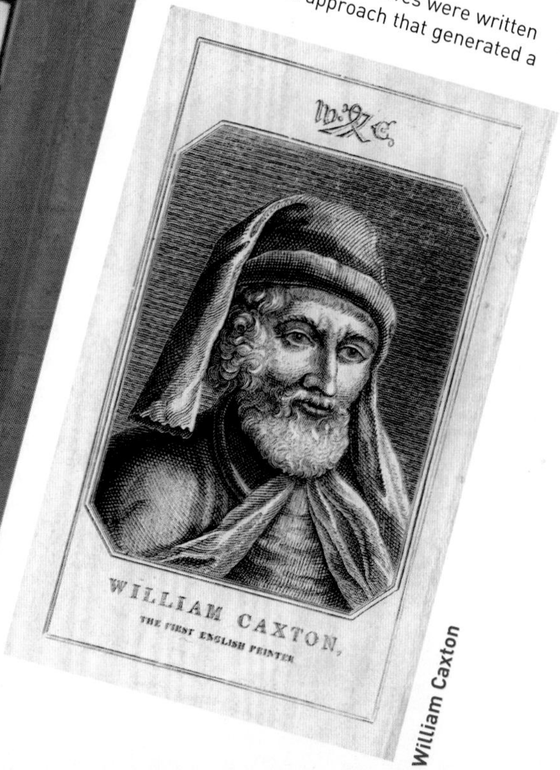
WILLIAM CAXTON,
THE FIRST ENGLISH PRINTER

William Caxton

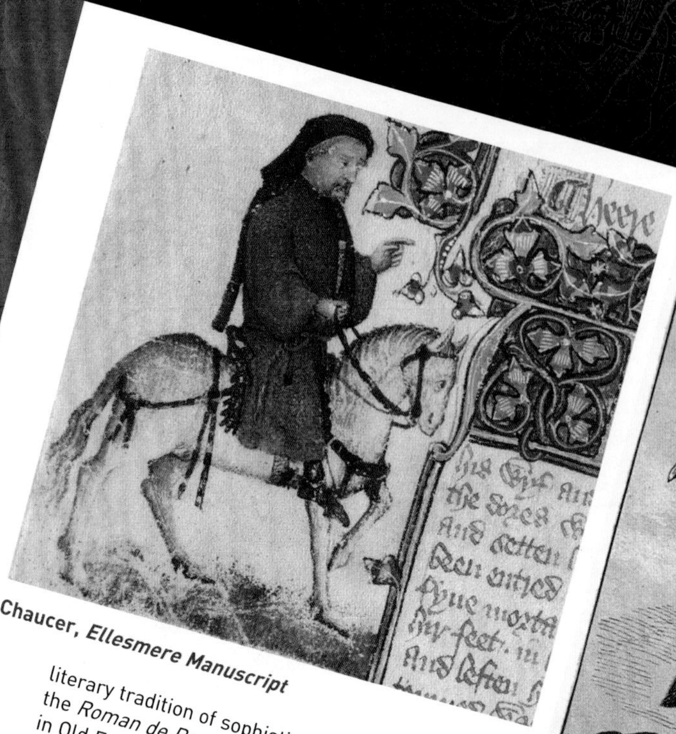

Chaucer, *Ellesmere Manuscript*

literary tradition of sophisticated texts organised as the *Roman de Renart*, 'branches' of which, written in Old French, date back to 1170. Using their anthropomorphic cast, these poems were daringly used to satirise and ridicule the aristocracy and the Church, the two principal powers in Medieval Europe. Reynard's popularity with the lower classes and that Robin Hood-like anti-heroism is then less surprising. Such were the poems' popularity that 'renard' soon replaced the Old French word for 'fox',

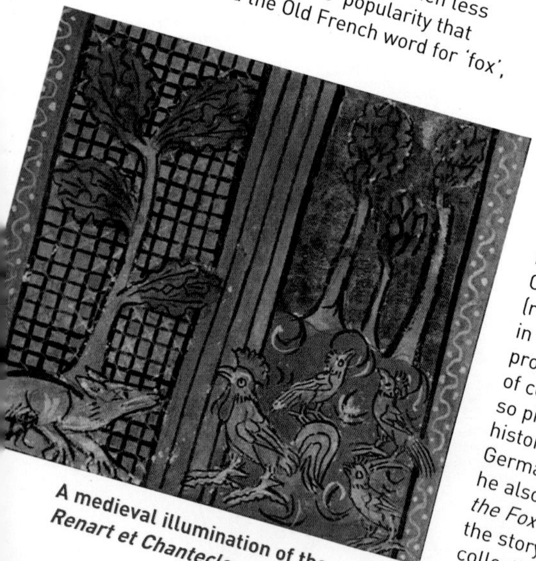

A medieval illumination of the *Renart et Chantecler*

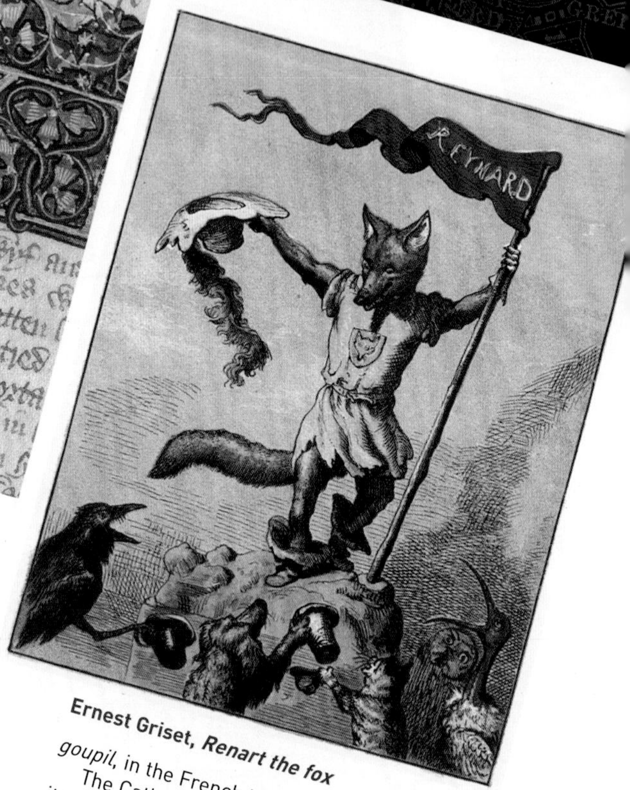
REYNARD

Ernest Griset, *Renart the fox*

goupil, in the French language.

The Catholic Church was keen to use Reynard in its own war of heretical words with the Lollards, an English movement that began life in the 14th Century. Their beliefs pre-dated Protestantism, in that they felt many Catholic beliefs and practices fell outside the teachings of the Bible, but Catholic authorities used the image of a preaching fox in their own anti-Lollard propaganda artwork.

Printed versions of Reynard's stories began to appear in the 15th Century, thanks, largely, to William Caxton. Originally from somewhere in the south-east of England (records are ironically hazy), he had moved to Bruges in 1453, where he became a prosperous merchant. A prodigious reader and translator of classics, he tired of copying by hand the weighty tomes he enjoyed and so pioneered the art of printing. His first volume was a history of Troy, but soon he was producing Dutch and German adaptations of the French tales of Reynard, which he also translated into English as *The Historie of Reynart the Foxe*. The basis for these adaptations was a version of the story written in Middle Dutch (not actually Dutch but a collection of Germanic dialects) during the 13th Century, by Willem de Madoc maecte.

THE FOX'S TALE

Another of Caxton's first titles was his edition of Chaucer's *The Canterbury Tales* – the first book to be printed in England, after he had set up shop in Westminster Abbey in 1476. Chaucer's tales are themselves stylistically and thematically not dissimilar to the *Roman de Renart* – satire and commentary on issues of concern to the general populace – so it is no real surprise that Reynard appears in 'The Nun's Priest's Tale' as Rossel. A sophisticated fable of jousting egos and the 'sly iniquitee' of the fox, Rossel flatters the protagonist, the cock Chauntecleer, into crowing rather than escaping, despite the latter's dreams of his own downfall. The cock then uses the same appeals to the fox's ego to initiate his own escape.

Another Englishman also made good use of the 'sly fox' mythology. Playwright Ben Jonson's *Volpone* – Italian for 'sly fox' – premiered at London's legendary Globe Theatre in 1606. In terms of literary figures to emerge during the English Renaissance, Jonson is considered second only to Shakespeare, and while the Great Bard only used animals to comedic effect in *A Midsummer Night's Dream*, Jonson follows the *Roman de Renart* tradition of using anthropomorphic characters to satirise the gentry and the rich in a sizzling tale of desire, both for wealth and sex. Typically, as with many of Reynard's tales, Volpone ends up losing out.

Whilst not overtly laying down his cloak for Reynard, Shakespeare seems to have been familiar enough with the *Roman de Renaut* to pay it lip service to them in *Romeo & Juliet*; Tybalt, the eponymous heroine's cousin, was so named after Tybalt (sometimes referred to as Tibert), the Prince of Cats and one of the characters in *Roman de Renaut*. Mercutio scathingly refers to Tybalt as such.

By what might be considered modern times, Reynard was a regular in satire but, harking back to Catholicism's artistic assault on the Lollards, also in propaganda. This time it was against another religion very familiar with persecution – the Jews. Unsurprisingly, this caricature had its origins in National Socialism – but more surprisingly, it was not in a German story, but a Dutch one (returning Reynard to his Low Country roots). Rather more insidiously, *Van den vos Reynarde* was a children's story first printed in *Nieuw-Nederland*, the publishing organ of the Dutch Nazi Party, in 1937. Curiously, in this tale, the Reynard character is more or less the hero, instrumental in overthrowing the crazy ideals of race mescegenation introduced by the rhinoceros Jodocus – a variation on 'jood', the Dutch for 'Jew' but also slang for 'betrayer'. An animated film version funded by German Nazis in 1943 never got off the ground, due to objections by the Dutch propaganda department in using a fox as a hero figure.

Reynard's list of appearances in recent times is broad and varied. Disney did indeed plan a version of Reynard's epic but it was abandoned and the characters wound up in *Robin Hood* instead; less surprisingly, there was a French cartoon series made in the 1980s. Foxes, in one form or another, often adaptations and variations on Reynard, have appeared in children's stories for centuries, usually portrayed less sympathetically than Reynard. There's been a Stravinsky ballet, and Reynard has appeared in comics, and even the occasional movie. In the 1986 adaptation of Umberto Eco's novel, *The Name of the Rose*, Sean Connery adds William of Baskerville to the entire diocese-worth of monk turned investigator. Studying an illuminated manuscript, William finds beautiful artwork of a fox as the Pope – no doubt harking back to *Roman de Renaut* and underscoring Reynard's influence through the centuries. •

Heaton, Butler and Bayne, *Reynard the Fox*

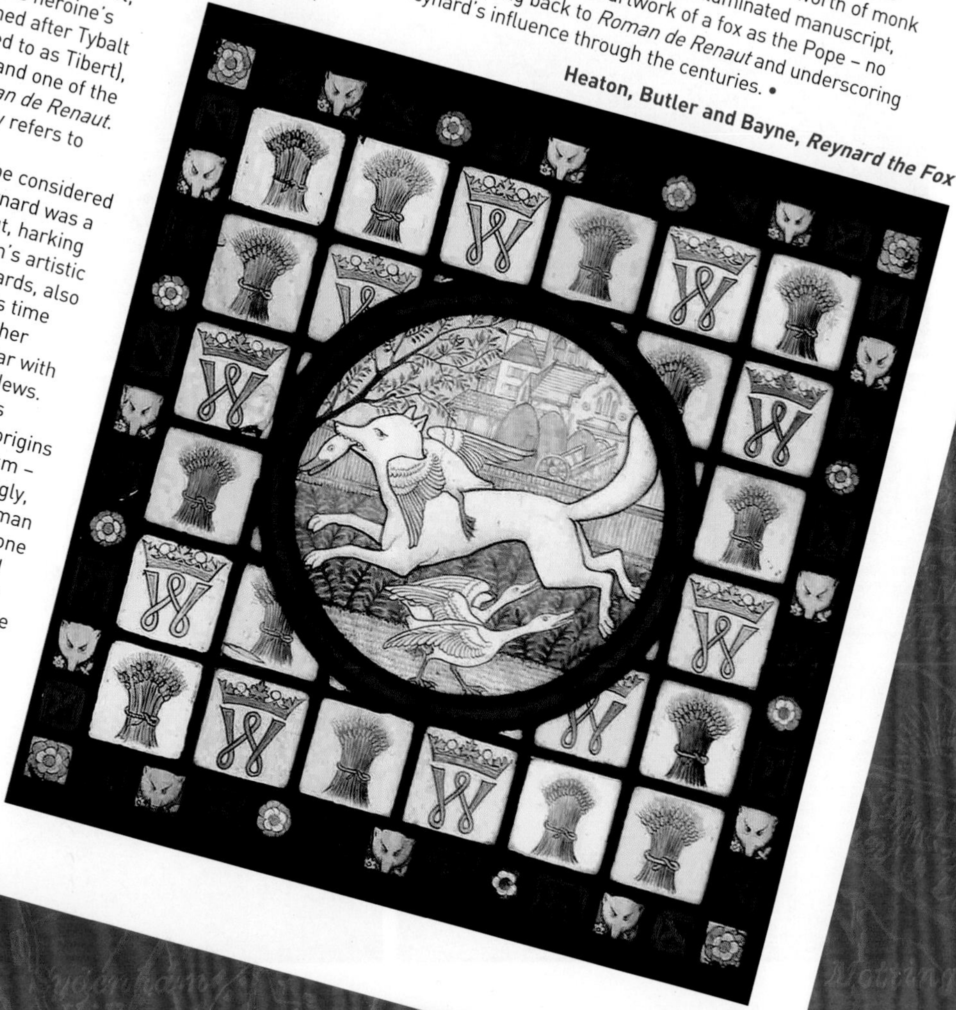

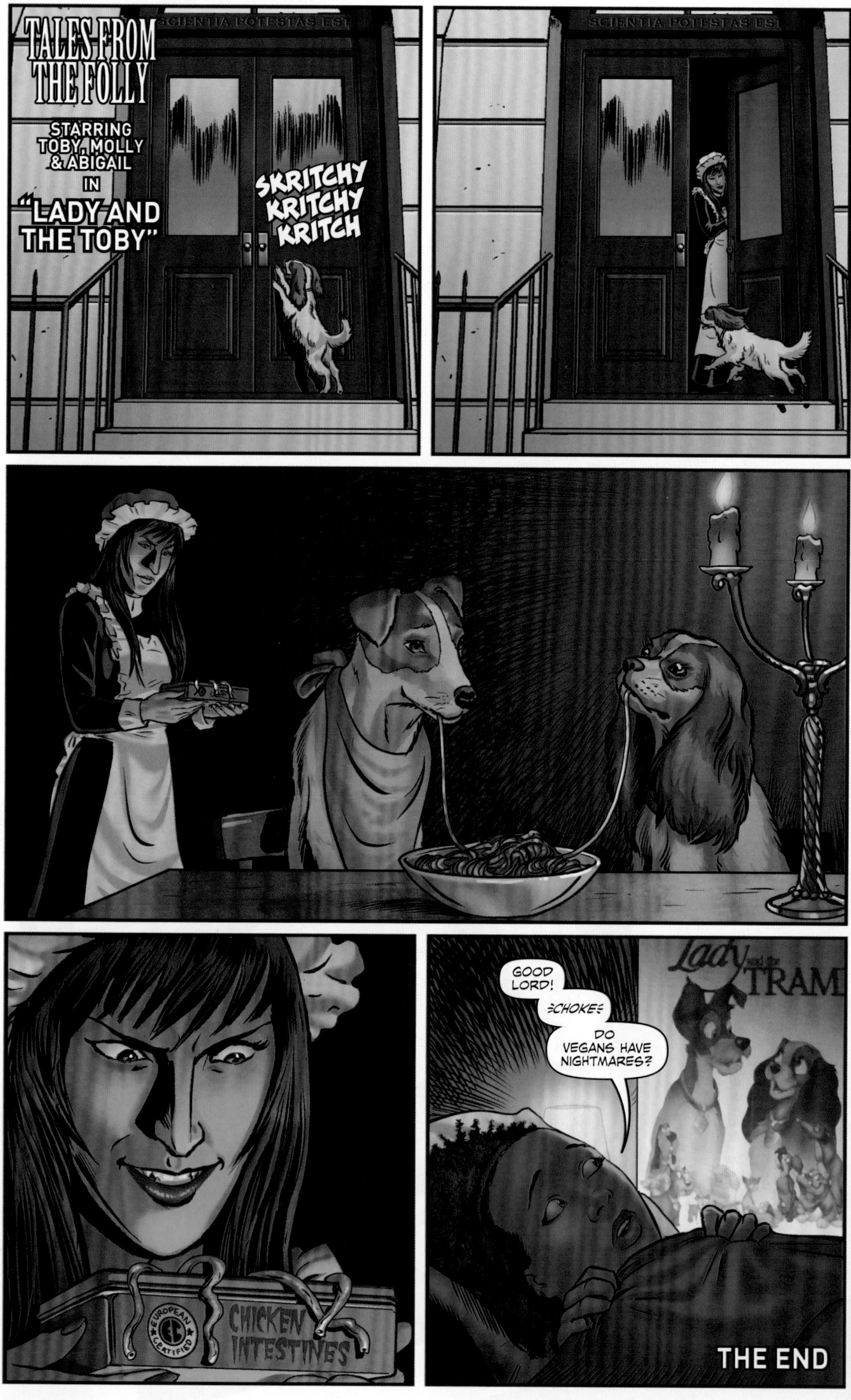
TALES FROM THE FOLLY
STARRING TOBY, MOLLY & ABIGAIL
IN
“LADY AND THE TOBY”
SCIENTIA POTESTAS EST
SKRITCHY KRITCHY KRITCH
SCIENTIA POTESTAS EST
EUROPEAN CERTIFIED
EC
CHICKEN INTESTINES
GOOD LORD!
=CHOKE=
DO VEGANS HAVE NIGHTMARES?
THE END

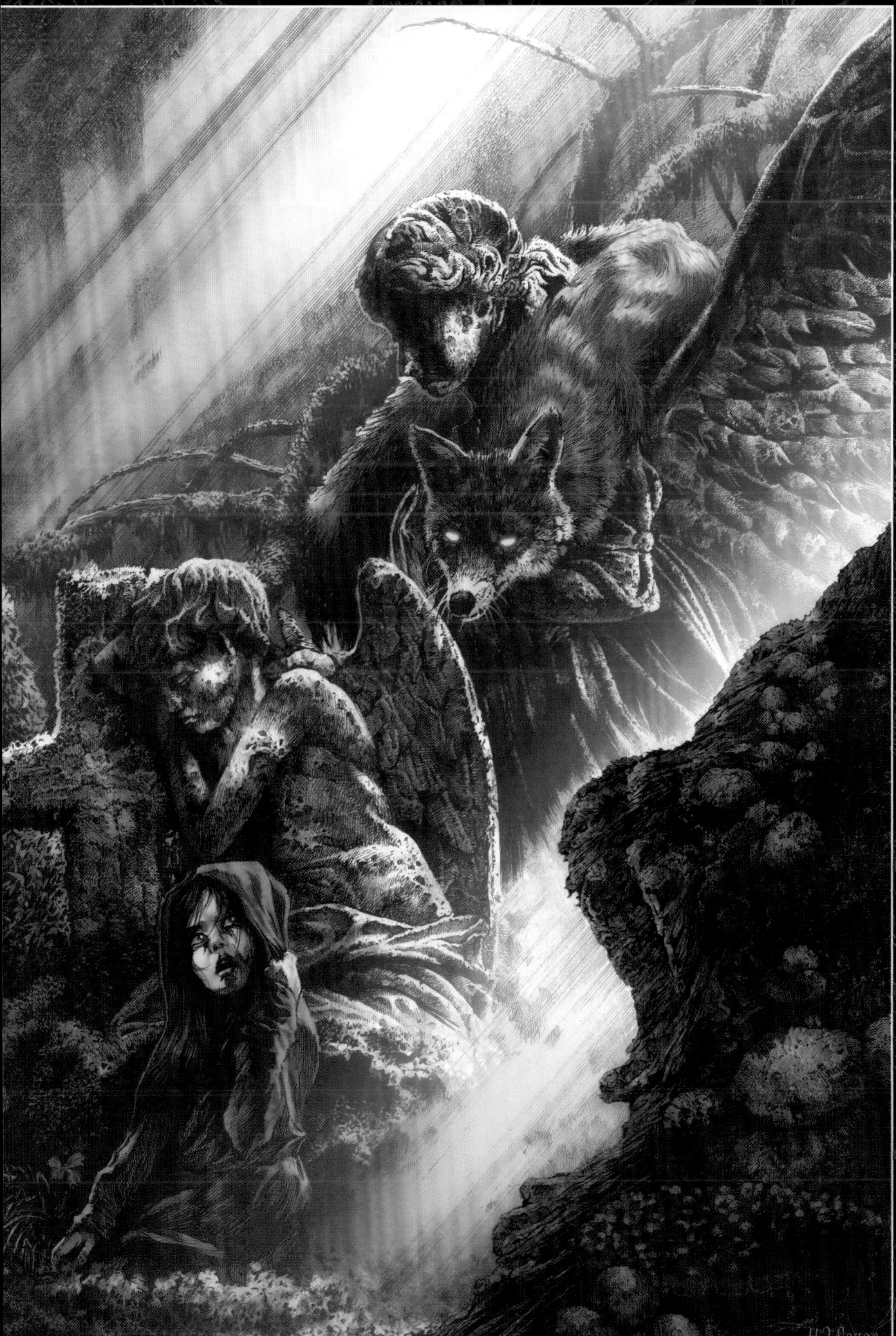

#3 Cover
Steve White & Luis Guerrero

COVERS GALLERY

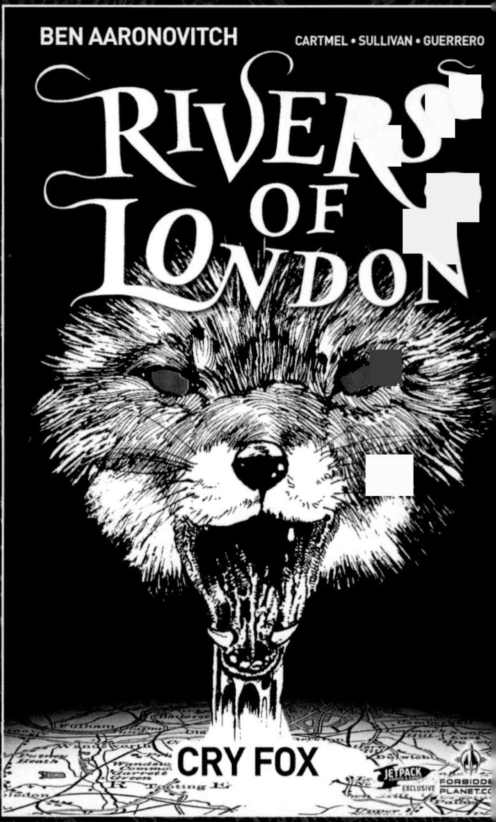
BEN AARONOVITCH
CARTMEL • SULLIVAN • GUERRERO
RIVERS OF LONDON
CRY FOX
JETPACK EXCLUSIVE
FORBIDDEN PLANET.COM

ISSUE 1 - Variant Cover
Steve White

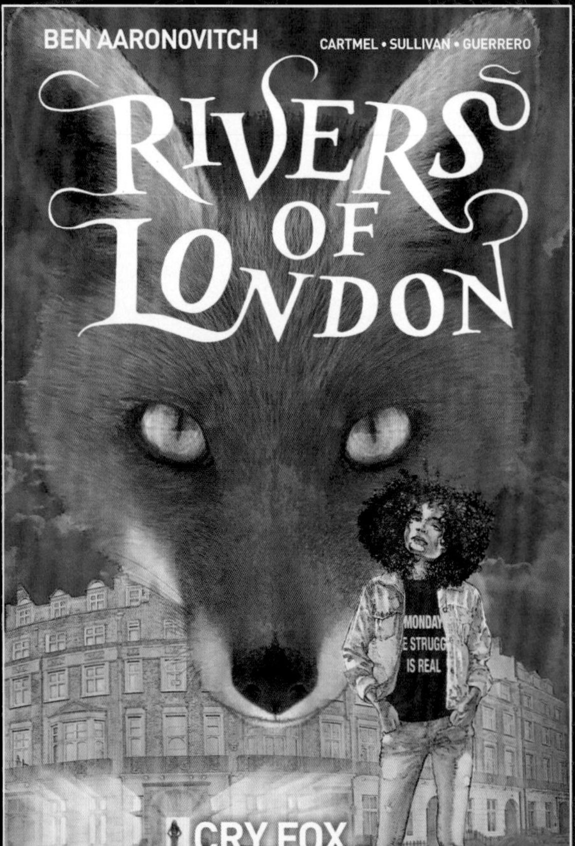
BEN AARONOVITCH
CARTMEL • SULLIVAN • GUERRERO
RIVERS OF LONDON
MONDAY
E STRUGG
IS REAL
CRY FOX

ISSUE 2 - Cover
Illeighstration

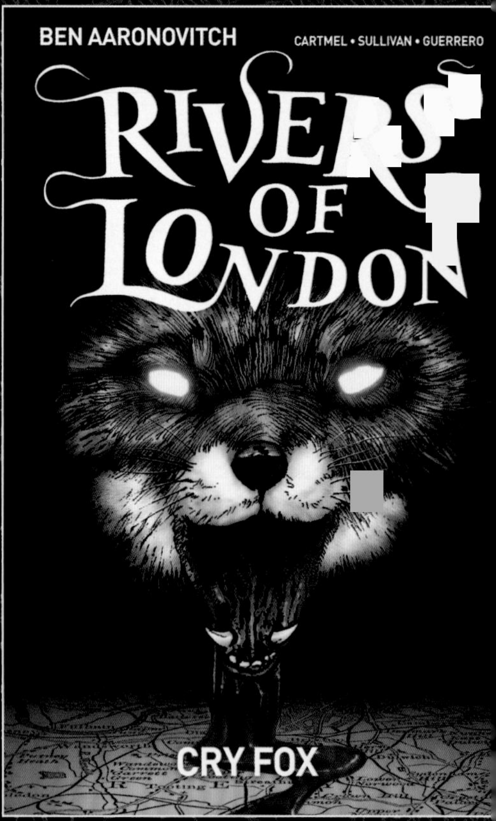
BEN AARONOVITCH
CARTMEL • SULLIVAN • GUERRERO
RIVERS OF LONDON
CRY FOX

ISSUE 1 - Cove
Steve White & Luis Guerrero

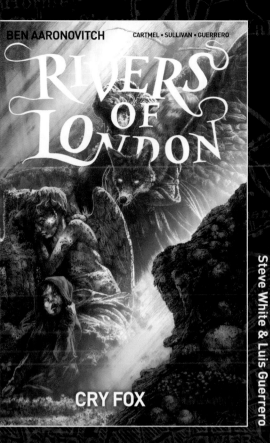

BEN AARONOVITCH　CARTMEL • SULLIVAN • GUERRERO

RIVERS OF LONDON

CRY FOX

Steve White & Luis Guerrero

ISSUE 3 - Cover

BEN AARONOVITCH　CARTMEL • SULLIVAN • GUERRERO

RIVERS OF LONDON

CRY FOX

ISSUE 4 - Cover
Illeighstration

RIVERS OF LONDON
READER'S GUIDE

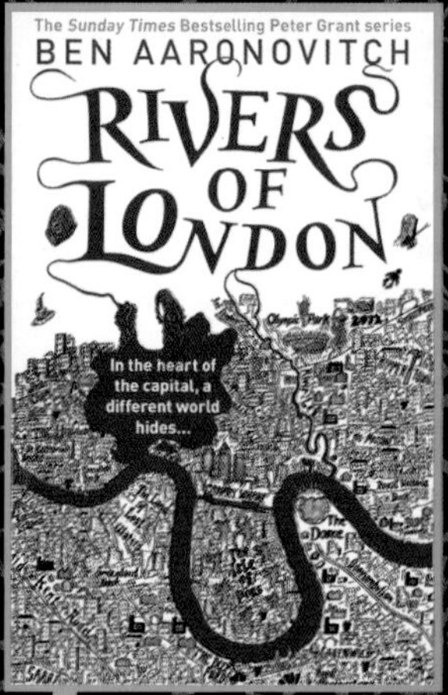

RIVERS OF LONDON / MIDNIGHT RIOT
Novel 1

MOON OVER SOHO
Novel 2

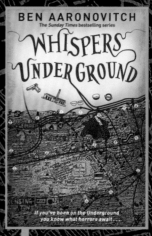

WHISPERS UNDER GROUND
Novel 3

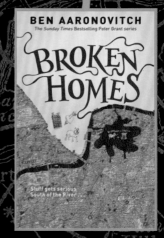

BROKEN HOMES
Novel 4

The *Rivers of London* comics and graphics novels are an essential part of the saga. Though they each stand alone, together they add compelling depth to the wider world of Peter and the Folly!

This helpful guide shows where each book fits in the ever-growing timeline of the *Rivers of London* universe!

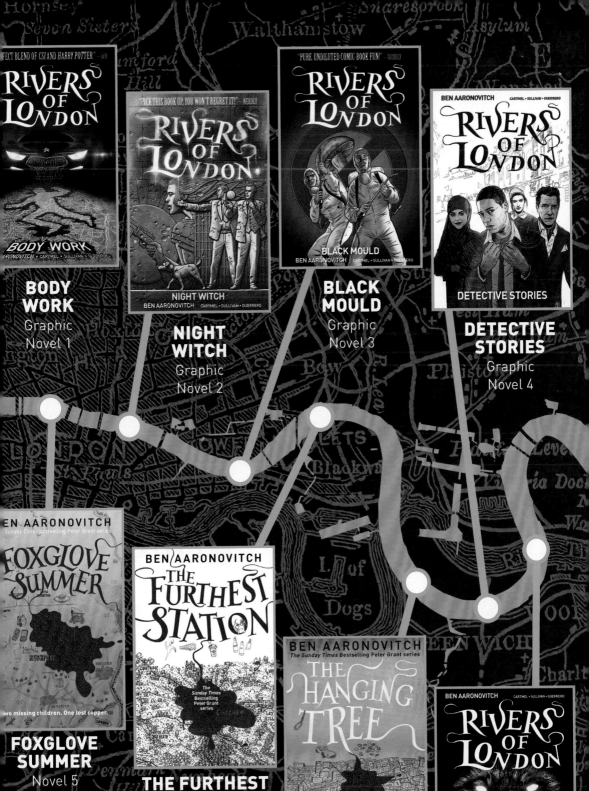

**BODY
WORK**
Graphic
Novel 1

**NIGHT
WITCH**
Graphic
Novel 2

**BLACK
MOULD**
Graphic
Novel 3

**DETECTIVE
STORIES**
Graphic
Novel 4

**FOXGLOVE
SUMMER**
Novel 5

**THE FURTHEST
STATION**
Novella 1

**THE HANGING
TREE**
Novel 6

CRY FOX
Graphic Novel 5

Murder. Mystery. Magic.

Forget everything you think you know about London.

OUT NOW

*Get on the case with PC Peter Grant
in the Sunday Times bestselling series.*

*'An incredibly fast-moving magical
joyride for grown-ups'*
THE TIMES

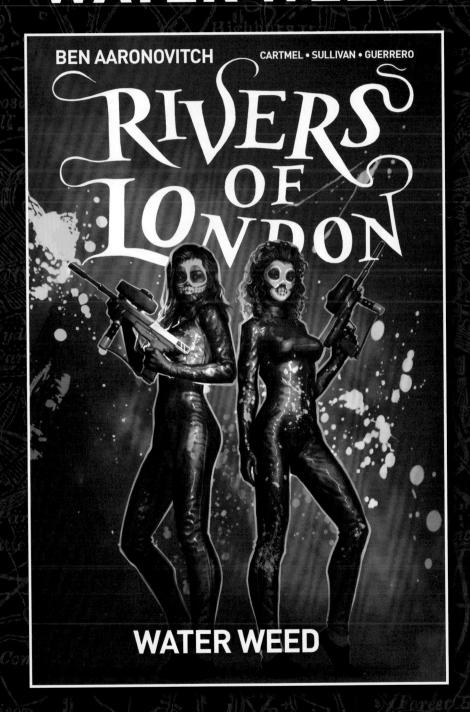

CREATOR BIOGRAPHIES

ANDREW CARTMEL

began a long and varied career in TV and publishing when he was hired as script editor on *Doctor Who* in 1986. He had a major (and very positive) impact on the final years of the original run of the TV show. He has recently completed a comedy for the London stage, Screwball, and is also writing the *Vinyl Detective* series of crime novels for Titan Books; the third, *Victory Disc*, is available now. In his spare time, he likes to do stand-up comedy.

LEE SULLIVAN

began his comics career at Marvel UK, drawing *Transformers* and *Robocop* for the US before moving on to *Judge Dredd* and *Thunderbirds* – and *Doctor Who*, for which he continues to draw, for a variety of publishers.

He played saxophone in a Roxy Music tribute band for a decade. He has dotted various Roxy Music-related gags through this series!

LUIS GUERRERO

Luis is a relative newcomer to comics. A native of Mexico, he has become a regular fixture at Titan Comics, colouring interiors and covers for a number of series including *Doctor Who, The Troop,* and *Mycroft Holmes,* as well as *Rivers of London*. Recently he has coloured for DC Comics on *The Flash*.

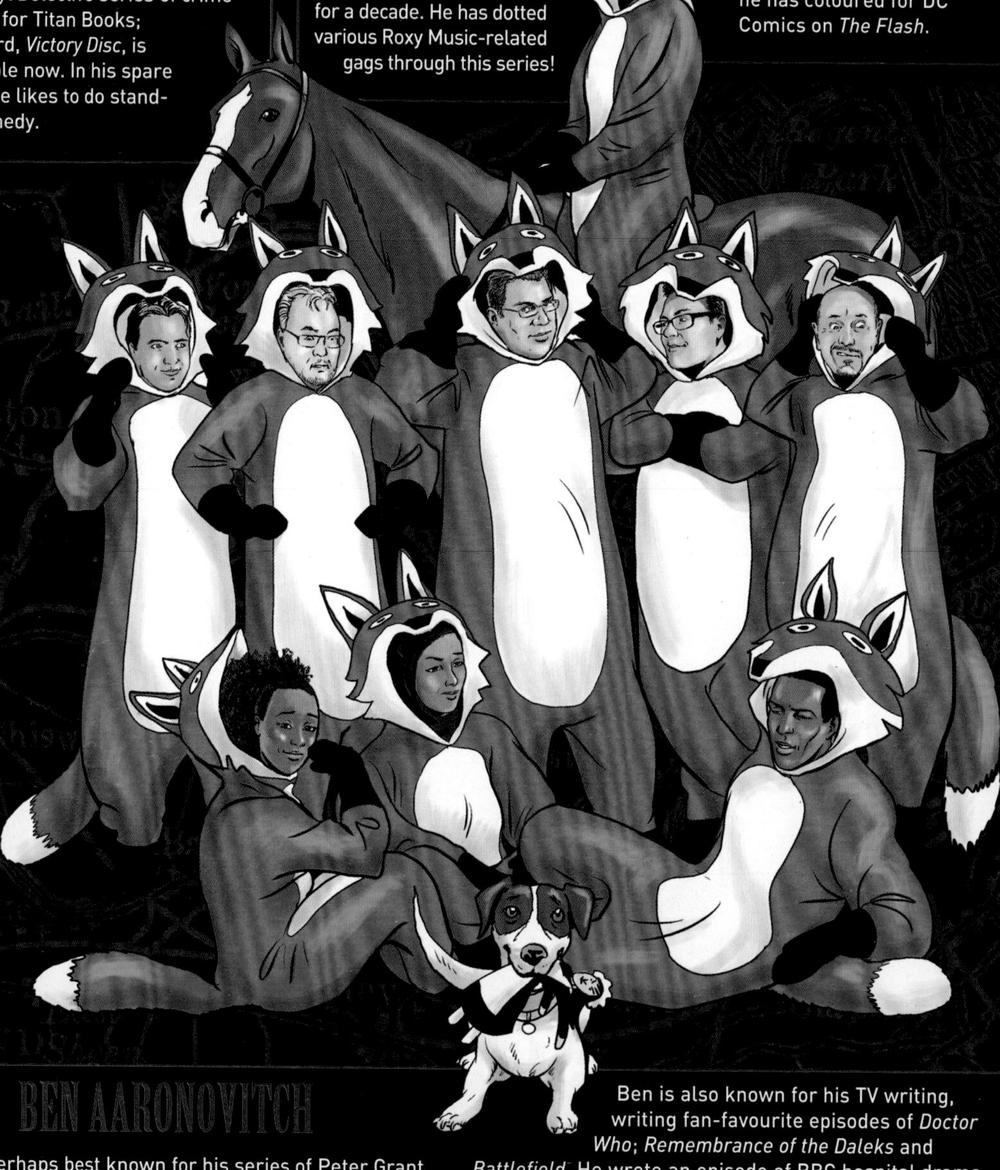

BEN AARONOVITCH

Ben is perhaps best known for his series of Peter Grant novels, which began with *Rivers of London*. Mixing police procedural with urban fantasy and London history, these novels, the latest of which is *The Hanging Tree*, have now sold over a million copies worldwide. A new Peter Grant novella, *The Furthest Station,* is now available.

Ben is also known for his TV writing, writing fan-favourite episodes of *Doctor Who*; *Remembrance of the Daleks* and *Battlefield*. He wrote an episode of BBC hospital drama, *Casualty*, and contributed to cult SF show, *Jupiter Moon*.

Ben was born, raised and lives in London, and says he will leave the city when they prise it out of his cold, dead fingers.